The Home Chef

Transforming the American Kitchen

Blessings,
Chef Perry

Perry P. Perkins

Published by:

Elk Mountain Books
Battleground, Washington

Copyright © 2016 by Perry P. Perkins
ISBN Print Edition: 1533350337
ISBN-13: 978-1533350336

*Elk Mountain Books titles are available for special promotions and premiums.
For details contact: **homechef@perryperkinsbooks.com***

It would be my *very* strong suggestion, before delving too deeply into *my* book, that you watch the amazing 4-Part series, Cooked (*available for streaming on Netflix*) or read the book of the same title, by Michael Pollan.

I've read the book, and watched each episode several times, and am still learning new techniques with each viewing.

It is, in my not-so-humble opinion, the best resource available for understanding why and how we have reached the point we are at in food and cooking, in our society, and our world.

Consider it your unofficial first assignment.

How do you write a book on how to save the world?

When I started this project, over two years ago, I had no idea how all-encompassing it would become. Unlike my blog, or the "Caja" cookbooks, which practically write themselves, this was more than just how-tos and recipes (*though, rest assured, there are plenty of those*), this manuscript included deep, wide, unpredictable rivers of philosophy and conviction, unexplored dark chasms of learned opinion, personal bias, and (often cynical) worldview, as well.

It was easy to get lost. The sheer volume of hubris, required to assume such a goal is, alone, exhausting.

Every idea, it seemed, birthed two more, and each of those two more again, growing exponentially into a fertile rabbit-warren of thoughts, questions, arguments, and hundreds of hours of research, fact-checking, testing, photography, formatting, and more than a dozen re-writes (*In fact, I ditched the whole damn thing, twice, as just being too much of an information dump.*)

The toll on myself and my family was much higher than I could have expected in the beginning, but it would have been impossible without their amazing patience, support, and occasional kick in the ass.

But here we are. Today, the book releases, it is done...

Consummatum est.

So, how do you write a book on how to save the world?

As someone once said, it's a bit like watching hippos have sex. Scary in places, hilarious in others, a little awkward, and once it gets going, you want to stay out of its way.

Most of all...you'll know when it's done.

It's done.

Enjoy...

Table of Contents

Dedications

This book is dedicated to my father, my mentor, my friend...**Chef Frank Leon Perkins**

Alexander the Great said, "I am indebted to my father for living, but to my teacher for living well." I had the unique good fortune to find both in the same man. Thank you pop, for passing along your passion so freely.

No matter what else was going on, we could always talk about the food.

To my dear old friend and brother, **Ed Bjorklund,** my mentor, fellow foodie, kindred spirit, and cast-iron cooking guru.

I'd give a hell of a lot to have one more dinner with you, even if I do cook a better steak!

(Wow, I finally got the last word in...) ;)

And, lastly, to my sweet, amazing hero in the faith, Teri Gant. Who taught me, more than anyone in my life, what it really means to be Jesus to the least of these...and what joy it brings.

I miss you, my sister, my friend. Keep an eye on me, will'ya, pal?

If more of us valued food and cheer and song above hoarded gold, it would be a merrier world.
~ J.R.R. Tolkien

Author's Note

---

moral imperative [mor·al im-per-uh-tiv]

noun

1. something that must happen because it is the right thing

2. a principle originating inside a person's mind that compels that person to act.

synonyms:

reinvigorate, revitalize, refresh, energize, reanimate, resuscitate, revivify, rejuvenate, regenerate, enliven

---

Today the average American spends a mere 27 minutes on food prep each day (*another four minutes, or so, cleaning up*); that's less than half the time that we spent in the kitchen when Julia Child arrived on our television screens.

It's also less than half the time it takes to sit through an episode of "Chopped" or "Cutthroat Kitchen." As Americans, we're are spending considerably more time *watching* cooking than we are cooking ourselves — an "old fashioned" activity that today's hustle and bustle world will tell us we no longer have the time for.

We are standing at the edge of a cliff.

Our health, our finances, even the very fabric of our families are poised to plunge over the brink. At our backs is the home kitchen, the family…time.

Before us nothing less than total destruction.

We have an obligation, a moral imperative if you will, to regain control of our children's health, our planet's sustainability, even our nation's greatness.

And I believe it starts in the kitchen.

Introduction

I was seven years old when I tasted Boeuf Bourguignon for the first time. Standing on a milk crate at the six-burner in one of the many kitchens in which my father sweated, and laughed, and cursed.

I had some trepidation, I recall, as the steaming spoon was brought to my lips. I had tasted from the big pot hours before, and found the winey bitterness of the raw dish not at all to my liking, which had garnered my father's approval (*not the easiest thing*) and a lesson (*and there was ALWAYS a lesson*), so I was unsure what my reaction was supposed to be this time.

In that moment, as the spoon touched my lips and with a shiver of pure pleasure I tasted that uniquely perfect French peasant's stew, I had an awakening. I loved the kitchen, having played among the pots and spoons and rushing feet since before I could remember.

I loved the heat, the chaos, the naughty words that I was *never* to repeat at home, all of it. But it was that moment, etched so deeply in my brain that even now, forty years later, I can remember exactly the smell of the eye-watering pungency of raw onions in the kitchen, the greasy grey steam from the dish-washing station, my father's pleasantly familiar aroma of Old Spice and Camel cigarettes, and...especially, the moment I tasted that broth and realized what it was, exactly, that my father, and his scruffy crew of morally-questionable pirates really did.

They made magic.

At seven, I didn't know the word "alchemy", that mythical process of turning lead into gold, but for the first time I realized that such a thing was possible.

That is what I experienced in that moment...alchemy. A dented old pot of cheap, unpleasant tasting ingredients combined in a proper way, for a proper amount of time, touched by fire and transformed by a wave of my father's hand into something...magical.

For the rest of my life, my time in the kitchen has been a ripple, ever widening and leading outward from that first taste from my father's spoon, pushed forward by a single desire.

I wanted to make magic.

It's been more than forty years, since that life-changing sip of soup, and I now find myself in a society that is standing at the edge of a cliff.

Our health, our finances, even the very fabric of our families are poised to plunge over the brink. At our back is the home kitchen, the family dinner table, before us nothing less than total destruction.

If that sounded hyperbolic, trust me, it's not.

Growing up in the Rockwood slums outside of Portland in the early 1970's, with an invalid mother, and a father living out of state, I never heard the term, "food insecure."

We were just called *poor*.

Times were good when there was money to buy enough boxed and canned processed food to fill our bellies. Times were tough when there was nothing left but a bag of potatoes and a brick of government issued American "cheese".

Times were bad when the cheese ran out.

Most months ended somewhere between tough and bad.

In the winter of 1975, my parents divorced. My mother had a chronic heart condition that made it impossible for her to work and the two of us couldn't quite make ends meet that first year on our own.

In previous years, Christmas had been a grand event in our home.

Money had always been scarce, but my parents scrimped and saved for the holidays. My first memories are of bright lights, rich smells, and a pile of gifts with my name on them. That year, however, would be different. My mother received a meager social security check each month that almost, but not quite, covered the bare essentials, with nothing left for the luxuries of Christmas.

My mother, alone for the first time in her life, found it difficult to put aside her own hurts and fears and participate in the holidays.

I do remember that we had a small tree and brought a box of decorations down from the closet shelf, but there wasn't much joy in our home that year.

One thing that did worry my mother was that there was no money for gifts. She fretted over this for weeks but the funds just were not there for presents.

One day, a neighbor told her about a local toy charity, an organization dedicated to providing donated presents for children in need.

My mother applied for the program and visited their office, bringing home a small box of gifts, which she wrapped and hid under her bed.

The night before Christmas, we ate our baked potatoes, and Mom read to me from a book of children's Christmas stories. Just before bedtime, there was a knock at the door, and my mother answered to find a young woman who had just moved in next door to us.

She was Hispanic, speaking very broken English, and had twin sons who were my own age. She was also divorced and was in as bad, or worse, financial straits as we were. She came to the door asking to borrow some flour and looked so exhausted that Mother invited her in and made her a cup of tea. I was hustled off to bed, lest I still be up when Santa made his appearance, and they stayed up and talked awhile.

I remember my mother coming into my room and gently waking me up, then sitting on the side of my bed and asking me if I minded if we had company for Christmas. I said no, unused to have my opinion asked in such matters.

Then she took my hand and asked if it would be all right with me if Santa gave some of my presents to the two little boys next door.

I thought about this for a while, wondering why Santa couldn't bring them their own presents, but somehow my young brain sensed that it would make mother happy, and she hadn't seemed happy in a long while, so I hesitantly agreed.

Mother kissed my forehead, and I went back to sleep.

The next morning I awoke to the most wonderful smell wafting under my bedroom door. Hunger banished even the memory of Christmas from my mind, and I ran from my room to the kitchen to find the source of that glorious aroma. I skidded to a stop as I rounded the corner into a strange, dark-faced woman standing at my mother's stove.

She was rolling out tortillas and dropping them into a smoking pan, while a large pot bubbled noisily on the back burner.

I blinked one or twice in confusion, until my mother walked in, then remembered that we had company, and even more importantly, that today was Christmas!

I spun on my heels and ran into the living room to look under the tree. Two little Mexican boys sat, looking uncertainly around them, on our couch. Several small wrapped packages lay beneath the tree.

Mom followed me in and began to pass out presents, there were just enough for one gift each.

I gazed longingly at the brightly wrapped packages in these stranger's hands, knowing they should have been mine, clutching my solitary present tightly to my chest.

I unwrapped the box to find a GI Joe action figure, the old fashioned kind with the moving knees and elbows, the kind that came with a little rifle and a little backpack and a string that you pulled to make them say cool army things.

Except...mine didn't have a rifle, or a backpack, and there was only a hole in the back where the string had once gone.

I stood there in the middle of the living room, my lip trembling, clutching my broken toy.

I looked to see what the other boys had gotten, what gifts I had missed out on.

One package revealed a cap pistol (*without caps*) and a worn plastic holster (*I had a much nicer set in the toy box in my room*), the second box revealed a plastic bag full of Legos, in various shapes and sizes.

I stood there and watched these two boys whooping and laughing like these were the only toys they had, turning their meager gifts over and over in awe, and suddenly I realized, that these *were* the only toys they had.

Soon I would learn that these two, who would become my closest pals, each had exactly two shirts, two pairs of pants, and a worn sleeping bag that they shared on the floor of their room.

As I watched my mother talking to this strange woman in our kitchen, tears running down their cheeks, I was suddenly happy that she had woken me up, that Santa had shared my presents with these boys, for how terrible would it have been to wake up with nothing under the tree, no presents to play with, no Santa *at all?*

The boys, Jay and Julio, followed me to my room, where I showed them, to their amazement, the wealth of my toy box. Soon we were playing like old friends, until called out for a breakfast of seasoned eggs and potatoes wrapped in fresh, warm tortillas. *(Recipe follows)* It was the best breakfast I could ever remember having.

I've never forgotten that morning, nor my pals from Mexico who taught me that there is always something to be thankful for, often much more than we think. It also taught me that amazing food isn't always about expensive or fancy ingredients, but often…even usually, it's about the hands that prepare the dish. It's about the basic knowledge of what makes food good, and how to do it.

And, of course, it's about love.

Patatas y Huevos Burritos

4 large servings

Okay, so this is a little touched up from that Christmas breakfast, but even if you leave out the sausage, poblano peppers, and toppings, it's pretty darn good!

1 lb. breakfast sausage	2 large russet potatoes
1 large ancho chili, diced	2 Tbsp. oil
8 eggs	3 Tbsp. milk
2 Tbsp. flour	1 cup Pico de Gallo
1 cup Mexican Crema	1 cup cheddar cheese
10-12 flour gorditas, warmed	
1/2 tsp each: salt, pepper, cumin, chili powder	

Preheat oven to 350 degrees.

Take sausage out of casing and cook in a separate pan, breaking it up, until no longer pink. Drain, if needed.

Slice potatoes very thinly (*I use a mandolin slicer*) without peeling and heat oil in an ovenproof skillet.

Place potatoes and diced poblano chili in a single layer in pan and cook potatoes until golden brown, seasoning with salt and pepper to taste. Beat together eggs, milk, flour, and spices with a whisk.

Add sausage to cooked potatoes.

Add egg and milk mixture to pan; heat until almost firm, folding once or twice with a wooden spoon. When egg mixture is almost firm, add cheese, cover, place in oven and bake until eggs are firm and cheese melts.

Divide evenly between gorditas and serve with Pico and Crema.

Number of Servings: 6

NOTE: *To take this recipe up another notch — substitute 8oz chorizo for half of the breakfast sausage. Just make sure to drain the meat before adding it to the potatoes.*

When my father moved back to Oregon a couple of years later, things got much, much better, and I began to learn not only what good food was, but how to cook it...not in my mom's tiny apartment kitchen, but on the line at Dad's restaurants. I learned how to cook out of six pans at once on a Wolf gas range, how to sear steaks at the grill station, and double-dunk fries at the deep fryer. I learned the principles of *mise en place*, the importance of fresh ingredients, and many of the little tips and tricks that had always been the privilege of the professionally trained cook. With a mother who couldn't cook (*at all*), and a father who cooked a couple of hundred dinners every night, it was many years before I realized the gap that existed between the home cook and the professional chef.

That's what this book is about...that gap, because something amazing has begun to happen in the last two decades, something that has never before happened in the history of cooking...instead of growing wider, the gap between the home cook and the professional chef has actually begun to narrow, and continues to narrow exponentially with each passing year. We are entering the age of the "Home Chef", a title that's available to nearly everyone, regardless of age, gender, or financial standing.

> *All the information you could want is constantly streaming at you like a runaway truck - books, newspaper stories, Web sites, apps, how-to videos, even entire magazines devoted to single subjects like charcuterie or wedding cakes or pickles.*
>
> ~ *Mario Batali*

The time when these specialized skills were limited to those who could afford the cost and time required for culinary school are quickly passing into history. The time when the sole requirement to elevate your cooking skills to this level...*passion*...is emerging.

It's an amazing time to become a Home Chef...and if you have that passion, I'll show you how to get started.

Welcome!

Chef Perry

How to use this book

Highlight or underline any terms or techniques you're not familiar with. If the term is not included in the Cooking Glossary, then search for it online, preferably on one of the educational resources** provided.

Circle the word(s) in the book, and then write in your own definition, based on your research, in the extra pages at the end of the Cooking Glossary.

When all else fails, email me at chefperryp@gmail.com, and I'll track down an answer for you.

Homework:

This book is about learning and improving cooking skills, and you can't do that by just reading.

Throughout the chapters you'll find homework assignments, and blank pages to write in your own notes. If you really want to learn, stop at each assignment, and complete it before moving on.

Videos & Weblinks

 This is the video icon, when you see this icon it means there is a video that further describes that recipe or technique at www.thehomechefbook.com Password: **homechef**

 This is the weblink icon, this icon it means there is a webpage or blog post with further description on the topic, either via a Google search of the term provided, or at www.thehomechefbook.com Password: **homechef**

Back to School

Cooking is about joy and comfort.
Cooking in a restaurant is about business.
~ Anthony Bourdain

Okay, here's what the book is all about. Here are the resources and lessons that can take you from a "recipe cook" to a true Home Chef.

To start out, let's take a look at an example of what I was talking about regarding culinary school

This is the 18-month "Culinary Arts" degree class schedule from one of the most prestigious cooking schools in America.

In bold are the classes which (*in my opinion*) do *not* pertain to the required skills of the Home Chef:

Freshman Year, First Semester	
Culinary Fundamentals	**Culinary Math**
Externship Prep Seminar I	**Externship Prep Seminar II**
Food Safety	**Professionalism and Life Skills**
Introduction to Gastronomy	Nutrition
Product Knowledge	

Freshman Year, Second Semester	
Introduction to Management	Meat ID, Fabrication and Utilization
Seafood ID and Fabrication	**Modern Banquet Cookery**
Intro to À La Carte Cooking	**High-Volume Production Cookery**
Culinary Practical Examination	**Externship Prep Seminar III**
College Writing	**College Writing for ELLs**

Sophomore Year, First Semester	
Baking and Pastry Skills	**Intro to Catering**
Garde Manger	Cuisines and Cultures of the Americas
Controlling Cost and Purchasing	Cuisines and Cultures of the Med
Cuisines and Cultures of Asia	**Menu Development**

Btw, <u>Garde Manger</u> (*French for "keeper of the food"*) covers cold dishes such as salads, hors d'œuvres, appetizers, canapés, pâtés and terrines.

So, of twenty-seven classes, seventeen of them have to do with cooking professionally, and do not pertain to the Home Chef.

This leaves ten:

Culinary Fundamentals	Food Safety
Introduction to Gastronomy	Nutrition
Meat Ident., Fab., and Utilization	Seafood ID and Fabrication
Garde Manger	Cuisines/Cultures of the Americas
Cuisines and Cultures of the Med	Cuisines and Cultures of Asia

Please note: *I left out "Baking and Pastry Skill Development" not because these are not important skills, and worthy of study by the Home Chef, but because covering even the basics of baking and pastry would require a whole 'nuther book! Maybe next time...*

Now, once we take away optional foreign cuisine classes (*consider these options further study based on personal interest*), this leaves seven classes that I would consider essential:

Culinary Fundamentals	Food Safety
Introduction to Gastronomy	Nutrition
Meat ID, Fab., and Utilization	Seafood ID and Fabrication
Garde Manger	

These seven classes and the recipes, tips, and techniques relative to each, are what we well be covering in the rest of this book.

Along with way I'll provide some additional online resources that I've researched and feel cover these points the best.

 Additional videos and links for these topics are available, free, at **www.HomeChefClasses.com**

These will help your take your kitchen skills to the next level, but more importantly, I'm hoping that by the time you work your way through these classes you'll be comfortable with the process of researching and finding ongoing instruction online.

Also, many of these videos are parts of individual series of classes, so if you find an instructor you really like, you can branch out and see what else they have to offer.

Once that happens...you be able to cook anything you can dream of!

*To access these videos and blogs, do the recommended Google searches, or go to **thehomechefclasses.com** (password: **homechef**) and find this list, as well as many other recipes and techniques mentioned throughout the book, with click-able links. ~ Chef Perry*

Pay to Play Classes

The websites and videos I tag in the book are all free to use/view.

However, there's certainly nothing wrong with paying a reasonable amount for some dedicated courses from a reputable chef.

If that interests you, be sure to check the "Pay to Play Online Resources" page (*under resources*) at the back of this book!

FoodTV
(or..."pay no attention to the ad-man behind the curtain...")

My wife likes to say that every pancake has two sides, no matter how thin. In this book we'll talk a *lot* about what a great resource that food television has been for expanding modern food awareness, and as an educational resource for those who cook at home.

And I believe that...really...or I wouldn't be recommending specific shows. But, don't think for a minute that FoodTV is all pink rainbows and dancing unicorns...for every minute of decent, serious instruction on the art and science of food preparation, our health as a society, and the importance of sustainable diversity in the world's diet, there are twice as many minutes (*that's two...for those who are counting*) of mindless gameshow drivel, completely unrelatable cooking situations, and chemical-laden, "pre-made crap" commercials.

Worse, there's a subtle, unspoken marketing message being fed to us in heaping spoonful's, which is in absolute contradiction to the warm fuzzies we're hearing from the apron-wearing talking-heads...

Food Television does NOT want us to learn to cook for ourselves.

Let me repeat that...

Food Television does NOT want us to learn to cook for ourselves.

Seriously, grab a pen and an empty pizza box, and watch a few shows. Note the commercials.

Our favorite "celebrity chef" may be showing us the step-by-step of an amazing, healthy, "farm to table" recipe, one that looks almost too good to eat, but as soon as we fade to black, we're being hawked pre-packaged, over-priced, preservative-chocked meals (*literally* "*TV dinners*") by the smiling, reassuringly familiar face of some *other* "celebrity chef!"

The unspoken message to us being, "Sure that homemade, healthy dish looks amazing, but C'MON...we *both* know that *you* don't have the time, the patience, or the skill to do what a *celebrity chef* does...but doesn't *this* look almost as good? And...you can make *this* is just a couple of minutes! How awesome is *that?*" It's the old shell-game, and...the house is usually going to win.

In this Chef's opinion, this is the moral equivalent of starting a network featuring the works of the best African American writers, directors, and movie stars...and then running ads for the KKK.

(Yeah...I just said that...)

The message from these culinary snake-oil salesmen may be unspoken, but it's being heard loud and clear. The more minutes each year that are being spent watching Bobby, and Emeril, and Rachel...the less that are being spent on actually *cooking* ourselves. Is that an accident? I think not.

FoodTV makes its money the same way any other for-profit TV makes it money...from advertising dollars. Those number-crunching sociopaths in the advertising department know perfectly well that if they can make our mouths water for the gourmet dish that takes two hours to prepare, we'll still be hungry when they offer us the frozen enchiladas that take two minutes. And, let's face it, is there anything, ANYTHING, America loves more than instant gratification?

Again, I believe whole-heartedly that, used correctly (*and "use" is an action, not a passive act of sitting on the couch snorking cheeze-doodles, while Nigella yaps away about the importance of organic vegetables...*) food television can be a great tool in the Home Chef's toolbox for learning new techniques, and advancing our cooking skills. Without action though, it's like sitting and watching an uncooked chunk of meat.

It starts with great potential, but in the long run...all it's going to do is stink.

A Note on "Foodies"...

First, some definitions:

"Foodie is an informal term for a particular class of aficionado of food and drink. The word was coined in 1981 by Paul Levy and Ann Barr, who used it in the title of their 1984 book The Official Foodie Handbook." (From Wikipedia)

Nicole Weston, in her article, *"What is a foodie, anyway"* (February 10, 2006), says, *"Although the two terms are sometimes used interchangeably, foodies differ from gourmets in that gourmets are epicures of refined taste who may or may not be professionals in the food industry, whereas foodies are amateurs who simply love food for consumption, study, preparation, and news."*

UrbanDictionary brings the conflict to a whole new level:

"A person that spends a keen amount of attention and energy on knowing the ingredients of food, the proper preparation of food, and finds great enjoyment in top-notch ingredients and exemplary preparation. A foodie is not necessarily a food snob, only enjoying delicacies and/or food items difficult to obtain and/or expensive foods; though, that is a variety of foodie."

So...back to the original article. The author states:

"I'm surprised by a prevailing assumption I often come across that being a foodie means having an overwhelming desire to cook — to recreate the work of masters in one's own kitchen. I think that's pretty presumptuous and in some ways, devalues the art of fine dining. Being a foodie is more about appreciation than recreation. It's about being adventurous enough to try new things and to savor flavor combinations you never dreamed of."

Unfortunately, the comment box was closed.

Here's my completely subjective two cents...

If you've seen the Pixar classic, *Ratatouille*, then you may remember one of the critic Anton Ego's lines, following his "enlightenment" near the end of the movie. *"Not everyone can be a great chef, but a great chef can come from anywhere."*

I think that the foodie/cook issue may be a similar juxtaposition – in that, you don't have to be a great chef (*or even like to cook*) to be a Foodie, but most Foodies *become* passionate about cooking.

I do know one thing…of the dozen or so friends and acquaintances that I consider to be hardcore foodies in my own little world, every single one of them loves to cook.

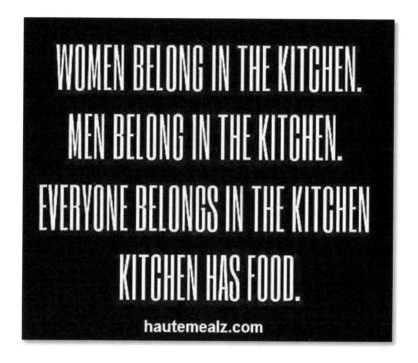

You know you're a foodie when...

- You plan vacations based on the local restaurant scene.

- You've stayed up till 2am reading...a cookbook.

- You take notes at the movies during "food scenes".

- You carry around your own condiments...you know, just in case.

- You have a 60" Plasma TV and pay for cable...but the only channel you watch is Food Network.

- You've used the term "food porn" in front of your mom.

- It no longer seems strange to take pictures of what you eat.

- You become obviously aroused at the mention of the word, "Tapas."

- You've woken your spouse up at 3am to read them a recipe.

- Friends apologize when inviting you to fast food restaurants.

- Dogs follow you because you smell like bacon.

- Your 4 y/o won't eat boxed mac & cheese, but begs for foie gras, goat cheese, and caviar.

- You have a specific menu planned for your own memorial service.

- You never get invited to dinner because your friends are scared to cook for you.

- You've rearranged food on *someone else's* plate, to take a picture...

- When the answer to any problem is to make dessert.

- You're on a first-name basis with the butcher at your favorite store, but you can't remember your babysitter's name.

- You've registered for your wedding AND baby shower at WHOLE FOODS.

- You have fantasized about being locked in a kitchen with Alton Brown

Part One: Chefs

Some people are just born to cook and talk.

~ Guy Fieri

Chapter One
The Chef

> *Cooking is not about convenience and it's not about shortcuts.*
> *Our hunger for the twenty-minute gourmet meal, for one-pot ease and prewashed, precut ingredients has severed our lifeline to the satisfactions of cooking. Take your time. Take a long time.*
> *Move slowly and deliberately and with great attention.*
>
> *~ Thomas Keller*

What is a *Chef?*

Now…before I get all preachy, please understand…call yourself whatever you want to call yourself, as long as you can back it up in the kitchen. However, I'm also not a fan of elitism…which I (*personally*) feel is creeping more and more into the cooking scene, thanks in no small part, I'm sure, to Food Network stars with sheepskins from places like CIA and Le Cordon Bleu.

NOTE – I think those are GREAT institutions, and I think they have a lot to offer. But…can you only call yourself a chef, if you have a degree from one of these places. This guy's opinion? – No.

My grandfather was a professional chef in many kitchens, including the opening of Timberline Lodge (*thanks WPA*), but he never went to school for it (*in fact, I'm not sure he ever went to school, period.*)

My father did have a degree, but he ran kitchens for MANY years before he decided to go to school for it.

Me?

I've done an awful lot of cooking (*some of it pretty awful, lol*) both in and out of restaurants, but I've only taken a couple of college courses.

I did most of my learning in my dad's kitchen (*as he did in HIS dad's kitchen*)…which was sort of a cross between Marine Boot and a war-time concentration camp…but with better food.

So, believe me, I learned.

chef *[shef]* —noun

1. the chief cook, <u>especially</u> in a restaurant or hotel, <u>usually</u> responsible for planning menus, ordering foodstuffs, overseeing food preparation, and supervising the kitchen staff.

2. any cook.

1826, from Fr. chef de cuisine, lit. "head of the kitchen," from Fr. chief "leader, ruler, head" (see chief).

I noted the words "especially" and "usually" in the first definition, as they seem to leave an awful lot of wiggle room, and the second definition even more so. Still, it seems to me that the maximum requirements would include some or all of the following:

1. Menu planning
2. Food ordering (shopping)
3. Food prep and/or the overseeing of food prep
4. The supervision of kitchen staff, if any

I don't see any requirements for getting paid or for having a degree.

On that note, I checked the Oregon State licensing website, and there is no educational requirement (*or any requirements*) for the position of "Chef", save the generic food handlers card.

Also, and I think many folks don't know this, a culinary school diploma does not grant one the title of chef. It's simply an associates' degree (*sometimes just a certificate, depending on the school*) in culinary arts, hospitality, pastry arts, food service, etc.

Grandpa (Chef) Perkins, front and center, with his crew at Timberline Lodge, preparing to cook for President Roosevelt.

No title is conferred with the degree. While the degree is a lot more common than it used to be, it's still neither a requirement nor an automatic conferral. Here's a great comment I found on a similar post, that looks at the title in a different way:

"IMHO, a 'cook' is someone who has a good mastery of basic cooking/kitchen techniques and can follow a recipe and turn out really good food. A 'chef' takes cooking to the next level by creating new dishes, new combinations of flavors, etc. Kind of like the difference between someone who can read music and play an instrument vs. a composer."

So, I guess I just don't see a "chef" being a solely professional position, as much as a position of accepted, or granted, responsibility.

At the same time, a little education can go a long way. Not everyone is lucky (well, *mostly lucky*) enough to come from a multi-generational professional cooking family, and if you're going be great at anything, you have to learn somewhere, right?

Classically Trained

I think that if I hear one more cooking school graduate brag about being "classically trained" I'm going to beat him to death with a hotel pan (*I'm joking…I'm joking…I wouldn't ruin a perfectly good hotel pan…*)

In 1895, French journalist Marthe Distel wanted to create a method of training women in culinary arts, for use in the running of their households.

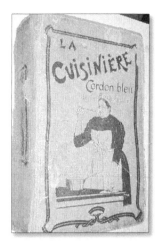

She began *'La Cuisinière Cordon Bleu'*, a publication which revolutionized the world of culinary arts, until then the preserve of men. (*Go Marthe!*) Such was the success of her magazine, she decided to take the next step: offering her readers cookery lessons.

She founded Le Cordon Bleu school of Culinary Arts in Paris in 1895.

So, 1895…that's pretty much the beginning of the "professional cooking school" and a pretty cool story, however, to call that "classical training" would ignore the fact that people had been learning to cook, as a profession, for many, many centuries (*you don't think all those inbred blue-bloods cooked for themselves, do you?*)

No, cooks and chefs had been trained the same way since time out of mind..

Dad, behind one of Grandpa's restaurants (about age 6), that's the "smoke house" behind him, and I have it on good authority that there's a moonshine still behind that.

Apprenticeship

The modern idea of a restaurant – as well as the term itself – appeared in Paris in the 18th century. For centuries Paris had taverns which served food at large common tables, but they were notoriously crowded, noisy, not very clean, and served food of dubious quality.

In about 1765 a new kind of eating establishment, called a "Bouillon", was opened on rue des Poulies, near the Louvre, by a man named Boulanger. It had separate tables, a menu, and specialized in soups made with a base of meat and eggs, which were said to be *restaurants* or, in English "restoratives". Other similar *bouillons* soon opened around Paris. Thanks to Boulanger and his imitators, these soups moved from the category of remedy into the category of health food and ultimately into the category of ordinary food.

Much like myself, young boys were turned over to a grouchy, heavy handed task-master of a chef in these restoratives, and came up through the ranks starting out (*unpaid, btw...another thing we have in common*) sleeping on the floor of stock rooms (*to discourage rats*), and starting fires in the ovens before dawn. From there they graduated to janitors and dishwashers, then to prep-monkeys, peeling potatoes and onions for years before they were allowed to so much as toast bread.

By the time they were actually working a station in the kitchen, they knew it inside and out, it was in their blood, and they had experienced (*and likely been clouted for*) every possible problem and disaster as they came naturally, and learned how to solve them.

That...is a *classically* trained chef.

By comparison, a 2-year culinary-arts program is more like a crash course in high-speed, high volume cooking and the business of running a restaurant kitchen. Now, please don't take this as a bash on schools like CIA or Le Cordon Bleu. If the latter was good enough for Julia, it's good enough for me.

I just hesitate at the (*often knee-jerk*) opinion that you can't be a chef, or aren't properly trained, unless you've been to culinary school, when there are many, many fantastic cooks out there, running the kitchens in some great restaurants, who's entire culinary education started at the dish-washing station. Many of them don't speak much English, either...but that's a different soapbox.

For me, maybe the real question is...is *anyone else* calling me *Chef?*

The Mystique of the Professional Chef

In my Dad's time, coming home and telling the folks that you wanted to cook for a living garnered about as much excitement as saying that you got a job in the euthanasia room at the local animal shelter.

Probably less, depending on your part of the country.

Nowadays, it's considered a skilled occupation to be proud of (*true*) with the possibility of stardom and riches (*probably not true*) in the future.

The job itself actually hadn't changed much.

There's also a lot of Hollywood fan-boy, backstage door rock star mystique these days about the professional chef.

It's a load of crap.

Let me repeat...**it's a load of crap.**

For some reason, our society wants to worship those we feel we can never be. Our heroes, through the generations are those who are the very best at what we, at best, might be a little bit good at.

I say cog's wallop.

(That's Shakespearean for bullshit, *btw...)*

Ignore the man behind the curtain *(yeah, that's him...the one in the white jacket and funny hat.)*

He's got 'nuthing you don't have, he can do nothing you can't learn to do. He's not a god come down from Olympus, he (*or she*) is just another schlep, just like you and me, who did the work.

There are no Wizards...or maybe we're all wizards, either way.

You can be the cowardly lion, or you can be Toto.

Does it take years of cuts and burns and 12-hour shifts, grinding it out in a steaming kitchen? No. In fact, many chef's skill level actually declines over the years, once they're out from under the scrutiny of a drill-master Chef instructor.

Don't believe me? Watch a few episodes of *Restaurant Impossible!*

It's about *learning* and *doing*. Learning as much as you can, then doing it over and over to hone your skills until they're as sharp as...well, a chef's knife,

There are only two people out there who want you to believe that fine cooking is an art, a gift from God bestowed on a select few, and unattainable to the lovely average peasant.

Television executives and insecure chefs.

(In all fairness most chefs are insecure, and most of us are fairly neurotic to boot, but my point still stands.)

Why is the title *Chef* important?

So, given all of that, why is it even important to have a category of "Home Chef", and moreover, why is it important to consider yourself one of them?

It's about self-recognition and opening the door to self-discovery. It's perceiving and acknowledging that you have "graduated" to a higher skill level in your cooking. The difference between considering yourself a home chef, and just being someone "who cooks for my family", is that it gives you permission to explore.

To take responsibility for your own growth, and to acknowledge in yourself the value of possessing a passion beyond the norm.

PS - Why I don't work in restaurants any more…

I don't have to be the general, but I make a lousy foot-soldier.

I've been in the business long enough that I can eat the occasional crap-sandwich from the boss if I must, but it's not in my nature to smile and ask for another.

My wife likes to say that I *"do not suffer fools well"*, and whether this is from a type-A personality, or just blatant hubris, it's still a fact.

The option of bottling it up, and living in a home with holes punched in most of the walls *(welcome to my childhood)*, was not especially attractive to me either.

"Listen to your appetite...
    And play with your food."
                    -- Alton Brown

Dad

Being raised in the kitchen, if the dishwashers were my delinquent older cousins, sharing nips from the flask, and drags from their back-alley smokes with the adoring pre-teen son of their boss, then waitresses were my doting aunts and big sisters, quick with a dessert, a free soda, *(and the occasional over exuberant hug)*. In my father's kitchens, if you survived long enough to have your name remembered, you were family.

And, as with the rest of his family, while HE might a merciless bastard to you on a daily basis, God help the stranger who presumed to do so.

It was a busy New Year's Eve, and the entire dining room was, of course, ripped to the gills. Food was flying out and tips were rolling back, the din in the kitchen was deafening, and everything seemed it's perfect mad happy chaos.

A chef unconsciously keeps one ear in the kitchen, and one on the front of house, and he can sense, on a psychic level, when the mood in the dining room slips off the rails.

I saw Dad look up from the roast he was tying...once, twice, towards the pass, his brow furrowed. Just as he straightened up, there was a crash from the other side of the wall.

A moment later the doors swung open and a young waitress, Candy, I think her name was *(this was thirty years ago, after all, so that might not be her name, but I do remember that she always had root-beer barrel candies in her apron pocket, so we'll call her Candy)*, burst into the kitchen.

She was in tears.

"I...I spilled his drink... He said to go find him a waitress that wasn't too stupid to do her job. He threw his glass."

My father trimmed a last bit of butcher's string, and set his knife down on his board. "Which table?"

The kitchen became a mausoleum. The clanging, slamming, cursing cacophony of a moment earlier, now an echoing marble tomb, as dad removed his apron, hung it on the wall, and walked out into the dining room.

I distinctly remember a young dishwasher whispering, "Oh, shit..."

Peeking through the pass *(my nose stuffed into the door crack with about a dozen others)*, I watched as dad walked up to the table, picked up the man's current drink *(which had just been replaced)* and casually upended it in the tipsy businessman's ample, wool-suited lap. Then he set both knotted, scarred, steam-burned fists on the tabletop and leaned forward until their noses very nearly touched.

"You ever throw another glass at my waitress, asshole, and I promise...you'll be having dinner in the hospital...through a tube."

As the man sputtered, my father peeled three twenties off of the gangster roll of tips he kept in his pocket *(likely for occasions just such as these)* and tossed them on the table. Then turned to the waitress.

"This gentlemen" he said, "will be eating somewhere else tonight."

Then he walked back to the kitchen, smiling and nodding to the other guests. He paused at the doors, looking back *(and this is where he became the coolest guy ever)*...

"And Candy? If his fat ass is still in my restaurant in sixty seconds...come get me, and then call an ambulance."

How could you not live in awe of *that?*

Chapter Two
Cooking at Home

"A good cook is the peculiar gift of the gods. He must be a perfect creature from the brain to the palate, from the palate to the finger's end." – Walter Savage Landor

Honestly, I don't much care for the term "home cook".

(Which may seem strange for someone who does meal planning for a living...but I'll explain...)

Despite it being descriptively accurate, IE: "a person who cooks in their home", what should be a badge of honor has become a caste term to designate someone who is "lower" or less skilled than the professional chef.

The glitz and glitter of the recent explosion of food television's popularity has, for many, created a level of misunderstanding and misinterpretation as to what "cooking" really is, and that is having a dangerously undermining effect of home cooking in our society.

But, for lack of a better title *(and because I despise the phrase "amateur cook")*, I'll use the term home cook, and do what little I can to elevate it back towards the status it deserves. It's no secret that many home cooks have skills and experience that matches and even exceeds that of their professional counterparts.

In fact, many of the "celebrity chefs" that are well known and beloved in our new food culture, were never really "chefs" at all.

Rachael Ray and Nigella Lawson are two of the biggest names in the culinary world, but neither are professionally trained chefs.

> *...no one is born a great cook, one learns by doing.*
> *~ Julia Child, "My Life in France"*

Self-trained and having never worked in a commercial chef position, they are just two examples of skilled and famous "home cooks" who have hit it big.

Oh, add to that list Julia Child, of course. *(Julia did attend Le Cordon Bleu in Paris, but except for her own cooking shows, never cooked in a professional setting.)*

Some would say that the title of "chef" has to do with formal education, which is, again, a ridiculous argument, as culinary schools have only been around for a couple of hundred years *(remember, there wasn't much in the way of a "restaurant industry" before the French revolution of 1789)* and even then, they teach and revere the methods developed by chefs who never attended any form of culinary school...or in some cases, any school at all.

Many of our modern chefs never received any formal cooking education either, including *Paula Deen, Gordon Ramsey, Rachel Ray, Charlie Trotter, Thomas Keller (!), Ina Garten, Jamie Oliver, Ferran Adria, Alice Waters, Wolfgang Puck*, and the list goes on.

The point is that if you take away all that "other stuff", then YOU have, or can develop, all of the same *cooking* skills in your home kitchen, to cook great food, and you can do it as good as anyone I've mentioned here.

If fact, without the pressure of high volume cooking, the drive for turn-over, the constraints of menu, the need to multitask, and the need to cook at a profit...you should be able to cook BETTER food than a chef in a commercial kitchen!

> *I can teach a chimp how to make linguini and clams. I can't teach a chimp to dream about it and think about how great it is.*
> *~ Mario Batali*

One of the best arguments we have for the legitimacy of the home chef comes, ironically, from the same cable networks that seek to elevate the term "chef" to a level of celebrity.

If you've ever watched a food-centric show that involves travel outside of the United States, you know what I'm talking about. Every time a chef or "host" visits a home and is offered a meal, it is invariably the best meal of the trip, regardless of how many world famous chefs or restaurants they've visited.

Hosts ask chefs where they learned to cook, and the answer is almost always in their mother's, or grandmother's kitchen.

Even that age-old kitchen game *"If you have 24 hours to live, what would your last meal be"* is answered with simple yet beloved dishes from the childhood home kitchen, and not some fancy Michelin star restaurant's tasting menu.

What then makes a "home chef?"

The home kitchen is the primal hearth from which all cooking was born.

It is where most of us first watched, and touched, and tasted, and smelled the delicious alchemy of earth and water and fire and flesh, and it deserves a higher honor in our society than to have become the repository of canned "food", frozen "meals", and boxes of fill-in-the-blank-Helper.

My daughter Grace learning the ropes

If we are to reverse the current trend of disdainful disregard, we must first agree that the definition is NOT anyone who cooks at home.

My nine-year-old daughter Grace could pour boiling water into a cup of noodles, or spread peanut butter on bread, if we agree that this makes her a "home cook", then we are as responsible for that disdain, as anyone. *(BTW, she's a pretty darn accomplished cook in her own right, and I never even made her sleep on the pantry floor…)*

Just as a "home mechanic" can have as good, or even greater skills than a professional mechanic, they still both must know how to take an engine apart, put it back together, and have it run, to be considered a competent mechanic…a home chef must know how to cook. Not thaw and nuke, not dump and stir…but COOK.

When I say I can cook, I mean I can melt cheese on stuff.

If we do not hold the term to a certain standard, then we are part of the problem.

Here is one of the best descriptions I've found for what, beyond financial compensation, makes a chef…and I would say the same goes for what I consider a home cook…

"A chef has to be responsible for the soul of the food. A chef should have a deep understanding of how to cook many types of food, what flavors go together, how to handle kitchen equipment (knife skills, etc.,), and so on. A chef should not require the directions part of a recipe, and usually shouldn't require the amounts in a recipe, either."

In other words, it's all about the *food*, knowing what to do with it, and having a *passion* for making it great…just like the home cook.

The Home Chef

Home Chef: One who actively purses a deeper understanding of food and cooking, who constantly seeks to broaden their culinary experiences, who tenaciously studies new styles and techniques to improve their skill, and who finds their joy in sharing good food with those they love.

Home Chef…it's a new term, one that has not, until now, had precedence in history.

For hundreds of years, since the first "restoratives" (*i.e.: restaurants*) opened in France, following the toppling of the French monarchy (*and their heads*) and the world's first "professional" cooks who worked for them suddenly found themselves without employment, the commercial chef and the home cook have eyed each other distrustfully across a wide abyss of training, technique, mythology and methodology.

That began to change on November 23, 1993 when **TV Food Network** was launched.

Okay, that's not exactly true, Julia Child paved the road for Emeril, Bobby, and all of the other "celebrity chefs" with The French Chef in 1963, as did Graham Kerr with the introduction of The Galloping Gourmet in 1969, but the globalization of food-related television really exploded in the early nineties.

The point being that starting back then, and increasing exponentially over the last two decades, the line began to blur.

Techniques and terminology what were previously only available and comprehensible to those who indentured themselves to a restaurant kitchen at a young age, or shelled out the bucks to attend culinary school, have become commonly and easily available to anyone who is willing to watch and study what is being offered for free (*or at least for a minimal cable television subscription*) and cares to pay attention.

> ***Please take note*** *of that last paragraph…words like "watch", "study", and "pay attention" are key. Sitting on your rear-end, sucking down Doritos and staring vapidly at a chili throw-down, ain't what I'm talking about here.*

I'm talking about people who watch the right shows (*more "Good Eats", less "Hell's Kitchen" please*) on Food Network, Cooking Channel,

Travel Channel, and an increasing number non-cable channels, with a pen and notepad in hand, and then test and practice what they learn in the "lab" of their own home kitchen, treating the medium more like correspondence courses, and less like a mindless hybrid of foodie game shows and kitchen soap operas.

Knife skills, French techniques, building on mother-sauces, deglazing, *mise en place*...

We can take what is actually about the *cooking* from these shows, and winnow the gold nuggets from the falderal of high-pressure, turn-and-burn techniques designed specifically to keep you alive and cooking through a 300-cover night, and not necessarily about creating two, four, or six perfect plates of food for your family.

Another amazing resource, possibly an even better one than the cable network shows, that has helped bring about this cooking evolution are online video sources like YouTube.

A note on videos: When researching a technique on YouTube or other video channels, watch the same technique done by several different people (all with high scores) and watch for what they do the same, and what they do different. This will help you glean the "best practices" for that specific technique.

Here, instead of being at the mercy of a television show's production calendar, you can actively search out short "how to" videos on specific techniques, often presented by professional chefs, on thousands of culinary subjects and recipes.

It's like having a free, private cooking instructor in your own kitchen!

The Home Chef vs. the Professional Chef

Understand this: one is not more or less than the other, or at least it doesn't have to be.

There are those who aren't interested in being a "home chef", just like there are those of us who couldn't care less about knowing how to change our own oil (*sorry, Dad!*) And, as the hippies say...*that's okay.*

Nobody really has to know how to Sousvide an egg, or chiffonade parsley, or blanch a duck, to put a fresh, healthy and delicious dinner in front of their family...as long as they can do the latter, that's all the skill anyone really *needs* to have.

Chefs are a little...different. Note the look on the lady's face when my friend Chef Chris Renner open the immersion circulation we got him for his birthday.

The Home Cook, and the Professional Chef are each their own animal, and now the *Home Chef* is an evolving hybrid of the two...someone who cooks nearer a "professional level" of quality (*if not quantity*) using and improving on the classic "Mom's methods" with two-plus centuries of techniques and styles perfected by professionals. I point out "quantity" because this is a large part of what you're paying for at culinary school...

It's not just the techniques, it's how to perform them on a massive scale very, very quickly, in such a way as to conserve costs and maximize profitability, the business of professional cooking...but none of which are skills required when cooking at home.

With the availability of online (*or on-air*) education, these are really the only factors that will separate the professional chef from the dedicated home chef of the future. It's an exciting time to cook in, and those of you who are willing to research study, and practice, practice, practice are ushering in a new age of food in the home kitchen.

You are the new home chefs!

Homework Assignment #1

Trying New Things

Below, list nine dishes you wish you could cook, or cook better, and one food you don't like, but are willing to try in a new way...

Take your time, look through some cookbooks, think of some dishes you almost ordered at your favorite restaurants.

Now, go to your planner, and commit to learning one of these dishes every two weeks, or once a month.

Remember, YouTube is your friend!

1._____

2._____

3._____

4._____

5._____

6._____

7._____

8._____

9._____

One food I don t like:_____

Being a Home Chef isn't about what you have to know, or what you have to do. It's about pursuing the skills and techniques that allow you to do what you want to do, whenever you want to do it. It's about freedom, not rules, enjoyment, not legalism.

~ Notes ~

My little sous chef Grace checking out a key ingredient...

Chapter Three

The Adventurous Chef is an Adventurous Eater

Before you raise people's expectations, you must change their preconceptions" ~ Jonathan White

There are those who might disagree with the title of the chapter, but I believe it with all of my heart. And, as it is my soapbox (and my book), you're going to hear about it too. ;) Being a chef is being a *lover of food*, and by which I mean twenty-two year old, sex-on-the-beach, tropical island honeymoon kinda lover. Show me a chef who doesn't want to try new things, experience new ingredients and flavors to share with their diners...and I'll show you a chef who's lost their passion...and likely their way.

Book knowledge and technique expertise are fine and good (*and important*), but love is about *passion*, and passion creates a yearning for adventure, for discovery, and for unique experiences...like watching my long-suffering and completely fearless Sous Chef, Sarah Bjorklund, eat her first *balut*.

[47]

Wondering for a moment if she was going to reverse engines, and then finally seeing her grin and mumble, around a mouthful of baby duck parts...

"That's *really* good!"

People ask me, quite a lot surprisingly, why I enjoy and get so excited about some of the "bizarre" foods I research, cook, write about, and eat.

I sat down and thought about that for a while (*with a nice headcheese sandwich, of course*) and I think it comes down to this...

Firstly, I refute that there are any "bizarre" foods, period. There are foods that may seem strange and alien to you and I, just as some of *our* favorite things to eat may seem just as strange to people in other parts of the world (*ask a native of China about cheese sometime, or an Amazonian child about peanut-butter...*)

I never cook or eat anything for shock value, and would never encourage anyone else to try something that I'm not at least optimistic that they will like, even if that enjoyment often comes with equal parts trepidation. Food is not dare...food is *gift* that I can give in one of the few ways that are unique to me.

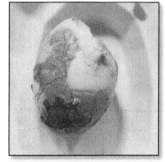

If I cook for you, I like you. End of story.

> *To me, life without veal stock, pork fat, sausage, organ meat, demi-glace, or even stinky cheese is a life not worth living.*
>
> ~ *Anthony Bourdain*

Secondly I am, in my own nature, a hedonist. I enjoy pleasure, and one of the pleasures I enjoy most is eating good food, and the idea that there might be something out there, in some other society, culture, or time period that might bring me new pleasure or even more gastronomic enjoyment than I've experienced up until now, drives me to explore and experiment, always looking for my "new favorite food."

For all intents and purposes, I'm a junkie…always looking for the next, bigger, high. This is common among chefs, known as "chasing the dragon…" Plus, based on my (*still limited*) exposure to these new foods, at least nine out ten that I try are enjoyable, and fully half are downright delicious…let's face it, nobody eats food they don't like, if they can help it. If whole societies enjoy something, or at least find it palatable, the optimist in me has to wonder if I might too.

Based solely on those numbers, it would be foolish, given my accepted hedonistic tendencies, to NOT want to find and try new things.

Gracie and a "friend" getting ready to cook dinner.

Lastly, I see the obvious ignorance and prejudice of deeming something outside of my own experience as "weird, gross, or bizarre."

What Chef Andrew Zimmern (*Bizarre Foods*) refers to as "contempt prior to investigation."

> *"There is no sincerer love than the love of food."*
> ~ *George Bernard Shaw*

Many folks I know think of kimchi, a cherished and epitomic food of Korea, as "bizarre", but if they had, through chance, or providence (*or just good luck*) been born Korean...or even been raised in Korea, they would, in all likelihood, have grown up loving kimchi as much as most native Koreans do, where it's about as bizarre as French fries.

The only thing that makes a food, any food, "bizarre", are the memories, experiences, and cultural bias that one grows up with. It's not nature, it's nurture. It's all just neurons firing this way and that, telling me what to like and not like based on nothing more than the rut they've formed in my brain.

Now you may not like a food once you've tried it (*tripe and century eggs are on my own list, lol*), or at least tried one preparation of it, but not liking a flavor or texture, which is a perfectly justifiable conclusion to an experiment, does NOT make a food "bizarre" or "gross", which could be considered an ignorant judgement on those who DO, it just means you don't like that one preparation of it.

Nothing tells us "who we are" more than the foods we eat and, frankly, I don't like to be told who I am. It's arrogant presumption...even when it's myself doing it.

> *I love simple food. I like to serve the entire animal, not only because it somehow provokes a customer to think about it, but also because to honor of the animal that has been killed for us to eat, you have to eat the whole thing. It would be silly to just eat the chops and throw everything else away.*
>
> *~ Mario Batali*

Pork and Prejudice

"Pa skinned it for them carefully, and into the long end he thrust a sharpened stick. Ma opened the front of the cookstove and raked the hot coals out into the iron hearth.

Then Laura and Mary took turns holding the pig's tail over the coals.

It sizzled and fried and drops of fat dripped and blazed on the coals. Ma sprinkled it with salt...At last it was done, it was nicely browned all over, and how good it smelled! They carried it into the yard to cool it, and even before it was cool enough they began tasting it and burned their tongues. They ate every little bit of meat off the bones, and then they gave the bones to Jack.

And that was the end of the pig's tail. There would not be another one till next year."

– Little House in the Big Woods, Laura Ingalls Wilder

During a recent trip through our local WinCo, which, like most large grocery stores that cater to a wide variety of ethnic groups, has a meat department that is stocked with practically everything you need to assemble your own pig or cow...(*I love that!*), I found, nestled innocently between the trotters and tripe, were these beauties...pork tails!

My inner *Zimmern* instantly leapt forward. I mean, how different could they be from chicken wings, pope's noses, and lamb neck bones...all of which I love?

Except…they're pork…that most loveliest of meats, most noble of beasts, and the divine proof that God loves us and wants us to be happy. Besides, they were a buck a pound. Into the cart they went.

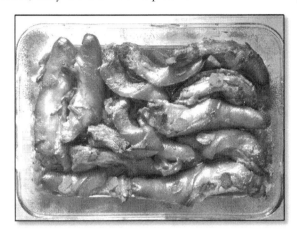

Getting home, I didn't have a recipe for pork tails handy *(alas, my copy of Fergus Henderson's The Whole Beast: Nose to Tail Eating, has not yet arrived)* nor did I bother with The Google. It's pig…I know how to cook pig:

Salty/Savory Dry Rub + Assorted Pig Parts + Low & Slow Roasting = Perfection

So, a loving massage with a liberal blanket of my favorite bbq rub, and into the oven at 250. Two hours covered in foil, another two hours uncovered.

How'd they turn out?

Well, let's come back to that in a second.

> *Food is symbolic of love when words are inadequate."*
> *~ Alan D. Wolfelt*

Foodies have long grumbled about the lack of quality *(and variety)* of meat available in the local supermarket, outside of the standard steaks, roasts, and assorted bird appendages, if you wanted anything different, historically, you either had to visit an ethic "specialty shop"…or raise it yourself.

With the growing food movement, and increasing acceptance and demand for traditional ethic dishes (*and not just the Americanized versions of them*)…well, the times they are a'changing.

In addition to a desire for variety, there's also a growing concern with the issue of wastage. Because consumers today like their meat packaged up in those easy-to-cook cuts, much of the carcass is thrown away — *the sign of a rich and disinterested society, IMO* – even though, with a little time and attention, much of it is not only edible but delicious.

With hunger, especially child hunger, becoming an ever-increasing tragedy in our country, and around the world, the ability to feed twice as many people from a single animal is more than a no-brainer, it's a moral imperative.

Thus, the "nose-to-tail" movement, endorsed enthusiastically by a new generation of "celebrity chefs" is exploding in popularity.

> *He was a bold man that first ate an oyster.*
> ~ *Jonathan Swift*

Let's face it – you can eat the same delicious and interesting foods, prepared by the "stars" of the culinary world, for cheap, all while feeling smug and superior as part of a "counter-cultural movement". In my hometown of Portland, this is enough to make your wool-clad toes curl up in your Birkenstocks…

In other words, it's about as close to foodie heaven-on-earth as you can get.

Ironically, this "new way of eating" is really just a return to how the entire pre-industrialized world ate, as a necessity, from the dawn of mankind all the way up to "Little House on the Prairie" days (*and is still the norm in much of the world.*)

One leader in this movement is Fergus Henderson, an English chef who is noted for his use of offal (*organ meat*) and other neglected cuts as a consequence of his philosophy of Nose To Tail Eating.

Celebrity chefs such as Anthony Bourdain and Mario Batali, and many others, have praised Henderson for his dishes, which optimize British food while making full use of the whole animal.

Henderson's restaurant, St John, was awarded a Michelin star in 2009.

In 1999 Henderson published *Nose to Tail Eating*, in which he provides recipes incorporating trotters, tripe, kidneys, chitterlings, and other parts.

Henderson also explains the philosophy behind his cooking explaining that "it seems common sense and even polite to the animal to use all of it."

In 2007, he published the sequel, *Beyond Nose to Tail*.

"On other pages," writes Henderson, "I have sung the praises of how the pig's snout and belly both have that special lip-sticking quality of fat and flesh merging.

This occurs in no part of the animal as wonderfully as on the tail.

Like an ice cream on a stick, a pig's tail offers up all of the above on a well-behaved set of bones."

By the way, if you have access to pork tails, and a desire to eat them, you're the kind of serious eater who needs this book!

The tails they use are referred to as "long tails" as opposed to the docked version you typically find *(as I did)* here in the States.

Food for Thought...

"People who love to eat are always the best people." - Julia Child

joinmykitchen.com

So, how did my own experiment turn out?

Holy Smokes!

These pork tails are the reason I roast whole pigs…that amazing combination of chewy/crispy/fatty/intensely porky flavor you find in a perfectly cooked bit of pig skin. So full of collagen that your fingers and lips stick together and your teeth feel deliciously gummy after you finish. Seriously, this is one of the Top 10 best bites of food I've ever had. It's the chicken-wing appetizer version of a whole roast pig. Awesome! And, I'm not the only one who thinks so.

Here's a great description, which I whole-heartedly concur with…

"Unlike oxtail, the tails of pigs come with the skin intact so that each segment is a perfect cross-section of skin, fat, tendon, and meat. Fried or roasted, the skin of the tail is chewy and crisp, with a gelatinous layer underneath. Tail flesh is fork-tender like that of the neck bones, but meatier in composition than trotters. There's a modest amount of tendon around each bony hub—just enough to make the gnawing enjoyable, but not so much as to distract from the whole. All in all, a tail is a little porky universe unto itself, a powerful reminder that the discarded cuts of the animal are often the most delicious."

– *"The Nasty Bits: Crisp Fried Pig's Tail"* – by *Chichi Wang, serious eats*

My recipe is a pretty basic, "roast 'em and eat 'em with your fingers" *ala* Laura Ingalls. If you want to get a little more hoity-toity with your hog-waggers, Google *"Pig au Vin* recipe from Serious Eats", as well as the *Crisp Fried* recipe in Wang's article above.

Oh, and for those who are sensitive to such things, I would recommend cutting the finished tails into 3-5 "bite-size" sections each, as the whole tail can appear a bit *ahem* *suggestive*...if you know what I mean. Looking back, I can't sum it up any better than Ms. Ingalls did..."*even before it was cool enough they began tasting it and burned their tongues*"

Laura baby...you and me!

> *I don't seek out foods because they're "bizarre", I explore new foods because I refuse to live my life in a cage built of my limited experiences and culture, declaring in my own ignorance that beyond the edge of my tiny map of knowledge "there be dragons...and they're gross."*

Author's Rant: You would not believe (*or maybe you would*) the grief I got when I mentioned this adventure on Facebook. People who wouldn't hesitate to eat those mystery-meat and rat-feces mush tubes we call "turkey" hot dogs, were gagging and grossing out over the idea of eating a pork tail. One reader actually posted that she "threw up in her mouth" at the thought. Another commented that he agreed with his child's assessment that the tail was "too close to the poop."

When I asked him where he thought the ham was located, there was no response. I'm assuming his five-year-old didn't know.

Anyway, I'm not sure why I continue to be shocked and disappointed in the Pollyanna viewpoint that most Americans have about food, and their flat out refusal to eat anything that can't find on the menu at their local McDullards...it makes me sad. Although, with only one tail per pig, if this ever becomes the new *haute cuisine*, I'd probably never be able to afford them again. So there you go. On a similar note...

Recently, I posted a photo of one of my newborn rabbit kits, on Facebook. Even though I deliberated only shared it with those on my "Friend" list, the responses still took me aback.

"OMG to tiny and adorable." (*Okay, that one was true*)

"Cute, yes. Eat him up, No!"

"If you cook this, I unfriend you for life!"

"So does it at least get to grow up?" (*Seriously?*)

First of all, A properly roasted rabbit, from a classic French recipe, is one of the best things you'll ever eat.

Secondly...got some news for you folks...baby chickens, baby cows, baby pigs...all very cute, lol...if you choose to disassociate yourself with that reality by only seeing shrink wrapped "meat" at the grocery store, that's up to you.

The difference to keep in mind is that that "meat" you're buying spends it's short life in dark, crowded, filthy cages, being fed the cheapest materials possible. My animals have fresh air, fresh food, room to run, and one bad day. Perhaps the most enlightening of the dozens of comments I received...

> *"I'll take your word for it on the bunnies... Chickens, cows etc... they don't pull at my heartstrings. Bunnies, I will just eat in a restaurant so I don't have to see their face."*

I don't have to apologize for my food, or live in denial of its origins, and neither do you.

Why can't so very many of the very people who are fighting to protect "the natural world" not grasp the concept of the food chain?

Of predator and prey?

That the very thing that they're suggesting is the most unnatural thing we could ever do? As a hunter, I can also testify that, anyone who has seen what a pack of coyotes will do to a new-born fawn, might think twice about how "natural" they want things to be.

> *A gourmet once challenged me to eat*
> *A tiny bit of rattlesnake meat.*
> *Remarking, "don't look horror-stricken*
> *You'll find it tastes a lot like chicken."*
> *It did.*
> *Now chicken I cannot eat*
> *Because it tastes like rattlesnake meat.*
>
> — *Ogden Nash*
> *"Experiment Degustatory"*

Speaking of pork...

Two of my favorite "deep end of the pool" stories are from our annual church camp-outs stretching back over the last decade or more. Each year I roast a whole pig in camp on my La Caja China, as the centerpiece to a huge potluck meal.

The kids, of which there are many (my youth group peers were fruitful and multiplied), are also fascinated by the process and I seem to cook in the middle a small, ever changing, herd of grubby younglings, who want to watch the fire, peek at the piggy, or sweet-talk me out of something yummy.

As often as not, all three.

On year, I jokingly dared one of the older boys to eat the roasted pig eyeball from the finished beast, and not to be out-manned in front of the girls, he did so. Word got around. Within a couple of years my van would be swarmed even as I arrived at camp, with kids shouting to secure the bragging rights to one of these porky trophies, an act of bravado which was by now being carried out center-stage in from of all of the pot-luck attendees with pomp and circumstance.

It all started the first year, as I was carving up the hog for serving, and started teasing the boy about eating that first eyeball - which, after 8 hours of roasting was really little more than a chewy chunk of muscle. One of our best friends (*a fine cook herself*) wandered over to see what the commotion was all about. When she realized the origin of the nasty-bit in my hand, she grimaced, made a gagging noise, and declared my obvious bluff as, "Disgusting!"

There was, of course, only one thing I could do at that point. Before she had time to turn away, I grinned and popped the eyeball into my mouth, chewing noisily and groaning with pleasure (*and seriously...they're pretty good.*)

Jeni vapor locked, her face going the color of new-fallen snow as her jaw dropped. Her eyes glazed over, and I literally saw her mind "go away for a moment" in disbelief.

"That...that did not happen..." she stammered, mostly, I'm convinced, to herself. There are no words in the English canon to adequately describe the look on her face when I toss that eye into my mouth. It was one of the great moments of my life.

But, as they say, sometimes you eat the bear, and sometimes the bear eats you...

A few years later, one of the kiddos (an adorable elvish-faced little girl of about seven) secured her spot the instant I arrived. She was one of those littles that, on first glance, strangers automatically cant their heads and say, "Awwww..."

Anyway, as she popped the steaming morsel into her mouth, in front of a hundred-odd family and fellow parishioners, I watched in dawning horror, as her eyes went wide and her throat visibly constricted.

Once...twice...

In that moment, in a sudden wash of cold sweat, a thought occurred to me that I had not previously considered...I was about to be the man who made the cutest little girl in   camp toss her cookies (and likely cry) in front of the entire congregation.

She was a trooper and swallowed hard (literally) and I was spared a potential stoning to death, but it was a close thing. I seem to remember a couple of extra "thank you's" in my evening prayers that night. Pig eyeballs and me...we go way back.

And, don't freak out on me...no one's going to ask you to eat an eyeball. Adventurous eating is all about baby steps...you don't START with the eyeball, you start with the cheek and work your way UP to the eyeball!

The History of Denial

During the age of British exploration, it was common practice when officers brought their wives and families to remote corners of the world for extended tours, to rename the local meats so as to protect the ladies delicate sensibilities.

Thus, rice patty rat, jungle snake, or old camel, would be served as "Indian Pork", or "South American Hare."

Items that were too easy to distinguish the origins of, would be served to the lady (*and eaten from under*) a large white napkin.

(Hence, the name of our adventure-eating club, "The White Napkin Gastronome Society")

> **Looking to expand your adventurous eating, or just want to dip your toe in? Be sure to check out my "Deep End of the Pool" recipes in the "My Recipes" section under *Resources*.**

The Senses

Enjoying food is about more than just tasting.

We've all heard the old adage, "we eat first with our eyes" (*more on that later*), but I would say that our noses come a close second. The sense of smell is a powerful thing, able to conjure up memories and emotions, good or bad, that we've long forgotten…or create new ones.

One afternoon, while on our honeymoon in Victoria, BC., my wife and I stopped into a very popular English-style pub for lunch.

She ordered (*more sensibly*) the fish & chips, while I…ever the treasure hunter, chose the provocatively named *Steak and Kidney Pie*, which I'd heard of, but had never tried. Our plates arrived and a beautiful, mahogany crusted pot-pie was set before me.

My mouth watering with anticipation, I broke the crust with my spoon…and that's as far as I got.

As the hot steam wafted up from the pie, I glanced up to see my wife's face pale and her jaw lock. She suddenly looked like someone trying very hard not to say something.

I asked what was wrong.

"Nothing…" She replied.

"No, really…are you okay?"

"It, um…it…"

"What?"

"It…smells like hot cat-food."

My throat clamped shut faster than a politician's fist around a bribe, as my stomach flip-flopped.

I never did get a bite of it to my mouth and, after a couple of tries, gave up and ordered a burger. 20 years later, my wife and I still refer to that as the "Steak and Cat-food Pie" lunch.

Looking back I'm just glad that *Spotted Dick* wasn't on the menu.

Real food doesn't **have ingredients.** *Real food* **is ingredients.**

#LiveLifeJuiced

On the Media, Corporate Food, and other Scum...

Look, it's no secret to those who know me that I'm a hopeless conspiracy theorist. My dream in to have my own bunker, a lifetime of ammo, and an endless supply of tin-foil hats.

That said...just because it's a conspiracy theory, doesn't mean it's not true.

Take corporate food...that corrupt, duplicitous band of bottom-feeding vipers that spend their every waking moment trying to shovel poison down our throats while calling it honey.

Make no mistake...the media, like the bloated food corporations whose boots they lick, cares about one thing, and one thing only...money. It will say whatever it takes, as often as it takes, regardless of the consequences to us, our families, or our country to sell one more nickel of airtime, or inch of print.

They are Jim Jones selling Kool-Aid on the school playground.

And nowhere is this more prevalent and obvious than in the world of food. U.S. consumers spent $1.46 trillion on food and beverages in grocery stores and other retailers and on away-from-home meals and snacks in 2014 (and the numbers are going up.) Bottom line, food is BIG business....the kind of money that makes a little "collateral damage" seem...acceptable.

American advertising extolls the virtues of innumerable foods that have been banned in more forward thinking countries around the world including (but by no means limited to): farm-raised salmon, Hawaiian (GMO) papaya, artificial food dyes, arsenic-laced chicken, ractopamine-tainted meat, bromate-containing drinks and bread, Olestra, carcinogenic preservatives, and rBGH-laced milk.

Farmed fish can also exposed to pesticides, along with compounds such as toxic copper sulfate, which is typically used to keep nets and tanks free of algae.

The big bucks stem from turning government-subsidized commodity crops—mainly corn, wheat, and soybeans—into fast foods, snack foods, and beverages.

> *Each year, food companies use an amount of salt that is every bit as staggering as it sounds: 5 billion pounds.*
> *~Michael Moss, Salt Sugar Fat: How the Food Giants Hooked Us*

High-profit products derived from these commodity crops are generally high in calories and low in nutritional value. Ultra-processed foods, for example, lack fiber, micronutrients, and healthful plant substances called phytochemicals that protect against heart disease and diabetes.

More than 3,000 food additives – preservatives, flavorings, colors, and other ingredients are added to US processed foods, including infant foods and those targeting young children. The most popularly used dyes in the country – red 40, yellow 5, yellow 6, and blue 2 – have been shown in research to cause behavioral problems, as well as cancer, birth defects, and other health issues.

Skittles and M&M's, which are dyed with Blue 1, Blue 2, Yellow 5, Yellow 6, and Red 40, had the highest levels found in candies. Skittles Original had 33.3 mg per serving; M&M's Milk Chocolate had 29.5 mg per serving. Both candies are made by Mars, Inc.

Kraft Macaroni & Cheese was found to have 17.6 mg of artificial dyes per serving.

Again, these are based on the minimal "suggested serving", which is typically far less than actual consumption.

According to the Purdue researchers, the amount of artificial food dye certified for use by the Food and Drug Administration has increased five-fold, per capita, between 1950 and 2012.

The researchers estimate that a child could easily consume 100 mg of dyes in a day and that some children could consume more than 200 mg per day.

Most FDA studies were conducted in the 1970's and 80's, giving children 26 mg of a mixture of dyes. Negative results from these tests were minimal, and many doctors concluded that a dye-free diet was pointless.

"Until now, how much of these neurotoxic chemicals are used in specific foods was a well-kept secret. But now it is clear that many children are consuming far more dyes than the amounts shown to cause behavioral problems in some children. The cumulative impact of so much dyed foods in children's diets, from breakfast, lunch, dinner, and snacks, is a partial reason why behavioral problems have become more common." - Michael F. Jacobson, CSPI* Executive Director

In countries where these food dyes and colors are banned, companies like Kraft employ natural colorants instead, like paprika extract, beet root, and annatto.

Why don't they do the same in the American Mac & Cheese and other widely consumed products?

We all know why...

Natural dyes are more expensive, and therefore lower the margin of profit for companies, like the aforementioned Kraft, whose (US only) annual revenue is north of 18 billion dollars.

According to the Federal Trade Commission and the Journal of Public Health Policy , food makers spend up to 10 billion annually to reach children through the traditional media as well the Internet, in-store advertising, and sweepstakes.

On TV alone, the average child sees about 5,500 food commercials a year (or about 15 per day) that advertise high-sugar breakfast cereals, fast food, soft drinks, candy, and snacks, according to the Yale Rudd Center for Food Policy and Obesity.

Compare that to the fewer than 100 TV ads per year kids see for healthy foods like fruits, veggies, and bottled water.

And it's not all just "junk"...many "healthy" replacement foods are little better than the foods they replace.

In 2006, for example, major beverage makers agreed to remove sugary sodas from school vending machines. But the industry mounted an intense lobbying effort that persuaded lawmakers to allow sports drinks and vitamin waters that—despite their slightly healthier reputations—still can be packed with sugar and calories.

And lastly, let's not forget to include the lobbyists.

Those corporate hired guns who are greasing the palms and blackmailing our (already corrupt) law makers in Washington.

Unless you follow politics closely, you might not realize that a group with a name like the "Center for Consumer Freedom" has anything to do with the food industry at all.

However, this group has lobbied aggressively against obesity-related public health campaigns—such as the one directed at removing junk food from schools—and is funded primarily through donations from big food companies such as Coca-Cola, Cargill, Tyson Foods, and Wendy's.

It comes down to this: allowing ourselves to be influenced by the "lure" of the fast, cheap, easy options that are being hawked by corporate food and their media minions these days is the moral equivalent of hiring a meth-addicted homicidal, prostitute to babysit our children...and that's a bad idea.

Make no mistake, the enemy is out there.

The best way to win this war against our families and children is to arm ourselves with the knowledge of what "real" food is, what "fake" food is, and to keep our bunkers stocked with as much of the former as possible. In other words...to be a Home Chef.

Tin-foil hats are optional.

*The Center for Science in the Public Interest (CSPI) is a Washington, D.C.-based non-profit watchdog and consumer advocacy group that advocates for safer and healthier foods.

On Cookbooks

To the home cook, a cookbook is an encyclopedia, a card catalog of recipes, most of which they'll never make.

Often bought on a whim for a single recipe, or a sexy cover, and likely destined for the attic or the garage-sale table in a never ending cycle of unreadedness (*I just made that word up.*)

To the *Home Chef*, however, a cookbook is a novel, a Homeric epic of adventure, and travel, suspense and romance, in which the reader is both hero and villain.

It's an heart-stopping page-turner that can't be put down, leading to midnight cooking sprees, and red-eyed mornings.

The Home Chef's cookbooks don't gather dust on a shelf, but rather make up an untidy pile on the bedside table, stacked high to entertain, and inspire one's dreams...and, where favorite passages can be shared regularly to the captive audience of a long-suffering spouse, who does not, in unfortunate likelihood, share the reader's excitement over an ancient technique for crisping pork skin.

Littered around the stack are pens, highlighters, sticky tabs (*one does not dog-ear the pages of an epic, after all*) perhaps a small reading light (*hiking headlamps work great, just sayin...*) and ever-fluttering, oft lost, scraps of paper, and post-its.

Old envelopes that once housed the gas bill, now hold the secret codes of the culinary universe.

The cookbook, for the Home Chef, it is about love and suffering, joy and tears.

It is a treasure map, whose edges read, "*Here there be dragons...and this is how you cook them...*"

"Tis an ill cook that cannot lick his own fingers."
~ Romeo and Juliet: Act 4, Scene 2

A love note from my wife...

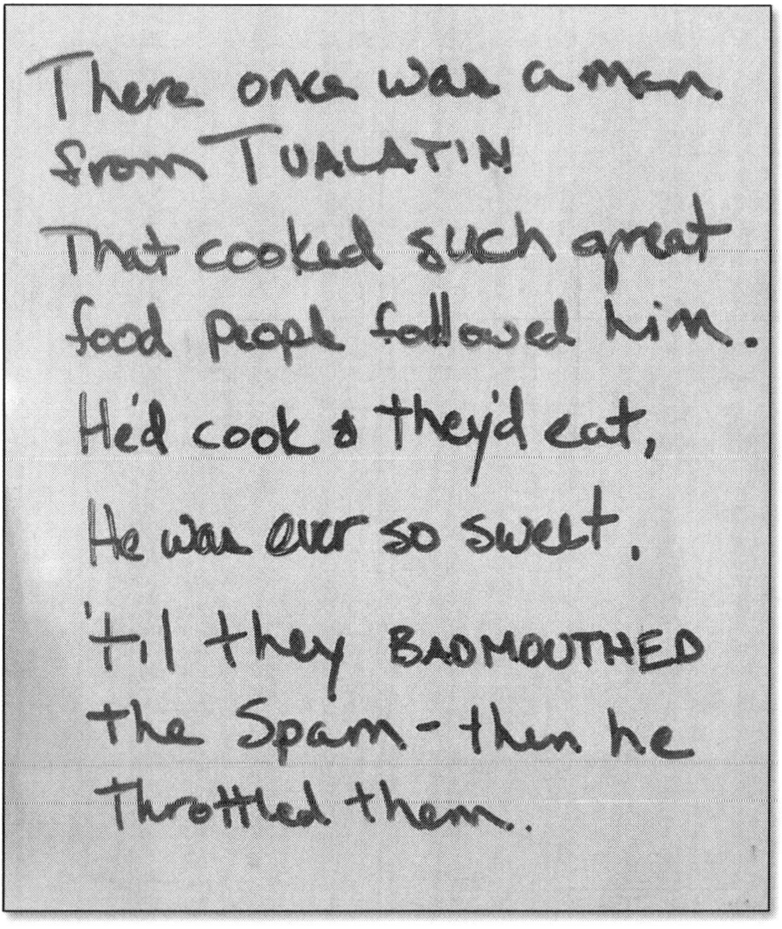

There once was a man
from TUALATIN
That cooked such great
food people followed him.
He'd cook & they'd eat,
He was ever so sweet,
'til they BADMOUTHED
the Spam - then he
Throttled them.

Homework Assignment #2

Kick-starting Your Palate

Okay, time for some more homework…

You didn't really think I was going to let you just READ about it did you?

Sorry, this ain't Food Network, you don't get to just sit on the couch and snork down corn-chips while watching (*or in this case, reading about*) food.

Suck it up, buttercup…it's time to put some preachin' into practice.

Luckily, this is a really fun way to start a dinner party or other small group get-together. For many, taste is the least finely tuned of all the senses. In our haste or our hunger, we eat without thinking about it. In fact, eating is one of the few activities that we all participate in regularly that touches all the senses. We all know that we eat first with our eyes, so that's vision, but what fun would a potato chip be without an audible crunch?

A bite of cheesecake without the silky mouthfeel?

Or spicy food without that pleasant burn in the back of our throats>

Finally, smell is perhaps the most important sense, and most of our sense of taste is derived from it, and we often prejudge our like or dislike according to what we smell. The aroma of campfire smoke and cooking bacon can set my mood for the entire day.

Ingredients (per person)

1 square high quality Swiss milk chocolate
½ large cherry tomato, sprinkled lightly with sea salt
1 half-inch sliced of fresh cucumber, pickled in rice wine vinegar and a bit of sugar.
¼ cup freshly made Miso broth
1 fresh strawberry washed and rolled lightly in fine white sugar.

(white miso is available in the refrigerated section of your local Asian market. Just dissolve 1 teaspoon in 1 cup boiling water.)

Put the items on a small plate, and sit at the dining room table.

No TV, no music, no chatter...you need to concentrate. From a health standpoint, it takes our stomach at least 5 minutes to signal our brain that we are full. By slowing down and really thinking about what you're eating, you'll find that you eat less before feeling satisfied.

> *"One cannot think well, love well, or sleep well, if one has not dined well."*
>
> ~ *Virginia Woolf*

Two hundred years ago, a typical family dinner took two hours to eat, now the average is 20 minutes and we eat 2 1/2 times as much food.

Okay, let's start...

Close your eyes and take an item one at a time (*no particular order*), smell the item, place it in your mouth, breathing in, and then chew slowly at least six times before swallowing..

Try to focus all of your concentration on what you're experiencing.

- o *What does it taste like?*
- o *Why did you like it, or not like it?*
- o *What is the texture?*
- o *What sense did it trigger most directly?(sight, smell, taste, feel)*
- o *Does it conjure a specific person, place, or event in your memory?*
- o *What does it make you want to eat with it?*

Now, take a sip of water, and repeat with the next item on your plate.

Without going full-bore food geek here, I do recommend having a small notepad to jut down your answers immediately.

Now your palate is up and running, and ready to eat a meal.

If you're in a group, talk about your answers to those questions, while you enjoy a good meal and maybe a glass of wine.

~ Notes ~

Part Two: The Food

Food for Thought...

"You don't need a silver fork to eat good food."

-Paul Prudhomme

joinmykitchen.com

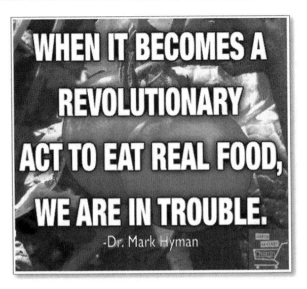

Chapter Four
Real Food

"A hundred years ago, chicken for dinner meant going out and catching, killing, plucking, and gutting a chicken. Do you know anybody who still does that?
It would be considered crazy! Well, that's exactly how cooking will seem to your grandchildren: something people used to do when they had no other choice."

- Harry Balzer

Someday I want to write a cookbook based on the premise that you can eat anything you want, any time you want, as long as you personally cook every bite from scratch ingredients. You see, I disagree that people "don't have time to cook" (*I kinda have to, right?*)...but really, I believe that:

1 ~ People choose not to prioritize home cooking (*we all have 24 hours in a day*), largely due to social pressures and media influence, and...

2 ~ People with little cooking experience don't understand that home cooking can be simple, healthy, fast, and affordable... a position of ignorance that corporate food has been more than happy to encourage and profit from.

In our **MY KITCHEN** program, I teach foster kids, many with ZERO kitchen experience, how to cook simple, healthy meals in classes lasting less than an hour.

Regardless of what Food Network (*and their frozen food sponsors*) would LIKE us to think…you don't have to be an Iron Chef to cook real food.

There's also the ever-growing trend towards convenience "foods", again much of it due to corporate marketing, who's been trying to push their C-Rations and "just add water" crap on us since they were forced to find a non-military market at the end of WWII.

One of my favorite anecdotes from this transitional period in American cooking has to do with the first "cake mixes" which hit the mass market due, in large part, to a glut in the flour market following the war.

Sales were…*disappointing.*

Psychologist Ernest Dichter, the man who coined the term "focus group," turned around the tepid sales of cakes mixes with his revelation that American women wanted to feel more involved in the cake-baking process, and that cake mixes that required them to add eggs would sell better. Said Dichter, *"The housewife and the purchasing public in general seem to prefer fresh eggs and hence the use of dried or powdered eggs is somewhat of a handicap from a psychological standpoint."*

In other words, despite the added convenience, if it didn't feel like "real cooking" even if that just meant cracking a couple of eggs, the home cooks of that time didn't want any part of them.

By the end of the 1940s, corporate food giants weren't in the food business anymore; now they were in the business of selling convenience.

"In the ordinary preparation of pastry products, there are a large and varied number of ingredients which must be used which means keeping a complete stock of materials on hand," Duff explained in what would become U.S. patent no. 1,931,892.

"This is not only expensive and inconvenient, but necessitates careful measurements and mixing and, therefore, the provision of suitable apparatus therefor. In addition to the above, unsatisfactory results or failure occur too frequently which represent a serious loss of time, of money, of materials and of energy." ~ U.S. patent for the first cake "mixes"

We're reaching a critical tipping point in history where it will no longer be a matter of IF I choose to cook from scratch, but that there won't be raw ingredients available to do so.

Lack of business and ever-tightening "regulations" are putting small farms, farmer's markets, and artisan food producers out of business in droves (*and not by accident*) while corporations are buying up larger tracts of farmland at a historic rate. As the supply diminishes, so does the knowledge, interest, and demand.

Retailers, of course, have a much more vested interest in moving people toward "meal assembly" than actual cooking.

There's less waste, it's easier to stock and store more "high profile" products in less space, and the shelf-lives (*i.e.: the amount of time they have to get it sold*) are vastly greater with frozen and pre-packaged foods. I'm not sure what the difference in mark-up is, but with 30% of our fresh produce ending up in the dumpster, the gap has to be pretty marginal.

Finally, how much responsibility should we place on the TV shows, magazines, and food writers of the past decade's "foodie movement" for possibly widening the rift between "us and them" (*i.e.: people who cook and people who don't*) by making it more about entertainment, game shows, and "food porn" than practical application?

You'll note that Food Network (*and all the others*) may be yapping incessantly about "farm to table" during the shows…but the ad time is filled with pre-packaged garbage and convenience food. Is the underlying message that…

"We both know you can't do what you just watched Bobby do…but doesn't THIS look almost as good?"

Change and education are the key to regaining responsibility for our family's health and nutrition, not conceding to a corporate food mentality that will always, ALWAYS place the security of their shareholders over the health of our families.

One of the biggest factors in cooking good food, is using good food to cook. This is a point we stress over and over, with every kid that comes through our cooking program.

Not *expensive* food, not even "fancy" food (*though that can be a lot of fun, when you can swing it*), but good, real, *recognizable* food.

Start small, instead of buying that can of diced tomatoes, buy three Roma tomatoes (*about the same price*), dice them in a bowl, and sprinkle a little salt and sugar on them.

10 minutes later you'll have the same, but far superior tasting ingredient: diced tomatoes in juice...and really, was it that hard? (*...and it doesn't taste like the can!*)

 Check out my video for a quick and simple method of dicing tomatoes!

Google: Chef Perry Dicing Tomato

Now, let's take that one tiny step further...now that you have your diced tomatoes, is it really that much harder to dice up an onion, chop a little garlic, and squirt some olive oil in a pan?

Sauté (*that means a low fry in a small amount of oil*) for 10 minutes.

Toss in some fresh herbs like basil, oregano, and Italian parsley (*which you can now buy pre-packaged in small amounts in just about any produce section*) and your diced tomatoes, and give a stir.

Throw some pasta in a pot of salted, simmering water...spaghetti, linguine, angel-hair, whatever, and let heat and water work it's crazy magic for you.

Meanwhile, grill a chicken breast, or cook and crumble some ground pork, or sauté some zucchini slices, or if you're feeling *really* crazy, poach a dozen little-neck clams in their shells with a little white wine...(*don't flip the clams*), and a generous sprinkle of salt and pepper.

Good food is very often, even most often, simple food.

~ Anthony Bourdain

Don't worry about a bunch of spices, see the what *food* tastes like first, and to quote a guy I know...

"Bam!" you've got a dish of pasta that probably cost less, and certainly tastes much better than you'll ever get from that bottled muck on the shelves. Sprinkle on a tablespoon or so of fresh grated asiago cheese (*it's in the deli section, it's expensive, and it's worth it. Plus, a little goes a LONG way*) and I promise you, I PROMISE you...

You will never, willingly, go back to prepared, bottled "spaghetti sauce." Why's it so darn good?

Not because it's harder to make (*it really wasn't, was it?*) Certainly not because it was more expensive...it wasn't, at least not much.

No, it tastes so darn good, because you used good food to make it!

Congratulations...you're a Home Chef.

> *"It's difficult to think anything but pleasant thoughts while eating a homegrown tomato."* ~ Lewis Grizzard

A last note on "real food"...

Here's the thing...

Every time I write something about butchering or eating the animals we raise, I get a bunch of guff on Facebook. Some of you, I know, are just teasing me, and that's fine, you crack me up, but some of you seem genuinely offended.

TO THE OFFENDED:

I have a farm, and our goal is to use it to become as self-sustaining as possible. We have pets...2 dogs (*and one spectacularly stupid duck*), besides those, any livestock (*chickens, ducks, rabbits, goats, steer, etc.,*) that I am paying to feed and sustain, I do so for a single purpose...to feed my family. They are not pets, they are not treated as pets, they are livestock.

If you are only comfortable letting someone else do your killing for you (*of animals that don't get a fraction of the quality of life that mine do*) I guess that's up to you. Regardless of what you may like to think, that plastic-wrapped meat at Safeway didn't die of natural causes, either.

But, if not looking it "in the face" assuages your guilt, that's between you and your butcher. If you don't eat meat at all, that's fine too, as long as you're willing to acknowledge the uncountable number of small animals that die every year to commercially raise your fruits, vegetables, and grains. As the man said, "Ain't nobody clean."

I'm not trying to change anyone's philosophy, regardless of how ridiculous or unnatural it may be, but if you really ARE offended when I write about the breeding, raising, butchering, or eating of my animals, I strongly suggest that you stop reading now.

'Cause, baby…it's only gonna get worse!

Ironically, MY daughter was quite put out the first year on the new farm, because I wouldn't shoot any of the wild rabbits and cook them for her.

One Chef's Opinion on GMO Labeling

I put off posting on this subject on my blog for a long time, mostly because I knew it would make some of my acquaintances VERY unhappy with me. I figure if you haven't tossed the book out the window yet...I can probably risk it now.

First and foremost, as someone who has had close, personal experience with *true* hunger, in areas of the world that deal with the real thing, I find it offensive and shameful that a bunch of fat-assed Americans *(and, in all fairness, I could be included in that group...so I'm speaking for my people!)*, with access to what is an unimaginable cornucopia of food choices for much of the planet, think they have the right to arbitrarily shut down companies that are developing grains and foods that can be grown in poor and arid conditions, providing nutrition for entire communities of people who are starving to death. *(You know they do that too, right?)*

Frankly, and I know there is much more to the argument than this, but coming from a guy who has been there, and feeds hungry kids *here*...until <u>you've</u> done the same, you should probably put down your sign, shut the hell up, and find a way, beyond smugly sharing the latest snarky, and largely inaccurate Facebook meme, to be part the solution.

If that seems harsh...well...watching a two-year old girl, with a bloated belly, and stick-figure arms and legs, die in front of you, tends to lessen one's tolerance for sugar-coated bullshit.

Okay...sorry...deep breath...happy thoughts...

Here's the deal. I don't have a problem with people knowing what's in their food. I like to know what's in *my* food. I think we SHOULD know. But...do folks know now?

Have they studied up on how much sodium is in that can of beans?

The processing standards for their store-bought chicken?

The Federally-allowed maximum amount of rat feces in their hot dogs and sandwich meats? Or, are they simply stroking their own egos and misguided sense of "standing up against the man", their need to feel important, by taking shots at the largest and easiest target they can find from their easy chair, with little or no idea who or what is standing behind it?

We used to have a term for a group of people with that kind of mentality...we called them a lynch mob. My problem (*and I think many of the farmers out there would agree*) is with the idea that it's (mandatory labeling) "just to give people a choice."

Unfortunately, I've helped enough people do their shopping to know that, all things considered, most of us are too lazy or too uneducated to know what a label like this means, or to find out...we simply default to "there's a label so it must be bad!"

That's like me being forced to wear a t-shirt that says, "*Potential Rapist*", on the front. From a purely analytical standpoint, it could be argued that, as I have the equipment and I fall within the highest demographic of assailants (*men*) the use of the word "potential" is an accurate and fair description when solely used to inform.

But...it's really not.

I know that it's not.

Most of *you* know that it's not as well...but what would be the immediate internal or even external reaction to those who have no idea who I am, and/or are uninterested in finding out? (*I.e.: uneducated or lazy.*)

Do you think it would be positive? Do you think that the majority would see the technical potential accuracy of the statement for what it is?

Do you see what I'm saying?

In a society of snap judgements and contempt without investigation, most people would see that shirt and instead of asking me *"What's up with THAT?"* would simply cross the street or walk the other way.

A label, any label, would have huge negative ramifications for any company's product. This is why so many of them are fighting so hard against labeling, because any marketing professional (*and I was one for 10 years*) knows that there is nothing truer that the old adage that you have only one chance to make a first impression.

These companies aren't cape-wearing baby-eating monsters (*though some are not saints by any means, either*). They're businesses, doing what businesses do...trying to sell as much product as they can.

And before you let anyone fall back on the "it's just for identification" argument, remember...

That was the marketing excuse behind forcing a people to wear the Star of David in the 1930's too...and, like most labels mandated by humans, regardless of intention (*true or otherwise*) it was a very, very, bad idea. And it's that, that will keep growers and corporations fighting the labeling advocates on this one subject to their dying breath, when there are so much more productive ways of achieving the same end results. Assuming, of course, that those end goals really are what they are claimed to be. Both camps rely on marketing and public opinion, after all.

So, no...I can't support product labeling, in its current form.

What I can and DO support is tighter legislation, testing, and banning of what DOES go into our food, and stricter penalties against PROVEN dangers. PROOF is all I ask, from respected, non-biased sources, in layman's terms.

What I support even more, however, are individuals taking personal responsibility for their opinions, and taking due diligence in studying the facts, and learning and understanding the truth (*and I'm not dictating what the truth is or isn't in this situation*), before slapping a smarmy bumper-sticker on the back of their VW Bus.

> *"This is how capitalism works: (speaking about "fortified" white flour) it creates a problem, and then instead of fixing the problem, it creates a new business to solve that problem."*
>
> *- Michael Pollan, "Cooked"*

10 Quick Grocery Shopping Tips

1. **Eat first.** Don't shop when you are hungry. You will come home with a lot less money and more food than needed.

2. **Store brands are okay.** Often times, if you compare the more expensive brand name versus the store brands, you will save money if you choose the store brand.

3. **Placement of food** in a grocery store is all about making money. You usually have to walk through a lot of other yummy looking items to get to the staple foods and healthy foods. In the aisles look up or down for better prices as more expensive items are placed at eye level.

4. **Watch the scanner.** Make sure you are paying the right price when checking out. The scanner can make mistakes.

5. **Read labels.** Is what you are buying the healthiest choice?

6. **Grocery lists.** Write out a grocery list before you get to the store and stick to what is on your list.

7. **Shop sales and grocery flyers.**

8. **Compare prices by portion.** How many servings/cost. Often times this is shown on the price sticker on the shelf, if not, calculate it yourself.

9. **Menu Plan.** Have a menu planned out and follow your grocery list.

10. **SHOP the perimeter of the store.** For the freshest, healthiest eating, and easy rule of thumb is to stick to the outside walls of the store. Typically this is where you'll find fresh produce, dairy, meat and fish, and the bakery.

Think of the inside aisles as "the badlands", you want to make an occasion targeted strike, typically for staples like flour, oil, spices, pasta, etc., and then get the heck out of enemy territory as quickly as possible. Also, always plan around what you already have on hand.

If you have a stockpile of staples like rice and beans, and buy meat in bulk at the wholesaler, you can plan around what meat and staples you have in the pantry. This means you only need to get a few fresh ingredients each week, and one or two things to restock the pantry.

If you buy cream (or other perishables) for one recipe, include another so that the cream is used before it spoils.

Example SSDP (*Simply Smart Dinner Plans*) Shopping List:

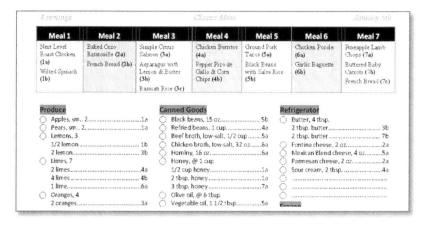

Sharing recipes and cooking advice for fresh produce with low income families at the local Farmers Market.

My good friend, and foodie extraordinaire, Diane Anderson, is small market/local market guru (*some might say it's an obsession, but not me – I want her to keep writing for us...*) So, here's an article that Di was kind enough to put together on making the most of your local Saturday Markets...

To Market! To Market!

by Diane Anderson

I'm excited for all the signs of spring I see and hear and smell each day. I know that with the arrival of the warmer weather, the Saturday Market and Farmer's Markets will start again.

I enjoy purchasing fresh fruit, vegetables, nuts, and meats directly from local farmers. Then, I use them in meals throughout the week or I can or freeze the extras.

The first Saturday of May brings the beginning of my small town's Saturday market. I love browsing the farmer's stalls to find fresh produce at wonderful prices. I hope I'll see my favorite family back this year with their yummy seasonal fruits and veggies. Also, the teenagers from a high school gardening club should be back with their produce and crafts. I love supporting their endeavors.

Yesterday, the market organizers announced that there will be new farmers at the market this year. Should be fun getting to know them!

When I first get to the market, I do a quick browse through of all the stalls to check the produce and the prices.

Then, I go back around to make my purchases. Produce is often up to ½ the price of the grocery stores and it's fresher—often picked that morning!

I usually carry reusable market bags with me (*some vendors will have bags, but don't rely on that*). It's good to carry at least two bags to prevent delicate produce from being crushed.

If you're visiting a very busy, larger, market, you'll want to arrive early as I've heard local restaurants purchase the best stuff first thing in the morning. I prefer the smaller ones and believe the prices are better.

Many vendors do not have credit card machines (*they might in the larger, more established markets*), so bring cash. I have a foster parent friend who received WIC vouchers to use at produce vendors in some Saturday markets. So, if you qualify, please check with the WIC office for more information. I've found that it's good to bring some extra cash in case there is something special to try.

My personal favorite farmer's market is in Jos, Nigeria. A bit of a drive...but totally worth it! – Chef P.

So, be adventurous this summer and check out the Saturday markets near you! You might make some friends and you'll be supporting your local small businesses and farmers. You might even be surprised at how much money it saves you in your grocery budget.

Most of all, you'll have fun exploring and learning more about your community. Not sure where to find your local markets? Give your local Chamber of Commerce a call – they'll know!

Of course, the very best, freshest, and most delicious are the veggies pulled fresh from your garden, moments before cooking or serving.

While not everyone is lucky enough to have the space for a huge backyard garden, my friend and fellow foodie, Christina, shows here how a little ingenuity and elbow grease can work wonders on a second-story balcony, when you have no yard...so, use what you've got! (*and...yes, that's a plastic kiddie pool in the corner!*)

Homework Assignment #3
Creating a shopping list

List the top items in each category that you find yourself picking up each time you go grocery shopping (milk, eggs, bacon, etc.,) This will be the "base" for your personal shopping list. Use this list, with plenty of blank space, to create your own custom shopping list.

Produce_____
_____
_____
_____

Bulk/Spices_____
_____
_____
_____

Deli_____
_____
_____
_____

Meat_____
_____
_____
_____

Dairy_____
_____
_____
_____

Frozen_____
_____
_____
_____

Bakery_____
_____
_____
_____

Dry Goods (canned, boxed, bottled)

_____
_____
_____
_____

Other

_____
_____
_____
_____
_____
_____
_____
_____
_____
_____
_____
_____
_____

> _**Chef's Opinion:** People who gather in clusters to chat in the middle of the aisles of the grocery store two days before Christmas, should be considered pins in a life-size game of bowling for morons..._

Chapter Five

The Problem with "Farm to Table"

Many of today's cooking programs rely unapologetically on ingredients that themselves contain lots of ingredients: canned soups, jarred mayonnaise, frozen vegetables, powdered sauces, vanilla wafers, limeade concentrate, Marshmallow Fluff.

This probably shouldn't surprise us: processed foods have so thoroughly colonized the American kitchen and diet that they have redefined what passes today for cooking, not to mention food. Many of these convenience foods have been sold to women as tools of liberation; the rhetoric of kitchen oppression has been cleverly hijacked by food marketers and the cooking shows they sponsor to sell more stuff.

So the shows encourage home cooks to take all manner of shortcuts, each of which involves buying another product, and all of which taken together have succeeded in redefining what is commonly meant by the verb "to cook."

~ Michael Pollan, "Out of the Kitchen, Onto the Couch"

Okay, I know that this title is going to be fightin' words for some folks, so before you start sharpening your pitchforks and hurling your organic, fair-trade, rotten tomatoes...let's be clear: *I love the farm-to-table concept.* I love my local farmer's markets, and I take every opportunity to support my local artisan food purveyors; in part because I believe it's the healthy and more socially responsible choice, but also because the food just tastes better! However, my love and support for the *ideal* of farm-to-table does not negate that, in practice, the system is flawed.

Maybe a more fitting title would be *"Farm to Table...the missing ingredient"*, because the farm-to-table model leaves out a critical step...creating a gap that is not just important, but imperative to fill, for the system to work. Functionally, the equation is actually "farm-to-*KITCHEN*-to-table"

The kitchen is the bridge (or, unfortunately more often the gap) *between* the farm and the table. What good is fresh, organic, sustainable, fair-trade food, if the end-user (*the home cook*) doesn't know what it is, or what to do with it, and so won't buy it?

> **Side note:** *my definition of "cooking" is turning raw, unprocessed ingredients into a finished meal with a minimum of pre-made additions.*

Part of the issue, I believe, is that foodies, farmers, and people who cook are often amazed at the extent to which other people *don't* cook.

When my wife, who did not grow up cooking, says to me, "I'm afraid to cook meat", my eyes tend to glaze over…but she's not alone. In fact, she's not even in the minority! Take a friend with you (*and no cherry-pickin' one of your foodie friends!*) to a large grocery store or farmer's market, and see how many vegetables they can name without looking at the label. Then, if you need further convincing, ask they how'd they prepare the ones they *did* recognize.

This isn't just about foodies loving good food, or hippies wanting to save the planet…this gap effects our country's health, ecology, finances…the list goes on.

In his article, **"Home cooking in decline as low-income households turn to ready meals"** (*5 September 2013*) Patrick Butler, social policy editor at theguardian.com writes…

"Spending on chilled ready meals is up 25-30% among working class groups, and our cooking skills and habits are in decline, with the least well-off consumers increasingly turning to a diet of calorie-laden convenience foods and fatty ready meals to beat austerity.

Despite our obsession with high profile chefs, cookery books, and foodie TV shows, data compiled by retail analyst Kantar Worldpanel shows that consumers, particularly those who are short of money, time or both, are spending a bigger share of their food budgets on unhealthy frozen and chilled products. Home cooking has declined most among those whose food budgets are under the most pressure, especially families earning under $30,000 a year, as poorer consumers opt for cheap and "filling" prepared foods on offer in supermarket price promotions rather than fresh produce.

In the past two years frozen food sales have grown by 11% (up 20% among skilled working class groups) and spending on chilled ready meals is up 19% (25-30% among working class groups) as hard pressed consumers seek "recession buster" value.

Partly as a result, the proportion of home-made food eaten by children is decreasing, fueling a further erosion in cookery skills.

Low-income families with young children on tight food budgets were most likely to buy food on cheap "special offer" promotions, and roughly a third of all sugar and saturated fat purchased by consumers were sold through these offers. Worldpanel added: "Consumers appear unwilling, unmotivated, and unable to alter their current eating habits. There is clearly confusion over how to ensure real, tangible changes are made and with whom the responsibility lies to deliver them."

Health

Fresh, unprocessed, (*or what I like to call "real"*) food is better for us, and better for the environment. Everyone knows this. The number one most effective method for battling the proliferation of processed foods, obesity, diabetes, celiac disease, GMOs, corporate farming, yadda yadda yadda…is to shop, cook, and eat with as few steps as possible between the dirt and the plate. True healthcare begins in the kitchen, not the gym. Most of us know this.

It takes 10 minutes to grill a pork chop and some fresh veggies. Some of us know this.

However, just *knowing* the truth is only the first step in slowing our society's descent into further slavery to the boxed, processed, artificially preserved, instant, easy-to-prepare corporate food masters.

We must increase that knowledge and spread it around.

Knowledge is power, and we've turned much of the power over to the fast-food corporations. If we don't know how to cook, believe me, they'll be more than happy to continue to make our lives "easier" by doing the "hard part". Why am I picturing Morlocks and Eloi?

These companies, btw, buy from the agri-conglomerates (*or own them outright*) many of them in other countries, and NOT from your local, small, organic, fair trade farms…perpetuating the spiral.

I take exception to the idea that it's "too hard" for us to make good food ourselves. I take exception to those who would try to manipulate our insecurities for their own gain, and who think I'll happily accept a plate full of crap, just because crap was easier to put on the plate.

In fact, I more than take exception; I take it as a challenge.

I can, like a long line of Perkins men before me, be a stubborn, contrary, pig-headed, pain-in-the-ass. Curled lips and clenched jaws are the secret handshake of my family. Tell us what we can't do, and we'll likely kill ourselves trying to prove you wrong. Maybe that's part of what I love about cooking…

Finishing a great dish, using real, natural ingredients, is a stiff middle finger to those Corporate Food marketing-pukes who want me to believe that I have to be spoon-fed pureed garbage, because is just too darn hard to do it myself.

Environment

One-third of food produced for humans (1.3 billion tons) is wasted somewhere along the food chain each year.

Food waste creates higher carbon and methane levels, so there are environmental, as well as economic benefits to wasting less food.

Finances

Where does a pervasive lack of basic cooking skills lead, from an economic standpoint?

Well, at the residential level, it leads to a reliance on instant, processed, or packaged foods, or eating in restaurants, which isn't financially sustainable for the average family, unless it spirals down to, as it often does, the local drive though dollar menu.

Even then, we're spending more than we think. The average cost of a "cheap" drive-thru meal here in Oregon, runs between $3-$4 per person. For a family of four "lite-eaters", we're looking at $12-$16 dollars. This is 20-30% more then we spend at our house, cooking quick, simple, healthy meals, often with enough left-overs for lunch the next day. "Value Menu"...really?

Oh, and we don't toss a big bag full of cardboard, paper and plastic in the trash afterwards, either. On a "broader" scale (*pun intended*) the nation's health care tab stood at $2.7 trillion in 2011, the latest year available.

I don't think I need to say anything more about that.

Education

This is the crux of this article. Laws, labeling, testing, etc., can all be good things, but they will never, *ever*, replace the ability of the educated consumer to "vote with their checkbooks" by knowing what to buy, and how to prepare it for their families.

We're moving into a third and fourth generation of people raised without a grasp of basic cooking skills or confidence in the kitchen.

In her article, "Bring Back Home Economics in Schools!" (*Cooking Light, 2012*) Hillary Dowdle refers to herself and her generation as "the 'lost girls' and boys', saying, "Public health experts , nutritionists, and educators are beginning to realize that the lack of basic life skills, like cooking, presents a serious problem: Americans are growing up ignorant about the *what's, whys*, and *how's* of eating healthy."

Basically, if no one cooked at home, today's young people's options are to (a) get a job in a "real food" restaurant kitchen (*plan 2-3 years, minimum, before you actually cook anything*), or spend thousands (*or tens of thousands*) on culinary school...which is a pretty deep commitment for someone who just wants to feed their kids a healthy dinner.

Where do most folks end up? Right back on the processed foods aisle, or in the drive-thru.

"(Food) is devalued generally in our education system . . . it's more than just learning how to cook. It's about food literacy, which means teaching children what foods to eat and why, how to understand food labeling information and how and why we need to prepare and cook food safely." says Griffith University School of Education and Professional Studies Dean, Donna Pendergast.

This leads me to a personal soap box…

In an article titled, "Compulsory home economics essential to fight childhood obesity", the home economics advocate blog, *HomeEcConnect*, states: "We are losing basic survival skills. Home Economics is essential for learning about the basics of growing, transporting, purchasing, preparing, nutritional values, cooking, presenting, enjoying, cleaning up and storage of food. 'Food literacy" is about learning food skills as a holistic concept."

Dr. Arya Sharma, *Director of the Canadian Obesity Network*, says "time to bring back home economics" because "the art of basic food preparation and meal planning may be a very real part of the obesity solution".

Our kid's need to learn to cook good food. Period.

Budgets are tight, and school days are long, we know.

Frankly, I don't mind a computer doing my math, or my science, but I don't want one cooking my food. If we're going to cut something from the curriculum, let's not make it the one thing that is at the core of our survival and well-being as a species, shall we?

If my daughter's lack of proficiency in trigonometry means she might live longer than her parents…I'm okay with that.

Speaking of which, my daughter started learning to cook at three, now, at nine, she is an adept omelet, salad, and soup maker, a savvy produce shopper, and could give Chef Gordon Ramsey a run for "kitchen tyrant." She loves to cook, and is more adventurous and open in her eating than most adults I know.

But, not every child has the (*sometimes*) good fortune of having a father who's a chef, whose father was a chef, whose father was a chef.

What do we do? We fill the gap!

While, in this author's opinion, mandatory home economics classes, for both genders, are vital…what do we do to help those who are already out of school; folks who have jobs, and families, and bills, and budgets? We started *SimplySmartDinnerPlans (our free weekly meal plans)*, in part, to help fill this gap. We believe that to help people make responsible changes in planning, shopping and cooking, that those changes, to be effective and lasting, must SIMPLIFY their already too-busy lives, instead of further complicating them.

As our subscribers cook their way through their weekly menus, they learn basic cooking and nutrition techniques and skills, sometimes directly from short video clips, blogs posts, and Q & A, but mostly passively, though the hands-on process of actually preparing easy, non-threatening, nutritious recipes.

They are introduced to new vegetables, healthier cuts of meat, etc., and soon have a grasp of what's available, and what to do with it.

We believe that folks who are already spinning a lot of plates need to *love it before they learn it*, in other words, they need to prepare themselves a simple, delicious meal, before they need to learn why it's good for them, and we hear this happening time after time from our subscribers.

We prepare a weekly shopping list of ingredients, organized by aisle, which saves them hours of planning and organizing, and we provide a color photo of each dish, so they know what they're shooting for.

We also encourage our readers to cook with their families, offering simple steps in the recipes that children of various ages can help with, and, hopefully, educating the next generation.

Lastly, we're here for them. Professional and home cooks ready to answer their questions, provide options, and give tips and advice for exactly what they're cooking.

Here are four things *you* can do to bridge the gap:

Learn to cook, and to cook healthier

Teach your kids, grandkids, or *any* kids to do the same

Become a regular customer of your local farmer's market and independent food purveyor

Fight for mandatory food science classes in our public schools, and volunteer at an after-school program. *(Those are your tax-dollars, you should have a say in how they're spent!)*

Daughter & Goddaughters Making Pizza

Bottom line: if we can help home-cooks prepare simple, affordable, healthy meals, in the time they have…we capture their attention, and can lead them towards a healthier, more responsible food lifestyle, one they will be explore with a sense of excitement, not guilt or frustration.

Become an advocate for people knowing their way around the kitchen, and you help bridge the gap between farm and table.

Let's cook!

> Dieting is easy.
>
> It's like riding a bike.
>
> Except the bike is on fire.
>
> And the ground is on fire.
>
> And everything is on fire
> because you're in hell.

Chapter Six

On dieting & healthy eating...

I would guess that I actually have less temptation than most, as I have a very detailed shopping list to follow each week, to plan menus for our subscribers. Given my issues with crowds, I try to shop late at night, and eat dinner just before going to the store, so I'm not shopping hungry.

Be adventurous...there are tons of great fresh produce, meats, etc., along the outside of the grocery store that you can experiment with.

Try new fresh herbs, and unusual fruits.

If you see something that looks interesting, write its name down, and Google some recipes until you find one that sounds good, then add that item to your next shopping list.

> *Eating pasta doesn't make you fat...it's how much pasta you eat makes you fat.* ~ *Giada De Laurentiis*

I'll tell you, a handful of chopped fresh Thai basil will rock just about anything! Sample some cilantro (*you'll love it, or you'll hate it*), and find a good recipe for roasting your own garlic.

Any of these will turn something as pedestrian as a *Cup O' Noodles* into a satisfying repast, and turn a good recipe into a next-level one!

Personally, I think that, in terms of a general style of cooking, it's hard to beat a great "traditional" (*not Americanized*) Italian cookbook for finding healthy, exiting new things to try (*disclaimer: yes, I am Italian, and totally biased.*) Greek cooking is pretty amazing, as well.

Brass tacks…if it's something you love to do…DO IT…just find a way to do it right. I think the biggest deal-killer to most folk's healthy eating, is that they believe that they have to deny themselves to eat healthy. We are, all of us, narcissists and hedonists by nature, and a deprivation mentality is a one-way ticket to a binge session. I speak from personal experience.

Make learning, exploring, and experimenting with healthy eating something you love to do…and then indulge yourself! Try something new at the grocery store… take a field trip to your local farmer's markets…throw a "healthy (*country of choice*) dinner for your friends or family.

Make it fun…make it something you want to do…and you'll do it.

Okay, perhaps one can enjoy their food a little too much…like after spending a long, cold day hauling up fresh crab on the Oregon Coast.

> *"Life moves pretty fast.*
> *If you don't stop and look around once in a while, you could miss it."*
> *— F. Bueller*

Why it's important to enjoy your food

Let's face it, we're all in a hurry, rushing from here to there, trying to squeeze more than 24 hours into each day, surrounding ourselves with gizmos, gadgets, plans, and books that promise to improve our "efficiency" (*i.e.: spin more, and drop less*).

How many breakfasts, gobbled in rush-hour traffic? Never mind *what* we're eating, just try not to spill it on ourselves! How many lunches snorked down at our desk, never glancing away from our monitor?

How many dinners from the drive thru, or delivered from the local pizza shop, because we're just always in a hurry? Let's look at three seriously good reasons why we should consider slowing down to smell the dinner…

Losing weight

Oh boy…everybody wants to tell you how to drop some pounds, right? Everyone's got a secret plan that lets you "eat whatever you want" and lose weight (*just spend $19.95 on their new book, and they'll give you the secret*). Here's a simple one that won't cost you a penny. SLOW DOWN!

It's not a race to chew our way to the finish line, the communication lines from the stomach take 20 minutes to signal your brain that it's full. I don't know about you, but I can stuff down a lot of pizza in 20 minutes. Ever wonder why you can be hungry one minute and stuffed to the gills the next? It's because your stomach finally sent that email to your brain saying, "Good Lord, STOP!"

A number of studies confirm that just by eating slower, we consume fewer calories; some say enough to lose 20 pounds a year without doing anything different or eating anything different!

- Pick up your fork
- Take a reasonable bite
- Put your fork down
- Chew your food
- Ask someone at the table how their day was.

It's simple math...if you take two bites per minute, instead of four bites per minute...you've cut you calories in half when the buzzer rings at twenty minutes!

Obviously, the better (*healthier*) the food you're putting in, the better your results are going to be, as well.

Relieving Stress

Anything that allows you to slow down and focus on one thing (especially something enjoyable), is going to lower your stress level.

As we mentioned before, breakfast and dinner are a great time to talk with your family, plan or look back on your day, or just enjoy the act of eating. Be present, be in the moment...

- What do you *like* about the food?

- What might you try differently next time?

- What, if any, memories do certain ingredients invoke?

Learning how to calmly focus on nothing but the present moment is a key factor in reducing stress, and what other activity do we have, daily, that so easily lends itself to doing so?

Taking Charge of Your Life

Stop paying someone else to look out for your best interests, because most of them aren't. Fast food, and processed/packaged food companies are not interested in your health and well-being, they're interested in keeping their shareholders happy.

That means getting you to pay as much as possible for something they spent as little as possible to provide. Is that really the philosophy you want your family's health and nutrition based in?

Me neither.

It's time we stop trading this so called "convenience" for our health, and took responsibility for ourselves again.

Cook your own food. Make time to eat. Savor the food you're putting in your body. Decide that your meals are going to be a time to relax and connect. Enjoy your meals and those you share them with.

Just...slow...down.

On Good Food

I don't understand people who don't love good food.

It's not that I don't like these people, or think less of them, some are in fact, dear friends, and I am on constant alert against the slippery slope of food snobbery, that most boorish and ultimately ridiculous narcissism of the joyless, insecure culinary Puritan.

If you're afraid of butter, use cream. ~ Julia Child

I mean, let's face it, the best of food is still only feces in waiting...how pharisaical can you be about THAT?

(By the same token. if you're too ashamed to admit that you really like Chicken McNuggets, a good dirty-water hotdog, or a cold PBR, even if not morally approving of them, you are nearing the base of the mountain...and that way leads to the dark side...or worse, veganism.)

I just don't, in my soul, understand them, those poor souls who mumble a litany of "food is just fuel" while ordering a plain lettuce salad with non-fat dressing (on the side) in a restaurant famous for dry-aged porterhouse.

Don't get me wrong. If you're an athlete, a model, actor, etc., something that requires you to restrict yourself, despite what you would RATHER do, that's a different story. I couldn't do it, but I respect those who do, lol.

It's beyond simply enjoying these things, it's a fundamental recognition that their absence would leave a void that nothing else could fill - a maddening itch between the shoulder blades that I would never quite be able to reach *(even with my dinner fork)*.

I couldn't live without the joy of good food, and the preparation thereof, any more than I could long survive without the wagging of dogs or the laughter of children in my life.

Perhaps it's not even so much about the food as it is about joy.

I distinctly remember this birthday. Sitting in front Mom's homemade (and slightly lop-sided) cake, surrounded by my pals, I glanced down the hallway of our tenement apartment to see two young boys, neighbors and also friends, standing in the open doorway, gazing longingly at the festivities within.

Their parents, Jehovah Witnesses, wouldn't let them attend my party.

I've had no truck for that particular religion ever since.

So many of the joyous occasions in my life have involved a groaning table, so much laughter has competed with the crash of pans, the bass beat of slamming oven doors, and the moment of closed-eyed euphoria garnered from the end of a tasting spoon.

So many more occasions of joy in the fevered expectations of planning a dinner party.

These things feed my soul, and my soul, like the rest of me, has an insatiable appetite.

We all eat, and it would be a sad waste of opportunity to eat badly.

~ Anna Thomas

Chapter Seven
Organic Ingredients

First of all…

What "Organic" Means…and Doesn't.

Organic food now represents a $16-billion business, with sales growing by as much as 20 percent per year. Sadly, the quality and meaning of "organic" is undergoing an equally rapid and exponential nose dive.

Organic foods, which used to be raised truly naturally, on small farms with pride and integrity, big business has tromped in and destroyed many of the principles on which the whole organic movement was founded. The sad truth is, much of the organic food we're buying is a complete and total scam. Once the US Government got into the labeling, or certification business there was bound to be trouble. Con-Agra, Tyson, Kellogg, Post, and all the rest have little respect for the organic label, and misconstrue it at the drop of a hat.. When a label says ALL NATURAL that should raise some very large red flags. They are even labeling GMO, as all natural.

Products labeled "100% organic" Must contain only organically produced ingredients and/or processing aids, excluding water and salt. No other ingredients or additives are allowed.

Products labeled "organic" Must contain at least 95 percent organically produced ingredients (*again, excluding water and salt*). Any remaining ingredients must consist of non-agricultural substances that appear on the NOP's *National List of Allowed and Prohibited Substances.*

Products Labeled "Made with Organic Ingredients" These are processed products which must contain at least 70 percent organic ingredients to use the phrase "made with organic ingredients" and list up to three of the organic ingredients or food groups on the principal display panel.

Chef Chris discusses the importance of reading labels with our students.

For example, a soup made with at least 70 percent organic ingredients and only organic vegetables may claim "soup made with organic peas, potatoes, and carrots" or "soup made with organic vegetables."

Regardless of what label may be on the product, it is important, as with any packaged food, to read ingredients carefully. Look for whole food ingredients that are not puffed, isolated, concentrated, hydrolyzed, crystalized. Make sure added sugars are not within the first two or three ingredients.

That said…

I love roadside vegetable stands, food fairs, and the farmer's market.

There are many, many opinions (*some informed, some not so much*), regarding organic foods, unending debates on how they are more sustainable and better for the environment, more naturally produced and safer from chemicals and processes, and how all of this effects our local communities…there are many, many arguments against, as well. So, why do I stress the importance of eating these foods?

I'd like to stand smugly on my pedestal and claim that my reasons come from an enlightened world-view, and deep concern for the environment (*and that is a part of it*) but to be perfectly honest, most of my reasoning comes from one position…I like good food…and good food starts with good ingredients. Produce that was picked yesterday, a few miles away, from a field that's never seen synthetic pesticides or fertilizers, have a fresher, more natural flavor than those that don't. No question. Okay wait, let's pause and get one thing out of the way first…yes, buying organic is often more expensive that the alternatives. So…shop smarter! I mean, don't just throw your money away, clip those coupons, watch for sales, and stock up the freezer when you find a good deal. Learning to can and preserve your own fruits and vegetables is another way of taking advantage of the great food when it's at a great price. And really…is it that much more expensive?

Recently I was comparing, literally, apples to apples. The apples in the organic section were $1.99 a pound, the same species of apple, in the "regular" section, was $1.79 a pound. I bought three pounds, and spent a total of sixty cents extra for apples that are safer for me, sustainably grown, and most importantly to me (*just being honest*) they just plain taste better! Sixty cents! Yes, I know it adds up…but let's say I buy ten produce items that each cost me an extra sixty cents…that means I spent a whopping $6 extra. That's one less trip through the fast food drive-thru, assuming I go alone! That is what we call a win-win, btw…trading flavorless, plastic-wrapped mystery "food" for something that's real and delicious.

Delicious.

As a chef and foodie, that last point is, again, huge for me. I've found, again and again, that we can buy a smaller amount of food, spend less overall, and get *much* more satisfaction from the flavors and consistency of locally grown, and organic meat, eggs, and produce. Let's face is, few of us need to be eating the portions we are, and this is one case where less is definitely more. Now, if you're not a hedonistic, narcissistic foodie (*and we still love you*), here are three more reasons. The depth and breadth of these points are endless, but I've tried to distill them down to their essence. You can find plenty more out there on the internet or, better yet, by striking up a conversation with a real-life farmer at your local Farmer's Market.

What you see is what you get.

Organically raised animals aren't fed antibiotics, rbGH - bovine human growth hormone (*if that term doesn't freak you out, it should*), or other artificial feed or drugs. These animals aren't fed genetically modified foods either. Further, animal products certified as organic cannot have their genes modified.

If you've ever stayed up late for "Classics Night" on the Sci-Fi channel…you know that this kind of thing is probably just a really bad idea anyway…

Farmers working on organic farms use fewer chemicals.

Synthetic pesticides and fertilizers aren't sprayed on crops or fields, which is good for both your veggies and your protein, as residue from chemicals like DDT, PCBs, dioxin, and others, can concentrate in animal fat. Eating organic protein reduces your exposure to these chemicals. Grass and water…that's what I want going into the cow that's going into my burger.

Chef's Note: *Balance in the key. "Moderation in all things, including moderation." The last thing you want to become is a zealot, that joyless gas-bag that is the bore of dinner parties, and the terror of wait staff everywhere.*

A concrete-jungle Gandalf, who will passionately decry the naked barbarism of eating the flesh of his fellow mammal as murder, while gleefully extolling the virtues of drinking the "live" kombucha.

Personally, I find the moral high ground of mercifully dispatching my food before subjecting it to the boiling death of my stomach acids, but perhaps that's just me.

Or maybe I just don't like hippies…

You get to be a good neighbor.

By buying and supporting local farmers of sustainable and organic operations in your local community you also support the sustainability of your own area. You put people to work in your neighborhood, who are going to put those paychecks back into your neighborhood.

Here's a favorite video recipe of mine that we demo'd at the Wilsonville farmer's market with fresh kale that was only hours out of the ground. SO good!

Google: youtube bacon kale slaw

You create local jobs, encourage economic growth, and help improve the financial as well as physical health of your community.

So, I encourage you to visit your local farmer's market, try out a few fruits and veggies from the organic section, and pick up some farm-fresh eggs (*you'll never go back, trust me*). Buy a little less, eat a little less, buy the good stuff, and see if you don't enjoy it even more!

Why I drink Raw Milk (and why you should too...)

My family and I drink raw milk from our own goats, and make our own cheese with the same. The US Government's stand on milk and cheese really pisses me off *(tho', in all fairness, lots of things about the US government really pisses me off...)*

- Pasteurization laws are based on century old technology, and held in place only by the massive bribes of big dairy lobbyists who want to keep smaller, local milk and cheese producers *(who can't afford pasteurization equipment and facilities)* out of the game. Don't be fooled for a minute. It has nothing to do with your health, but *(as usual)* everything to do with your money.

- Pasteurization kills protective enzymes that prevent spoilage and help humans digest milk.

- Heating milk destroys nutrients in it, particular vitamins C, some B vitamins, calcium and magnesium.

Raw milk is indeed healthier. Studies show that children fed raw milk have more resistance to TB than children fed pasteurized milk; that raw milk is very effective in preventing scurvy and protecting against flu, diphtheria and pneumonia; that raw milk prevents tooth decay, even in children who eat a lot of sugar; that raw milk is better than pasteurized milk in promoting growth and calcium absorption (*Ohio Agricultural Experiment Station Bulletin 518, p 8, 1/33*); that a substance present in raw cream (but not in pasteurized cream) prevents joint stiffness and the pain of arthritis (*Annual Review of Biochemistry*); and that children who drink raw milk have fewer allergic skin problems and far less asthma than children who drink pasteurized milk. Producers of raw milk are also better caretakers of cows, the land, and the milk, because they cannot "hide" bad practices by killing off all pathogens in their milk post-facto.

"In the 19th century, as cities grew, milk became one of the main ways that diseases like tuberculosis and typhoid were spread. It's not really surprising that milk was so badly contaminated then. <u>In the days before refrigeration, milk couldn't be shipped in from the countryside</u>, instead, cows were brought to the city.

They were <u>crammed into dark dirty cellars, and milked by poor people who were forced to live in similar conditions</u>...conditions that were ripe for the spread of infectious disease. The reason we first began pasteurizing milk, is because raw milk was killing lots of people." ~ Michael Pollan, *Cooked*

I've underlined what I think are the two important, and largely ignored, statements in that quote. These laws (*which were very necessary at the time*) where enacted doing a time when there was no refrigerated trucking, and due to unregulated and unsupervised conditions of cleanliness. However, we ae no longer living in 1901, we are living in 2016.

In France, there are no laws restricting raw (*unpasteurized*) milks and cheeses, instead, the government have very strict hygiene requirements for dairy facilities.

The French, who take their cheese very seriously, are meticulous about using only the very highest quality milk, as opposed to the direction we've gone here in the states, which is that milk that doesn't meet the standard requirements for being pasteurized for drinking, is labeled "manufacturing-grade" and is used for cheese making.

Think about that for a minute.

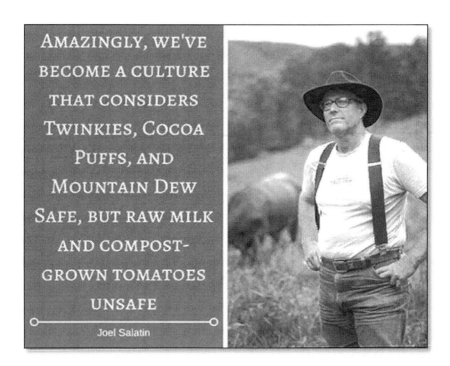

AMAZINGLY, WE'VE BECOME A CULTURE THAT CONSIDERS TWINKIES, COCOA PUFFS, AND MOUNTAIN DEW SAFE, BUT RAW MILK AND COMPOST-GROWN TOMATOES UNSAFE

Joel Salatin

Good food starts with good food

(and a pretty rockin' marinara sauce)

Not *expensive* food, not even "fancy" food *(though that can be a lot of fun, when you can swing it)*, but good, real, *recognizable* food.

Start small, instead of buying that can of diced tomatoes, buy three fresh, organic *Roma* tomatoes *(about the same price)*, dice them in a bowl, and sprinkle a little salt and sugar on them to release the juices and soften the flesh without making it pithy or sour.

10 minutes later you'll have the same, but far superior tasting ingredient: diced tomatoes in juice…and really, was it that hard?

And I'm not even going to bring up the subject of the health benefits of freshly made food, vs. pre-packaged.

So, let's take that one tiny step further…now that you have your diced tomatoes, is it really that much harder to dice up an onion, a little garlic, and squirt some olive oil in a pan?

Sauté (*fry with very little oil*) for 10 minutes. Toss in some fresh herbs (*which you can now buy pre-packaged in about any combination you could need*) and your diced tomatoes, and give a stir.

Throw some pasta and water in a pot...spaghetti, linguine, penne (*my favorite*), angel-hair, whatever, and let heat and water work it's crazy magic for you.

Meanwhile, grill a chicken breast, or cook and crumble some ground pork, or sauté some zucchini slices, or if you're feeling *really* crazy, poach a dozen little-neck clams in their shells...(*don't flip the clams*), with a generous sprinkle of salt and pepper.

And don't worry about a bunch of spices, see the what *food* tastes like first, and to quote a chef I know..."Bam!" you've got a dish of pasta that probably cost less, and certainly tastes much better than you'll ever get from that bottled and canned muck on the shelves.

> **Chef's Tip:** *Store spices and oils in a cool, dark place, NOT above your stove. Humidity, light and heat will cause them to lose their flavor quickly.*

Sprinkle on a tablespoon or so of fresh grated asiago cheese (*it's in the deli section, it's expensive, and it's worth it. Plus, a little goes a LONG way*) and I promise you, I PROMISE you, you will never, willingly, go back to prepared, bottled "spaghetti sauce."

Why is it so damn good?

Not because it's harder to make (*it really wasn't, was it?*) Certainly not because it was more expensive...it wasn't, at least not much.

No, it tastes so darn good, because you used **good food** to make it!

Fresh Herbs

Using fresh herbs in your cooking can easily change the flavors of your dishes in many ways, based which herbs you add. Fresh herbs are great in sauces, stews, soups or vegetables. Each time you add a new herb you've completely changed the flavor.

If you're a beginner take it slow, a little at a time, adjusting your recipe bit by bit until it's just right. In most instances individual herbs are associated with a particular food. Basil pairs superbly with tomatoes, Oregano with sauces, Rosemary is amazing with lamb, and Chives marry perfectly with butter or cream cheese. Obviously, none of these herbs are limited to these just items, but these are the ones you'll most often find them paired with.

Experiment, experiment, experiment!

Homemade herb vinegars make for lovely salad dressings, marinades, or soups. Herb oils are equally delicious in recipes that call for oil.

Fresh herbs can be used as a garnish on almost any dish, making it beautiful, while adding a fresh, delicious zip. I never send out a potato salad (*or almost any potato dish*) without a healthy sprinkling of fresh chopped parsley, and few Mexican dishes leave my kitchen without a similar treatment of freshly chopped fresh cilantro.

 The combinations are as endless as the outcomes are delicious.

Spices

Spices are something of a mystery for most people. Few people ever venture beyond salt, pepper, and maybe basil or garlic powder.

Spices are an art, and can change and enhance the flavors of foods in many, many ways.

With endless spices to choose from, how do you know which spices best compliment which foods, let alone each other?

The answer, of course, is EDUCATION.

Learn all you can, and practice what you learn. If you like the flavors of specific ethnic foods at a favorite restaurant, ask the wait staff what combination of spices you're tasting. Even if they have to ask the chef...do it! We love it when people appreciate and are curious about our creations.

We'll talk more about this in the chapter on spices.

There are many great YouTube classes on herbs and spices. For one of my favorites:

Google: YouTube "All About Spices"

How to shop for vegetables

Okay, so here are some tips on how to pick good produce while shopping for a few of my favorite veggies…

Artichokes: Compact, plump, heavy, with thick, green, tightly closed leaves. Avoid if leaves are dry, spreading, or hard-tipped.

Asparagus: Straight stalks with closed, compact tips and full green color, except for white ends. Avoid if shriveled or have spreading tips. Thicker stalks should be peeled before cooking.

Avocados: Shiny green or mottled purplish-black (depending upon variety); yield to gentle pressure. Ripen in a paper bag at room temperature.

Beans: Firm, crisp, bright color.

Broccoli: Dark green, firmly clustered buds on firm, but not thick, stalks.

Cabbage: Firm, heavy, with brightly colored (green or red) outer leaves and no black blemishes.

Carrots: Firm, straight, with bright orange color, preferably with fresh green leaves attached. Avoid if limp or cracked.

Cauliflower: Firm heads with tightly packed creamy white clusters and fresh-looking green leaves. Avoid those with black spots.

Cucumbers: Medium to small, with bright green color. Avoid any with soft ends, or wax coatings.

Garlic: Firm heads with tight, compact cloves. Papery skin should be soft, not brittle.

Leeks: Firm, white base with fresh-looking green leaves.

Mushrooms: Firm, plump with tightly closed caps and fresh-looking stems. Select carefully, avoiding mold.

Onions: Clean, dry, firm with papery husks, and no sprouts or soft spots.

Peas: Firm, bright or light green, with well-filled pods. Avoid swollen, wrinkled, or immature dark green pods.

Peppers: Firm, shiny, with bright color, green, red, orange, or yellow. Avoid soft spots, or darkened stem ends.

Potatoes: Firm, smooth skinned, well-shaped, with no sprouts.

Spinach: Bright green, fresh, tender leaves with no yellowing or wilted ends.

Squash: (*zucchini, yellow, straight neck, patty pan*) Smooth, bright skin, bright color, green or yellow, heavy and firm.

Sweet potatoes: Firm, uniform shape with even color. Avoid very large ones (*it's a sign of age*).

Tomatoes: Firm, plump with unbroken skin; color and size depends on variety.

Turnips: Firm, unblemished, heavy for their size with fresh-looking tops.

Shopping the Salad Bar

Here's one of my favorite "shopping" tips:

Often when a recipe is calling for a small amount of a fresh ingredient, like a 1/4 cup of diced onions or celery, some sliced mushrooms, a couple of tablespoons of chickpeas, etc., and that's all you're going to need of that ingredient for the week…you can save some trouble, money, and wasted food, by buying just the exact amount you need from the salad bar!

(If your favorite store doesn't have one, your local hospital cafeteria probably will. Don't cringe, it's likely to be cleaner and more sanitary than that salad bar at your favorite restaurant, lol.)

The higher "cost per pound" is mitigated by the small amounts you're actually buying for your recipes, and the fact that you're not paying for any waste or trim.

Plus, someone else has prepped it for you!

Chef's Tip: most salad bars stay stocked with the same ingredients all the time. Sneak a quick picture of yours, with your phone or tablet, and save it as a reference when planning your shopping.

The Flavor Profiles

Taste is the sensation that's produced when food (or any other substance) in our mouths react chemically with receptor cells located on taste buds (mostly on the tongue).

The tongue is covered with thousands of small bumps which are visible to the naked eye. Within each of these are hundreds of taste buds.

Others are located on the roof, sides and back of the mouth, and in the throat.

Each taste bud contains upwards of 100 receptor cells. The sensation of taste can be broken down into five general categories: sweet, sour, salty, bitter, and umami. Scientific experiments have proven that these five tastes exist and are distinct from one another.

Umami – from the Japanese meaning "pleasant savory taste", and popularly referred to as "savoriness," is one of the five basic tastes together with sweet, sour, bitter, and salty.

The Chinese characters for Umami, 旨味, are also used for a more general meaning to describe a food as delicious.

Umami (*my personal favorite*) is most often found in fish, shellfish, cured meats, vegetables (*e.g., mushrooms, ripe tomatoes, Chinese cabbage, spinach, celery, etc.*) meat broths, as well as fermented and aged products like cheeses, shrimp pastes, soy sauce, etc.

Anchovies are another popular umami food. In fact, they're often added to Italian red sauces as a "secret ingredient" to sharpen the other flavors in the dish. You've probably had them more than once like this and didn't even know it, as there's typically no detectable anchovy or "fishy" flavor in the finished sauce.

Humans' first encounter with umami is often breast milk. It contains roughly the same amount of umami as broth.

A key to great cooking is the ability to a balance one flavor with another. Flavors can compliment or contrast one another to create a deeper, uniquely flavored dish.

One of my favorite examples is combining sweet and spicy, as in bbq sauces, or Thai sweet chili sauce. Mexican hot chocolate, finished with a pinch of cayenne pepper, is another great example.

Think about what flavor type that most of your favorite foods have in common (*I love umami, but am not a fan of bitter*). This can help you find new foods and recipes that fall in your own sweet (*or sour*) spot!

The Truth about "Super-Foods"

In our over-priced, over-lit, over-hyped, media-crazed society, it should come as no surprise that there has been some serious lily-gilding on the subject of "super-foods."

Oh, it's not that these new and exotic foods from far-away lands aren't really, really good for you.

Acai and goji berries are loaded with phytochemicals, quinoa is a solid source of meat-free protein (*which, unfortunately has become so hyped that it's now too expensive for the native peoples who grow the stuff to eat anymore...*)

It's not that "super-foods aren't, well...super, it's just that there are lots and lots of amazing, if not quite so exotic, foods (blueberries, legumes, nuts, etc.,) that are every bit as good for you, with a much less over-hyped price tag, and a vastly smaller carbon footprint.

The only difference is that big-media isn't blasting us 24/7/365 with revenue-greedy hype over the amazing power of a kidney bean, while we stand, en-mass, mouths agape, credit cards in hand, nodding like a bunch of glassy-eyes children of the (*non-GMO*) corn.

RANDOM ACT OF KINDNESS
feeding pepperoni slices to our vegan
neighbor's toddler, through the mail slot.

On the Philosophy of Veganism

I spent a great deal of time writing and re-writing this chapter, which originally numbered 78 pages. Then I decided that I like you better than that. You seem like a nice enough person and, of course, you bought my book, so I didn't want to subject you to that. So, trimmed it down to a concise six pages, with 90% less snark.

You're welcome.

First and foremost, let me say this.... my comments here are about the *PHILOSPHY* of veganism, the Logan's Run meets 1984 totalitarian dogma of it, and not about a medical need, or personal dietary choice.

If you choose to eat a vegan diet for health reasons, or simply because it makes you feel better physically, emotionally or spiritually, and are willing to leave it at that, allowing others to make that same choice (*or not*) for themselves, then please understand that you have my 100% unequivocal support of your lifestyle choice.

[119]

I won't say I'd "die for your right to do so", but I'd probably write a snarky blogpost in your favor.

HOWEVER...My issue is with veganism as a *philosophy*, unsupported by anything more than bumper-sticker logic and lemming-esque Facebook meme arguments. I have, in my lifetime, seen veganism metastasize (*and yes, I use that word in the full cancerous definition*) through the typical liberal arch of:

"Live and let live" *to...*

"Really, everyone should feel the way I do", *to...*

The banner-carrying social bullying of "Anyone who doesn't agree with my enlightened philosophy is ignorant and/or morally evil."

That's social manipulation, and manipulation pisses me off. I don't like it in politics, in religion (including my own), or in the latest pseudo-intellectual fad philosophy.

> *"Vegans are the Hezbollah of the food world."*
> ~ *Anthony Bourdain*

So, instead of continuing with the other 77 pages of my rant, let me just point out the basic arguments and the obvious facts that discredit them... (*and yes, I will leave out my personal religious view on the subject, and the supporting documentation, though they be equally valid.*)

Argument #1: Cruelty to Animals.

This is probably the most popular (*and least logical*) argument.

Yes, cramming a bunch of chickens into a tiny cage and feeding them until they're too fat to stand isn't a particularly pleasant (*or culinarily smart*) thing to do. But, even if you give the animal the best life possible, as I try to do on my own family farm. there's no getting around the fact you're going to kill a sentient animal for dinner. Honestly, you can see why some people flat-out refuse to eat meat from this perspective.

However, refusing to eat meat because of industrial farming conditions is throwing the baby out with the bathwater.

It is intellectually and philosophically lazy. If your best and only argument is animal cruelty, then you are morally obligated to fight that system by supporting small, local providers who raise their animals in free-range, cruelty-free environments.

On a larger perspective, there are companies like *Humane Farm Animal Care*, a fantastic nonprofit organization created to improve the lives of farm animals by certifying their humane treatment. When you see the Certified Humane Raised and Handled® label on a product, you can be assured that the products in question have come from facilities that meet precise, objective standards for animal treatment.

> *When I met my wife 20 plus years ago, she was a vegetarian, so I was the closest thing to the devil that she had ever met.*
>
> ~ *Michael Symon*

Other organizations, like the *American Humane Association* (AHA), offer meat certifications to farms that practice humane farming techniques. Their standards are based upon the values of the Royal Society for the Prevention of Cruelty to Animals, as well as input from animal science experts and veterinarians.

If you don't want to eat animals that are raised in cruel conditions...don't! Put pressure on these corporate farms by supporting cruelty-free farms. Vote with your wallet, and when the big guys feel the pinch, they will change the way they do business. Your money is all they care about...use it to *be* the change you want to see.

Argument #2: Personal Health

This point has almost become a joke. Numerous studies have repeatedly shown that non-meat eaters who fail to supplement their diets with Vitamin D, B12 and iron often become dangerously anemic. Herbivores are also typically lacking in omega-3 fatty acids, which have been proven to slow the progression of atherosclerosis, reduce triglyceride levels, act as anti-inflammatory agents, and possibly help with depression and some personality disorders.

Oxford University recently followed 35,000 people from ages 20 to 89 for five years, and found that vegans are 30% more likely to break a bone than omnivores. Sydney's *Garvan Institute for Medical Research* has reported that vegan's bones are 5% less dense than meat-eaters, as vegans consume very little calcium due to the limitations of their diet.

Also, meat substitutes, like TVP are highly processed, and require considerable land and energy to produce.

Ironically, many vegans don't realize that they are not, in fact, eating "pure vegan" anyway...as many beers and wines contain dried fish bladder and gelatin made from pig and cow hooves, as do gelatin desserts and products. Candy contains cochineal extract made from crushed beetles, and many refined sugars contain bone char.

On a personal note, I have tried to bring this last point to the attentional of numerous vegetarians and vegans over the years, and the response I almost universally receive is..."Don't tell me...I don't want to know!"

Hmm...

Argument #3: We are not carnivores, evolutionarily speaking

From an evolutionary standpoint, we must keep in mind some blatant oddities of the human race. First, our brains simply shouldn't be as big as they are (*despite what reality TV in general, and the Kardashian's specifically, would seem to imply*...) The standard Earth primate's brains is comparative with its body size...except humans. There's also the much more advanced complexity of our brains, which are packed with neurons that are capable of storing exponentially more thoughts and memories, than any other species. Why?

Well according to a 2011 study...it's because of meat!

Honest. Studies suggest that as far back as 1.5 million years ago, cooking and eating meat, which provides vastly higher nutrition/calories to energy expenditure ratio than a herbivore diet, allowed the primate brain's complexity to go supernova.

In other words...if you don't have to spend all day grazing and chewing your cud to extract every last calorie possible from grass, your brain has time to grow and develop beyond the basic need to consume enough calories to survive.

In a nutshell, we're only capable of making intellectual choices like vegetarianism because we originally ate other animals. BOO-Yah!

Argument #4: Morality

This is, perhaps, the most ridiculous, and unsupportable argument for veganism. From the standpoint of "being one with nature" what would be more hypocritical than telling the human, the lion, the wolf, the coyote, the eagle...to not eat meat? Holding one species (*mankind*) to a higher standard of morality is to deny the very equality of nature that this argument predisposes.

To set mankind "outside of nature" is, well...unnatural. Also, does this food-morality extend to wearing clothes made by virtual slaves in third world countries; eating vegetables and grains that bring about the death of billions of sentient mammals (mice, rats, voles, moles, insects) in the farming and processing industry?

If my eating a few strips of bacon each day should produce a headache-inducing liberal guilt-trip, then perhaps it's time to look past your plate to the footprint the rest of your life, and lifestyle, is leaving on the world. Personally, I find the "food morality" argument to be especially hypocritical coming from a social group that tells me I have no right to "push" my personal religious morals on other.

'Nuff said.

Argument #5: Humans are the only Primate that Eats Meat

This is the absolutely unsupportable argument that humans are the only primates to eat meat. Ergo, it must be unnatural, is also the easiest to disprove. Jane Goodall observed chimps, clear back in the 1960's, hunting and eating other animals in the wild. Studies since have shown that many chimp communities eat as much as a ton of meat annually. IE:, this isn't as much about indulging occasional cravings, as it is a standard part of the primate's (*that's us*) diet. IE: we eat meat.

Argument #6: Carnivorism is Bad for the Environment

One of the big reasons for giving up meat, for many, is the supposed devastating environmental impact of getting, let's say, a rib-eye steak from Argentina to a New York City restaurant. Yes, we each have a carbon footprint, and we should be aware of our environmental shoe size.

BUT, (*and there's always a big butt*) before pointing that bony, anemic finger at the meat-eating diet, keep in mind that our furniture came from a tree that was killed and processed, disrupting animal and insect habitats. The gas that runs our cars comes from an oil company that has likely caused far more harm and pollution to marine and wildlife inhabitants.

Plastic bags pollute our marine ecosystem. Our sugar is rapidly destroying the Everglades wildlife, and, again, millions of animals such as mice and rabbits are killed every year when land is prepared for crops. If all life is to be protected, are these small animals any less valuable than the cow, pig, or chicken? If the argument is that all life matters, how can one support the idea that taking the life of an animal on a factory farm is in any way more immoral than the deaths of small animals in the growing of produce crops to feed vegans?

At what intelligence level is a "lesser" animal's death acceptable for a human's well-being? Vegans will argue that the cultivation of meat harms the environment, while they fail to research the fact that cultivating fruits and veggies can have an equally devastating environmental impact. Dangerous chemicals often leach into the water table, and can cause harmful neurological effects when ingested by humans and animals.

Produce farms also harm the environment through agricultural waste burning, and oxide emissions from nitrogen fertilizer.

The harsh truth is that life requires death. If we want to keep breathing, something else has to die. Everything else is semantics and justification. As the most intelligent (and dominate) species on this planet, it is our responsibility to not deny the natural process of predator and prey, of survival of the fittest, and to manage it ethically and responsibly. On the topic of environment, I gotta point out that the human body's inability to fully digest complex carbohydrates found in veggies results in a lot more gas from vegetarians and vegans produce a lot more gas than omnivores, increasing the production of gasses like carbon dioxide and methane.

Greenhouse-gas emissions be damned, I blame global warming on the growing number of farting vegans.

> *"You don't win friends with salad."*
> *-Homer Simpson*

I recently received what is, HANDS DOWN, the most ludicrous spam email subject line ever. Go home Nigerian inheritors; find a new job pyramid schemers, the contest is over...

"Try the new vegan taco recipe that's BETTER than pulled pork!"

For God's sake, America...we need to get these nutters off the streets. I mean, c'mon, the world is watching!

When I mentioned this to my Facebook tribe, one friend jokingly responded. "Why do vegans need food that tastes like meat, anyway?"

To which I, of course, responded, "Pretty sure you could shorten that sentence to just the first five words..." (Thank you for that softball, Nichole!)

Another friend, who I suspect may be a closet vegan, or at least have sympathies slanting dangerously in that dark, cold direction (I maintain a firm "Don't Ask, Don't Tell" policy with FB friends), interjected in a somewhat "Hitler was nice to kittens" voice, that "Jackfruit is actually pretty good. Just saying..."

Perhaps, but I maintain that whatever EATS the jackfruit probably tastes better.

In all fairness, that's just me enjoying the sound of my own voice (again). In truth, I find Jackfruit to be very tasty...but I'm still not going to slice it into a rectangle and say it's better than a steak.

And, just to clarify my position ('cause I know you were just waiting for me to do THAT)...I am NOT anti-vegetable.

I am simply anti-zealot, regardless of what's inscribed on the specific white-washed pillar they're standing. I despise mind-numbing laziness of character typified in contempt prior to investigation.

Anyone who would turn up their nose at a plate of fresh chanterelle mushrooms, a ripe Georgia peach, a cool tomato plucked from the vine, or a steaming hot artichoke dripping with garlic butter, is just about as afflicted by their own constipation of the brain and diarrhea of the mouth type of mental masturbation as any anti-meat man-bun-wearing hemp-headed hipster out there.

Hell's cafeteria is staffed with Vegans and Meatgans...and their nametags all read, "Douche."

Homework Assignment #4
Finding you umami

Here's my favorite umami recipe. Amazing on beef, pork, chicken, pasta, an old flip-flop…you name it!

Mushroom Duxelles

1 Tbs. unsalted butter	2 Tbs. minced shallots
½ tsp. minced garlic	10 oz. button mushrooms
¼ tsp. salt	1/8 tsp. ground white pepper
2 ½ Tbs. dry white wine	Toasted baguette, 1 in. rounds

Once the mushrooms are wiped clean, stemmed, and finely chopped, melt the butter in a medium skillet over medium-high heat.

Add the shallots and garlic and cook, stirring, for 30 seconds.

Add the mushrooms, salt, and white pepper, reduce the heat to medium.

Cook, stirring, until all the liquid has evaporated and the mushrooms begin to caramelize, about 12 minutes.

Add the wine and cook, stirring to deglaze the pan, until all the liquid has evaporated. Remove from the heat and let cool before using.

Yield: 1/2 cup

At the end of the day it's just food, isn't it?
Just food.
~ *Marco Pierre White*

Part Three
"The Home Chef's Kitchen"

Interior of a Kitchen.—Fac-simile from a Woodcut in the "Calendarium Romanum" of J. Staéffler, folio, Tubingen, 1518.

The evolution of the kitchen began with cooking over an open fire, on hot stones or sharp sticks which then progressed to an indoor stone "hearth" in the middle of the room which (usually) protected the rest of the house, which was built mostly with organic (*i.e.: flammable*) materials. Before the advent of modern pipes, water was brought from an outdoor source such as wells or springs.

In Ancient Greece, homes were commonly arranged around a central, partially covered courtyard, which served as group kitchen. Only the houses of the very wealthy had its own kitchen as a separate room. Romans, on the other hand, at least the commoners, typically had no kitchen of their own; and did their cooking in large public kitchens.

Some had small mobile bronze stoves, on which a fire could be lit for cooking. Again, wealthy Romans had fairly well-equipped kitchens, set apart for practical reasons of smoke (*there were no chimneys*) and with a raised fireplace, requiring the cook to kneel while cooking.

The Middle Ages brought spit roasting inside, in combination with an open fire (*still no chimney, just a hole in the roof.*) Similar designs can be found in the ancient Iroquois longhouses of North America.

In the larger homesteads of European nobles, the kitchen was sometimes in a separate sunken floor building to keep the main building free from smoke. European medieval kitchens were dark, smoky, and sooty places, and were referred to as "smoke kitchens."

The first stoves, invented in Japan, date from the 3rd to 6th century. Called "kamado", they were made of clay and fired with wood or charcoal through a hole in the front. A pot was hung over the fire through another hole in the top. This was pretty much the only option on modern kitchenware for centuries, until the invention of the chimneys, constructed in castles, in the 12th century. This brought the fire from the middle of the room to an outer wall, and in the first brick-and-mortar hearths

Using open fire for cooking was a risky business, and fires devastating whole cities were not uncommon.

Many of the wealthier homes used Leonardo da Vinci's propeller driven automated rotating spit (pictured, left) for spit-roasting in the chimney.

In the early New England colonies, kitchens were often built as separate rooms and were located behind the dining room.

In the southern states, specifically on the large plantations, the kitchen was separate from the big house or mansion.

The kitchen was operated by slaves, and their working place had to be separated from the living area of the masters by the social standards of the time.

> *The kitchen really is the castle itself. This is where we spend our happiest moments and where we find the joy of being a family.*
>
> *~Mario Batali*

The 1800's began a surge of innovation and invention that transformed, and continues to transform, the modern kitchen still today, beginning with Sir Benjamin Thompson's huge commercial "Rumford stove" in 1800, which was quickly transformed into the more domestic-friendly "Oberlin" style stove

Love your kitchen cabinets?

Thank the Hoosier Manufacturing Co!

Just over a hundred years ago, kitchens were frequently still not equipped with built-in cabinetry or storage (*as you can imagine...a problem*).

The Hoosier Manufacturing Co. of Indiana adapted existing furniture like the baker's table with some cabinets above it (*and frequently flour/grain bins beneath.*)

A little creative rearranging of parts and they were able to produce a well-organized, compact cabinet which answered the home cook's needs for storage and working space. The first electrical stove had been presented in 1893 at the World's Columbian Exposition in Chicago, but it was not until the 1930s that the "technology was stable."

I would assume that means it stopped starting fires and electrocuting cooks. Most of the factory working class in cities lived in deplorable conditions.

Entire families, often multi-generational, lived in tiny one or two-room tenement apartments up to six stories high, with little ventilation, and insufficient lighting.

The kitchen was often used as a living and sleeping room, and even as a bathroom.

Even buildings that had running water, often only had one tap per building or per story.

Brick stoves burned coal, while pots and kitchenware were usually stored on open shelves.

The "kitchen" was typically separated from the rest of the room using only a curtain.

For the wealthy, of course, things only got better.

Water pumps were installed, sometimes even with kitchen sinks and drains.

Everything became much cleaner with closed stoves with flue pipes connected to the chimney.

Kitchen floors were tiled; cooking gear was kept in cupboards to protect them from dust.

The Raytheon "Radarange" (1947), the first commercially available microwave oven was .5 ft. tall, 750 lbs., and cost about US$5,000 ($53,000 in today's dollars) each. In 1967,(Now Amana...) they introduced the first popular home model, the countertop Radarange.

A large table served as a workbench; there were at least as many chairs as there were servants, for the table in the kitchen also doubled as the eating place for the servants. (*Think "Downton Abbey"*.)

Following WWII, another surge forward came with the popularity of the gas stoves to replace the older coal-fired stoves. (*In workers' apartments gas distribution would go through a coin meter.*)

From there, the highlights are the electric range/oven (*and matching refrigerator*), the dishwasher, the counter-top microwave oven (*introduced in 1967 by the Amana Corporation*) and with our current boom of all things food and cooking...an endless string of toys from desktop salamanders, immersion circulators, and fatless fryers.

Food Safety

Here are just a few pointers that most cooks already know, to refresh and reinforce your common sense as you are preparing your current meal or storing it for future use.

- Food safety actually starts with your excursion to the supermarket. Pick up the packaged or canned foods.

  - ✓ Do the cans have dents? Don't buy them.

  - ✓ Is the jar cracked? Leave it.

  - ✓ Does the lid seem loose or bulging? Pick up another.

  - ✓ Look for any expiration dates on the labels -they are there for a reason. Never buy outdated food. Check the "use by" or "sell by" date on dairy products and pick the ones that will stay fresh the longest.

- After grocery shopping, put food into the refrigerator or freezer right away.

  - ✓ Make sure the refrigerator temperature is set to 40F and the freezer is set to 0F. Refrigerate or freeze perishables, prepared foods, and leftovers within 2 hours.

  - ✓ Raw meat, poultry, and seafood should be placed in containers to prevent their juices from dripping on other foods. Raw juices could possibly harbor harmful bacteria..

- Always cook food thoroughly until it is done. Chicken, when poked with a fork, should have clear juices. Fish, on the other hand, when poked with a fork, should flake.

- Be sure to use a food thermometer to check the internal temperatures of your poultry, meat, and other foods. Leave it in long enough to ensure an accurate reading.

- Wash your hands and cooking surfaces frequently. Bacteria can be spread quickly so this will ensure that it will not take hold and grow onto your food. A solution of one teaspoon of bleach in one quart of water is all that is needed to sanitize washed surfaces and utensils.

- Cooked foods should definitely not be left standing in the kitchen counter or table for more than two hours. Bacteria tends to grow in temperatures between 40 and 140F.

- Foods that have been cooked ahead and cooled should be reheated to at least 165F. (*This just so happens to be one of the most overlooked areas in food prep*).

- Chill Leftover Food Promptly. Place food in the refrigerator and don't overfill. The cold air needs to circulate freely to keep food safe.

Divide the food and place in shallow containers. Think about labeling some of these containers so you don't lose track of how long they've been refrigerating.

These are just a few pointers that you already know, but need to keep remembering. If you follow these basics you will avoid most of the 'disasters in waiting'!

One of the most prevalent illnesses today is food poisoning. It starts as a slight discomfort a few hours after eating, and grows into a life-threatening episode requiring hospitalization. The most common cause are the salmonella, e-coli, and listeria bacteria. And, these can be common problems in the kitchen.

Common breeding grounds for bacteria are kitchen towels, dish rags and brushes, cutting boards, kitchen sinks, door, drawer, and refrigerator handles. Little things like timers, whisk handles, pepper mills, and salt shakers also become breeding grounds for bacteria.

You can also add bottles of oil, spice jars, can openers, and the controls on your stove or ovens. Food itself can be storage places for bacteria with the culprits chicken and other poultry, eggs, raw meats, dairy products, and even fresh fruits and veggies.

In addition to washing your hands regularly while cooking here is a list of things you should do in your kitchen to reduce the likelihood of food poisoning:

1. Wash poultry in ice cold water when you bring it home from the supermarket and refrigerate immediately. Cook it as soon as possible.

2. Wash your hands and everything else that comes in contact with raw poultry.

3. Never reuse knives, cutting boards, towels or anything else that touches raw poultry without washing them. This means don't use the same cutting board or knives to chop vegetables or anything else that will not be cooked immediately.

4. Wash your hands after going to the bathroom. Your family is not immune to your personal e-coli!

5. Wash all vegetables immediately after you bring them home from the market. This includes all fruit including watermelons, strawberries, peaches, mangos, grapes, and almost every other fruit including bananas.

6. Keep your kitchen counters clean. Use a diluted bleach or disinfectant before and after meal preparation.

7. Refrigerate foods as much as you can, and read the labels on condiments, sauces, jams, and jellies to see if they need refrigeration after opening. DO NOT LEAVE MAYONNAISE ON THE COUNTER ON A SUMMER DAY! That goes for anything made with the mayonnaise as well.

8. Gently wash eggs in ice cold water before cracking them. There is nothing sterile about an egg that came from the chicken coop.

9. Buy your meat, especially hamburger, from a reputable butcher shop. (or, better yet, grind your own!)

10. Wash your hands!! I can't repeat this enough!

11. If fish smells like fish, don't buy it! If anything smells "off" or not what you are accustomed to, don't buy it.

12. Drain things over the sink, not in it. This place is teeming with bacteria. Sterilize it often, but still keep edible food out of it.

Now, keep in mind, I said "most cooks"… don't assume that the local corner restaurant with the pristine white tablecloths is a sterile environment either…

When I was fourteen, I worked one depressingly interminable summer in the greasy fly-blown, windowless washroom/sauna of a local (*and very popular*) breakfast chalet that was famous for platter-sized cinnamon rolls served in a huge pool of sickly-sweet icing which had probably killed more locals than crack (*and that's saying something in my neighborhood.*)

The head plongeur that I toiled with had a ritual of licking each and every fork (*the most commonly used utensil*) as it came steaming from the wash box, before placing it in the service tray.

Everyone knew he did it, and he had worked there for fifteen years without reprimand.

Very likely, he's still working there, washing pots and tounging cutlery with obsessive-compulsive glee.

The moral of the story being: don't be too quick to judge….

The guy who brings his own silverware to the restaurant might not be the craziest bastard in the house.

Chapter Eight
The Secret to Kitchen Success...

...is reading preparation! Preparation is reading your recipes. Read them twice...then read twice more!

Preparation is having all of your ingredients on hand and ready to use, having your gear clean and at hand. Professional chefs have a phrase they like to bandy around the kitchen, and it's one that has proved itself to me, both in success and failure, time after time.

They call it the *Six P's*:

"Prior Planning Prevents Piss-Poor Performance."

Sorry, but we *are* talking about chefs, lol. You can shorten that to five p's when working with kids. Let me explain...

Some home chefs find a recipe they'd like to try, often one with a pretty picture, and assume that all they have to do is buy the listed ingredients and they're ready to start cooking.

Honestly, I've done it many times myself.

This habit has probably led to more frustration and disappointment than any other single issue in the kitchen, and many a new home chef has thrown their hands up and said, "I'm just not a good cook!" when, in fact, what they're not is a good *planner*. Stumbling across a technique you're not familiar with, say reducing a sauce, or deglazing a pan, and being forced to do a desperate Google search for a how-to video is NOT something you want to be dealing with while your sauce is bubbling away to a black mess.

When trying a new recipe, read it at least twice from beginning to end before you even go shopping, then read it again before you start doing any cooking.

Chef's Tip: Recipes are only guidelines, not the Bible. Feel free replacing ingredients with similar ingredients that you like. If you like oregano but not thyme, use oregano.

Set up your *mise en place* (*more on that later*), organize the gear and utensils you'll need, maybe even jot down a quick timeline (*starting at the time you want to serve, and working backwards, step-by-step, to your start time*).

By reading the recipe twice, in advance, you'll know if there are any steps or techniques you're not familiar with, and either be able to research those, or decide if you need to put this one back in the box until you have more time.

You'll find out if you're missing a piece of gear (*it takes a LOT longer to mince 4 cups of veggies with a chef's knife than with that food processor that the recipe calls for – believe me, I know!*) By reading it again before you start cooking, you'll determine that you have all of the necessary ingredients BEFORE you reach for something that's not there.

Plus, you're a lot less likely to skip a step (*yes, it happens a lot*) which can be the ruin of even the simplest recipe. All of that said…don't be a slave to a recipe either, even one of mine. Unless you have a good reason to copy, exactly, the way the original chef prepared it, give yourself permission to add or remove ingredients, switch up a sauce, make it hot & spicy (*or not*).

In other words, feel free to experiment with your cooking – just be sure that you're making choices intentionally, not in a panic to fix something you missed.

> *Cooking isn't hard to do. Like most things, there's a learning curve, but it's one you can climb at your own pace.*

Cooking shouldn't be a frustration, either.

In fact, your best cooks will often say, in the midst of a seemingly chaotic kitchen, than the preparation of food relaxes them, puts them into an almost Zen state. Let's face it, chopping a bag of carrots is a heck of a lot cheaper (*and more interesting*) than an half-hour with a therapist.

So, enjoy the process, read and re-read, and remember…Prior Preparation…

"Mise en place"

Professional chefs use a system referred to as "mise en place" (*meez n plaas*) – or "*everything in place*" – getting their ingredients and tools organized and ready ahead of cooking time. This means setting up your kitchen so that everything is within reach.

The area where you do most of your prepping should have easy access to knives and measuring cups so that you're not digging around for the stuff you need. This means having wooden spoons near your stove, where you'll use them, instead of across the kitchen in a drawer; cutting board next to sink and disposal, knives near cutting board. Also, prep your food, open any cans, pre-measure dry ingredients into small bowls (a bio-degradable paper cup, kept in with the sugar, flour, salt, rice, etc...works great and saves on clean-up too!)

> *Always season meat and fish evenly; sprinkle salt and pepper from 12-16 inches above, as though it's "snowing."*
>
> *This will avoid clumping or ending up with too much seasoning in some areas and none in others.*

There are some key factors you need to know about how to read a recipe in regards to the list of ingredients. A list of ingredients is usually included at the beginning, but sometimes ingredients are listed within the recipe itself, as well. Sometimes directions are included within the list of ingredients.

For example; 1 onion, chopped, would mean you would need to chop the onion before adding it to the recipe. In a recipe, 1 ½ cups raspberries fresh or if frozen, thawed, means you will need to make sure your raspberries are thawed before adding them into the recipe. 1 ½ cups sliced bananas, means make sure you slice the bananas before adding them to the smoothie.

Another thing to look for in the list of ingredients is the word optional. Recipes sometimes include ingredients such as raisins or nuts that are not essential for the recipe but can be added in if desired. So, it will say 1 Cup raisins, optional. In some recipes, you will see ingredients listed, followed by "if desired." If desired or optional mean the same thing. You can add the ingredient, leave it out, or replace it with one of your own choosing.

> *Organizing ahead of time makes the work more enjoyable. Chefs cut up the onions and have the ingredients lined up ahead of time and have them ready to go. When everything is organized you can clean as you go and it makes everything so much easier and fun.* ~ *Anne Burrell*

Some recipes will only have a "C" or a "T" or a "t" which would stand for cup, tablespoon, and teaspoon. So, if a recipe called for 1 C sugar and 1/2 t of salt, then you would know that it's calling for 1 cup of sugar and 1/2 teaspoon salt.

- **Directions.** This will give you a step by step explanation of what needs to be done in the cooking process. Read these carefully and follow accurately:

  Finely chop boiled eggs. Mix in mayo 1 tsp. at a time, so not to add too much. Mix in mustard, salt and pepper. Put egg salad mixture on bread, crackers, on rolls, or on top of a green salad.

- **Time.** There are two times included in a recipe. Prep time, that is how much time is estimated it will take to prepare. Again this is just an estimate and may take a longer or shorter time depending on the chef's experience. The other time included in a recipe is total time, which includes the prep and cooking time. This is more accurate and should be followed.

With a proper *mise en place*, you should never have to stray for than a step or two from your cooking "station."

Trust me, this is a HUGE time and frustration saver!

Chapter Nine
The Home Chef's Pantry

Many folks, either when finally deciding to get healthy, or "gettin' back on the horse" have to do some major overhauls of the food they eat, and, therefore, the food they stock. In my business, I plan very different menus and recipes each week, and am often picking up foods or ingredients that I haven't worked with before.

I've learned (*mostly the hard way*) some tips to survive diet, menu, and pantry make-overs.

Here are my top three:

When changing up your pantry…

1. Don't go buy a ton of food you've never eaten.

   ✓ Try to stick to healthier versions of what you know (*1% milk instead of 2%, low-fat yogurt instead of full-fat, etc.*), and add 2-3 "new foods" each trip.

   ✓ This will keep you from finding your pantry overflowing (*and your wallet empty*) in a few months with a bunch of stuff you don't like, and won't eat.

2. Buy new foods in small portions. Based on tip #1 – if you like the ingredient, you can always go back and buy more, but a 25lb bag of brown rice takes up a LOT of space…especially if you won't eat it. The "bulk foods" section of your store, or your local farmer's market, can be a great place to get small portions!

3. Buy what you like to eat (*referring to "real food"*), and practice portion control instead of deprivation.

A little butter is NOT bad for you…pouring half a cup of it on your "steamed" veggies is. A baked potato is NOT bad for you…a bag of frozen French fries in one serving, is.

Don't be afraid to try new things, in fact, embrace new, healthy foods and ingredients. For many of us, variety and adventure are just as important as discipline (*maybe more so*) when it comes to sticking with a healthy lifestyle.

Organizing the Home Chef's Pantry

Confession time…while my on-again-off-again O.C.D. nature can (*sometimes*) keep my kitchen organized to near-military precision, everything else in my life often bears an uncanny resemblance to the living room in Sanford and Son.

That's one reason I picked up a copy of Julie Starr Hook's book **"From Frazzled to Freedom"** at a recent trade show. I need help, and I can admit it.

This is, of course, not my first book on the subject of getting organized, but what I like about this one (*enough to finish reading it, even*) is that it's not another self-righteous tome full of high-road theory (*like "never touch the same piece of mail twice"…if I could do THAT, I wouldn't need a book on getting organized, now would I?*)

No, "From Frazzled to Freedom" is a practical guide to getting (*and staying*) organized, filled with easy-to-follow, step-by-step instructions that I can start putting in place right now… and without making a $2,000 trip to Home Depot first. Best of all, after a brief chat with the author, I have permission to share some of the highlights, especially those related to turning your kitchen into a lean, mean, cooking machine.

Here are a few of the first tip that caught my eye, on the subject of pantries…

If you have a kitchen pantry, you know that it's one of the places in your kitchen that gets used often. A kitchen pantry can be a life-saver for storage. However, it can be an intimidating space to organize because there are so many different types of things you can store in this space.

I know that when you open the pantry door to begin your organization, it can be overwhelming. Don't feel defeated.

Getting the pantry organized, and having it stay as organized, is possible by using good storage organizers, and knowing how to be creative with shelf space. You can reach your goal of a beautiful pantry that is easy to use. Where to begin when organizing the pantry:

- Think in terms of categories and group like items together. The more space you have, the more categories you can include in your pantry. Some categories to consider: baking, breakfast, canned goods, snacks, pasta, rice and dry beans, picnic, etc.

- Keep more frequently used items at eye level.

- Position items you allow your children to use on their own on a shelf accessible to them.

- Instead of stripping down the entire pantry, try to work on a couple of shelves at a time.

- Clear plastic totes work great for organizing baking supplies (*cookie cutters, sprinkles, food coloring, and cake decorating items*), and picnic supplies such as paper plates and plastic eating utensils.

- If you have children, consider labeling the shelves so they know which items go where, this helping to keep the space organized.

The author goes on to offer another dozen practical, and easy-to-implement, tips for getting your pantry organized. Other areas of kitchen organization included in the book are: *Glassware, Cookware, Kitchen Utensils and Knives, Under the Sink, Appliances, Dishware, Kitchen Storage Containers, Recipes and Cookbooks* (um…yes, please!), *Junk Drawer, Spices Oils & Vinegars,* and *Other Kitchen Placement Tips.*

…and that's just the kitchen!

Hook walks you through every nook and corner of your home, offering simple and effective advice for getting them ship-shape and organized.

Here's what the author has to say about her book:

Are you embarrassed when friends show up unexpectedly on your doorstep? Do you regularly misplace important items like your car keys or the bills you need to pay? Would you like to entertain more, if only you could keep your house cleaner and more presentable? Are you ready to stop making excuses and get yourself organized?

If so, then look no further. In this book, author Julie Starr Hook will take you on an encouraging journey from frazzled to freedom – helping you get organized room-by-room and teaching you how to maintain the organized life that currently eludes you.

You'll discover:

- *How to identify the obstacles keeping you from having a more organized life*

- *How to begin the process of organizing both your day and your home*

- *How to organize each room of your house from your kitchen to your bathrooms, bedrooms, and even your closets*

Whether you're just starting out in life, downsizing after the kids have left home, or at any stage in between, the helpful hints in the book can help you achieve your goal of streamlining and simplifying your life. Read them, apply what you learn, and find the freedom you've been looking for!

I highly recommend this book!

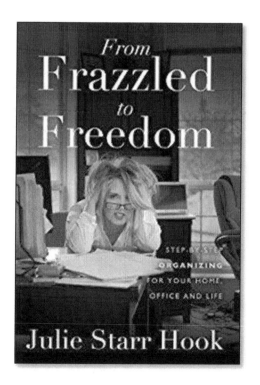

Spices

Spices and seasonings can take a dish from being as plain as cardboard to (*almost*) literally out of this world. Spices were discovered and have been used for hundreds of years in a number of combinations that is unfathomable.

> *She gave the king a hundred and twenty talents of gold, and a very great amount of spices and precious stones. Never again did such abundance of spices come in as that which the queen of Sheba gave King Solomon.*
> *~ 1 Kings 10:10*

The world of spices is wide open to explore, but we, as Americans, have been trained to use recipes to prepare dishes, and most of the time we are scared to stray. This can cause a problem when we want to try a new spice or seasoning, but do not know the proper way to use it. Unlike most Americans, other cultures around the world do not seem to be so intimidated using spices, chilies and dried herbs.

Many of these other cultures have grown up helping out in the kitchen and have no problem cooking by adding a pinch of this spice or a dash of that spice. Americans on the other hand tend to be much more apprehensive about making a mistake in the kitchen.

Master these few "rules" and you'll have much more confidence in experimenting and getting the most out of your spice cabinet.

You don't want to overpower the food with spices, you want to enhance its flavors, so except in a very few instances you want to use herbs and spices sparingly.

> *The secret of happiness is variety, but the secret of variety, like the secret of all spices, is knowing when to use it.*
> *~ Daniel Gilbert*

The Rules

Remember the ½ Rule - Start off with 1/2 teaspoon of spice for any dish that serves four to six people. And for herbs, use 1/2 teaspoon for powders and 1-1/2 teaspoon for dried or chopped.

Let Flavors Marry - During the preparation of salad dressings, blend the ingredients with the seasonings several hours before they are needed and then refrigerate. This allows the flavors to bond, or "marry"..

Chile Peppers are HOT! - Don't underestimate the potency of red peppers or any spice blends with red pepper (*or any chile pepper*) in them, as at first their tastes usually appear somewhat mild – but their heat will sneak up on you and you don't want them to overwhelm you after two or three bites! *PS ~ Never, ever, ever, go to the bathroom right after working with hot peppers...just trust me.*

Don't Let the Flavor Disappear - It's best to add ground or cut spices and herbs around the midway point or towards the end of the cooking process, so that their flavors won't disappear. This allows the spices enough time to marry with the food.

Make Your Fish Delish - With fish you want to marinate in lemon juice and herbs and then refrigerate for several hours before cooking.

You can also place the herbs across fish before steaming.

So there it is. Once you've nailed these simple steps, you'll start gaining confidence and begin experimenting with your favorite flavors. It's also very important to consider where you keep your spices. Spice cabinet? Counter-top rack? Some folks keep their spices in the refrigerator or even the freezer. Many cooks keep their spices in a cabinet above the stove, conveniently within reach. DON'T DO THIS! Exposing your dried herbs and spices to the heat and moisture that collects above your stove, will cause them to rapidly break down, leaching out flavor, and causing clumping in granular or powdered spices.

While counter-top spices racks are a better option, I don't like to use up that much of my coveted counter space. If you don't mind, just be sure that you place them in a spot that stays cool and out of direct sunlight. This goes for those cool magnetic boards as well.

As far as the fridge or freezer, unless it's long-term, one-time freezing, I don't advise it. Allowing spices or herbs to freeze and warm, freeze and warm will likewise deaden flavor and gather moisture and condensation.

So, what's ideal?

I keep my spices in the cabinet farthest from my stove (and, coincidentally the window) where it will remain at a fairly constant temperature (*right around 70°*), and in the dark, preserving the flavors.

Now, some will bristle at this idea, claiming that they don't want to have to be constantly running back and forth across the kitchen every time they need a spice.

But, of course *you're* not going to have to do that...*right?* Because the *Home Chef* practices diligent mise-en-place, so all of the herbs and spices come to the counter at the same time, get measured out according to our *previously read* recipe, and then get tucked back into the cool and dark, before we ever start cooking... *right?*.

Also, try to get out of the habit of shaking spices directly from the bottle into the pot or pan. The heat and moisture from the cooking food will get into the bottle and ruin the spice. In professional kitchens, if we need to add a little more of this or that, we always shake a small amount into the palm of our hands before adding it to a dish. Not only does this protect the spices in the bottle, and make for a nice tactile connection with the food we're cooking, but it also insures that we won't ruin our dish because some hungover knuckle-head on the line didn't screw the cap back on.

13 Spices the Home Chef Should Have

Chef's note: *I have omitted dried versions of herbs that I prefer to use fresh, such as: rosemary, basil, thyme, oregano, etc.) Rosemary, btw, grows as a bush, and is extremely easy to cultivate in your garden, or in a pot on the porch. It's hard, smells delightful, and is hardy. There is something profoundly satisfying about walking out and snipping your own ingredients for a dish. This list is not, obviously, exhaustive, and I have dozens and dozens of other spices in my cabinet. Some are regularly used staples, some are impulse purchases, but I love them all...*

Ground Cumin - For cooks in the Far East, Latin America, Mexico, the Middle East, and North Africa, cumin has long been a signature spice and is a key ingredient in various spice blends, and many bean, couscous, curries, rice, and vegetable dishes. Cumin flourishes when used with beans, bread, cabbage, pungent cheeses, chicken, eggplant, lamb, lentils, onions, potatoes, rice, sauerkraut and squash.

Cumin works well in combination with allspice, anise seed, brown mustard, cardamom, cinnamon, coriander, fennel, fenugreek, garlic, ginger, nutmeg, paprika, turmeric, and yellow mustard.

Saigon Cinnamon - Vietnamese cinnamon is highly prized among bakers and chefs for the high level of flavor that it brings to a variety of breads, cakes, cookies, dumplings, ice cream, pastries, pies, and puddings. You'll also find it in other more savory dishes as well - chutneys, pickles, meat glazes, soups, stews, squash and even vinegars. It's also an outstanding enhancement to hot drinks like coffee, cocoa, cider and tea. We even have some Microbrew customers who use cinnamon in their beer.

Bay Leaves - Bay Leaves are a staple ingredient in Mediterranean cuisine and are also found in many Armenian, Greek, North African and Turkish dishes. In Europe they're typically added to soups, stews, pickles and fish and meat marinades. The French add them to their popular bouquet garni blend and bouillabaisse. The Moroccans add bay leaves to their pickled fish, stews and tagines. In Turkish cuisine, they're added to kebabs, fish casseroles and grilled fish.

Bay Leaves are good with beef, chicken, citrus fruits, fish, game, lamb, lentils, rice, tomatoes, white beans, soups and stews. Bay Leaves work well in combination with allspice, garlic, juniper, marjoram, oregano, parsley, sage, savory and thyme.

Smoked Paprika - The smoky quality of this ground chile will seductively pull you in and even just a pinch or two adds a captivating smoky aroma and flavor to just about any dish. Smoked Paprika is customarily used in making Spanish sausage such as chorizo and lomo pork loin. Smoked Sweet Paprika works well in combination with allspice, caraway, cardamom, garlic, ginger, oregano, parsley, pepper, rosemary, saffron, thyme and turmeric.

Garlic Powder - Garlic Powder is especially good with just about anything savory. Garlic Powder works well in combination with most spices and herbs. For handy garlic conversions use: 1 fresh garlic clove = 1/4 teaspoon of granulated garlic or 1/8 teaspoon of garlic powder or 1/2 teaspoon of garlic flakes

Onion Powder - Onion powder provides terrific onion aroma and flavor, but not texture. Ideal for use in sauces and gravies, spice blends, canned foods, meats, spreads and soups. We like to use onion powder when we don't have fresh onions around and we can adjust the flavor of a dish by adding differing amounts of the dried onion. Other times we'll use onion powder to give a dish a more assertive flavor.

Red Pepper Flakes - While most of us in this country associate Red Pepper Flakes with Italian food, they can actually be used to give a nice zing to a variety of cuisines, and are an essential ingredient for many African, Chinese and Mexican dishes.

Red Pepper Flakes are ideal when you want to perk up chili, chowders, pizza, pickling, salads, homemade sausage, sandwiches, soups, spaghetti sauce, stir-fries or vegetable recipes. Red Pepper Flakes work well in combination with most spices, lemon juice, lime juice and coconut milk and because they're typically a member of the nightshade family they pair very well with potatoes and tomatoes (there's that pizza tie-in again).

Cayenne Pepper - Ground cayenne pepper is a reddish orange in color and may be used in any recipe that calls for ground red pepper.

This particular pepper comes in at 30,000-40,000 SHU (*Scoville Heat Units*) but don't let that lull you to sleep – I still recommend adding this spice to your dishes "one pinch at a time". This way you will be able to locate the ideal heat level for you.

Ground Cloves - Add a dash of ground cloves to baked beans, barbecue rubs and sauces, chili, tomato sauce and spaghetti. Cloves are an excellent compliment to apples, beets, red cabbage, carrots, chocolate, hams, onions, oranges, pork, pumpkins, sweet potatoes, squash, and in cranberry juice. Cloves work well when paired with allspice, bay, cardamom, cinnamon, chili, coriander, curry leaves, fennel, ginger, mace, nutmeg and tamarind. In our country, whole cloves are traditionally used to stud pork roasts and hams.

Curry Powder - Curry Powder is earthy, slightly floral, sweet and spicy with citrusy notes. It is not considered a hot curry powder and is ideal for adding magnificent color and unmatched flavor to seafood and chicken curries, and blended from fenugreek, turmeric, yellow mustard, black pepper, cardamom, cumin, coriander, fennel, cayenne, cinnamon, clove, nutmeg, ginger and saffron. As a general rule of thumb you'll get the optimum flavor from curry powder by frying it for 30 seconds or so in oil or butter (ghee is traditional in India). But you can use it in all types of dishes. Curry is excellent with eggs, chicken salad, and can be used as a secret ingredient in familiar soup recipes.

Chili Powder - Chili powder is used in many recipes, from barbecue sauces to tacos, but it's the signature seasoning of Chili Con Carne (chili with meat), the classic cowboy chuck wagon trail stew.

The best American chili powders have several layers of complexity and heat that come from the different types of chilies to form their base. Today chili powder blends are very popular in American cuisine and the first commercial blend of chili powder in the U.S. were created in 1894 by William Gebhardt for his chili con carne. Gebhardt had a saloon in New Braunfels, Texas and his chili was the town's favorite dish. Gebhardt's challenge was that the chile peppers he used were only available at certain times of the year. So as any resourceful businessman would do he imported some ancho chilies from Mexico and processed the peppers through a small meat grinder.

Ginger Root Powder - The first recorded use of ginger goes as far back as its appearance in the ancient Chinese book on agriculture and medicinal plants called "Shen Nong Ben Cao Jing". This text is estimated to have been written between 200 and 250 AD but the book is a compilation of oral traditions attributed to Shennong, the mythical ruler of prehistoric China, who is believed to have lived around 2500 BC.

Ginger is a quintessential ingredient of Chinese, Korean, Japanese, Vietnamese and multiple South Asian cuisines for flavoring dishes such as goat meat, seafood and vegetarian. Ginger plays a starring role in numerous Indian dishes. In Arab countries, ginger is combined with other spices to add flavor to couscous, tagines and slow-cooked meat dishes with fruit. Ginger works well in combination with cardamom, cinnamon, cloves, dried fruits, honey, nutmeg, nuts, preserved lemons, paprika, pepper, and saffron.

Star Anise

Star anise enhances the flavor of meat. It is used as a spice in preparation of *biryani* and *masala chai* all over the Indian subcontinent.

It is widely used in Chinese cuisine, and in Indian cuisine where it is a major component of *garam masala*, and in Malay and Indonesian cuisines. It is widely grown for commercial use in China, India, and most other countries in Asia. Star anise is an ingredient of the traditional five-spice powder of Chinese cooking. It is also a major ingredient in the making of *phở*, a Vietnamese noodle soup. It is also used in the French recipe of mulled wine : called *vin chaud* (hot wine).

With the explosion of cooking shows on TV, and more information on recipes from faraway places available on the internet, Home Chefs are more willing to experiment in the kitchen than ever before.

> *Once you get a spice in your home, you have it forever. Women never throw out spices. The Egyptians were buried with their spices. I know which ones I'm taking with me when I go.*
>
> *~ Erma Bombeck*

Spice Blends

Now, I'm not usually a big proponent of commercial spice blends, as I have no control over the amount of each ingredient that goes into the blend (*Yes, to be a Home Chef is to be something of a control freak...*)

BUT, that doesn't mean I don't love blending spices, which is the secret to many of the most amazing dishes in the world. So, get yourself a coffee grinder (*and label it "spices only"*) or, if you want to go old-school, a heavy mortar and pestle, and go to town. I promise you this – you will be amazed at the difference a palm-full of toasted, freshly-ground spices can make in your dish.

Cajun & Creole Spices

Allspice, basil, bay leaves, black pepper, caraway seeds, cardamom, cayenne, celery seed, chives, chile peppers, cinnamon, cloves, cumin, dill seed, dill weed, garlic, gumbo filé, lemon, mace, marjoram, nutmeg, onion, oregano (*Mediterranean*), paprika, parsley, saffron, savory, tarragon, thyme, white pepper, and yellow mustard.

Caribbean Spices

Allspice, achiote seeds (annatto seeds), black pepper, chile peppers, cinnamon, cloves, garlic, ginger, lime, mace, nutmeg, onion, and thyme.

Chinese Spices

Cinnamon, cloves, fennel seed, ginger, hot mustard, lemongrass, Sichuan peppercorns, star anise, Tien Tsin chilies, turmeric and white pepper.

Indian Spice Blends

Garam Masala, Panch Phoron, Madras Curry, Maharajah Curry, Vindaloo Curry, and Tikka Masala.

Indian Spices

Anise seed, ajwain, asafoetida, bay leaf, black cardamom, black cumin, black mustard seed, black pepper, black salt, brown mustard seed, chile peppers, cinnamon, cloves, coriander, cubeb berries, cumin, dried mango, fennel seed, fenugreek leaves, fenugreek seeds, garlic, ginger, green cardamom, lemon, lime, long pepper, mace , mint, nigella, nutmeg, onion, poppy seeds, saffron, sesame seed, star anise, turmeric, and white pepper.

Italian Spices

Basil, garlic, onion, oregano (Mediterranean), marjoram, and parsley.

Mediterranean Spices

Basil, bay leaves, black caraway, black pepper, cardamom, chervil, chile peppers, chives, cilantro, cinnamon, cloves, coriander, cumin, fennel seed, fenugreek seeds, garlic, ginger, juniper, mace, marjoram, mint, nutmeg, onion, oregano (*Mediterranean*), paprika, parsley, rosemary, saffron, sage, savory, tarragon, thyme, turmeric and white pepper.

Mexican Spices

Allspice, achiote seeds (*annatto seeds*), basil, Mexican cinnamon, cayenne, chile peppers, cilantro, coriander, cumin, epazote, mint, nutmeg, oregano (*Mexican*) , sage and thyme.

Middle Eastern Spice Blends

Baharat, Lebanese 7 Spice, Shawarma and Za'atar, Bazaar.

Middle Eastern Spices

Aleppo pepper, anise seed, caraway, cardamom, cumin, maras pepper, nutmeg, sumac and turmeric.

North African Spice Blends

Baharat, Berbere, Harissa, Piri Piri Seasoning, Ras el Hanout and Tunisian Five Spice.

North African Spices

Birds-eye chiles, cilantro, cinnamon, cubeb berries, cumin, garlic, ginger, grains of paradise, long pepper, mint, onion and saffron.

Spanish Spices

Basil, bay leaf, cayenne, cinnamon, cloves, garlic, mint, nutmeg, oregano (*Mediterranean*), paprika (*Smoked Sweet*), parsley, rosemary, saffron, sage, tarragon, thyme and vanilla .

Thai Spices

Basil , black pepper , cardamom , chile peppers , cilantro , cinnamon , cloves , cumin , garlic , ginger , lemongrass , lime , mace , mint, nutmeg , shallots , turmeric and white pepper .

This should certainly be enough to get you started, no matter which cuisine you want to try and my one guarantee – if you do it right there will be no such thing as a bland dish! A perfectly seasoned entree typically plays the starring role in an unforgettable meal. Achieving masterful balance is not always as easy as we'd like it to be (*or as you see on your favorite cooking shows*).

Here are a few tips for matching the spice to the main ingredient:

Beef - Basil, Bay Leaf, Black Pepper, Cayenne, Cumin, Curry Powder, Dry Mustard Powder, Garlic, Green Pepper, Onion, Oregano, Rosemary, Sage, Thyme

Fish - Bay Leaf, Cayenne, Curry Powder, Celery Seed, Chives, Dill, Fennel, Lemon Zest, Marjoram, Mint, Dry Mustard Powder, Onion, Paprika, Parsley, Red Pepper, Saffron, Sage, Sesame Seed, Tarragon, Thyme, Turmeric

Lamb - Basil, Cinnamon, Cumin, Curry Powder, Garlic, Marjoram, Mint, Onion, Oregano, Rosemary, Sage, Savory, Sesame Seed, Thyme

Poultry - Basil, Bay Leaf, Cilantro, Cinnamon, Curry Powder, Garlic, Mace, Marjoram, Mint, Onion, Paprika, Parsley, Rosemary, Sage, Saffron, Savory, Tarragon, Thyme

Pork - Allspice, Caraway, Celery Seed, Cloves, Coriander, Fennel, Ginger, Juniper Berries, Dry Mustard Powder, Paprika, Sage, Savory

Veal - Bay Leaf, Black Pepper, Curry Powder, Dill, Ginger, Lemon, Marjoram, Mint, Oregano, Paprika, Parsley, Saffron, Sage, Tarragon

Eggs - Basil, Chives, Curry Powder, Dry Mustard Powder, Green or Red Pepper, Onion, Paprika, Parsley, Tarragon

Cheese - Chives, Nutmeg, Oregano, Red Pepper, Sage, Tarragon, Thyme

Top 25 Spice Set

As you might imagine, I have a lot of spices in my kitchen and, while many of them I buy in bulk, for the harder-to-find items SpiceInc.com is my go to.

I'm not affiliated with these guys, and I don't get any kind of kick-back for recommending them, I just like their stuff.

If your spice shelves are a bit bare, the 25 Spice Set in a great place to start. To take a look at this set, and others (*I'm particularly fond of the "Taste of South America" set*) as well as some killer recipes, go to: **www.spicesinc.com**

From the website:

This is our premiere spice set and is the perfect starter package for any new kitchen – ideal as a wedding gift or as a house warming present. These spices are not only the most popular but also the most frequently called for in many recipes.

Now while this is called the top 25 "spices" we have also included key herbs, and some popular seasoning blends for the most well rounded selection.

What began as a simple question from one of our staff members of the top 25 spices needed to start a kitchen quickly turned into a spirited debate here at SpicesInc.com and then mushroomed into an avalanche of requests asking us to offer these spices at a special bulk package pricing – we are pleased to fulfill this request!.

We've recently added the perfect companion to this spice set our 25 Best Seasonings Spice Set which is loaded with exotic seasonings from around the globe. Best of all there are no duplicates to this spice set.

If you're looking to buy these to stock up your own kitchen or to set up someone's new kitchen we have a top 25 spice set that will do that for you and you can save a little bit of hard earned cash by buying them all at once.

"I have sprinkled my bed with myrrh, aloes, and cinnamon. Come, let us drink our fill of love until morning; Let us delight ourselves with caresses." ~ Proverbs 7:17-18

Author's note: *Yowza!*

Ps – Just so you know...I am not affiliated with these guys in ANY way, nor do I received ANY form of payment or gratuity from them for anything I've written

I just like their stuff! ~ Chef P

The Best Fruit and Vegetable Seasoning

Many folks are so accustomed to familiar foods and flavors that they forget that there are many, many delicious ways to season even the most humble foods.

In most homes, vegetables are often just tossed with butter, seasoned with salt and pepper and served. What a shame, as the flavor of most veggies can be taken to the next level with just a little fresh perspective on seasoning.

Vegetable and seasoning combinations are infinite, but here are some of my favorites to help you look at your veggies in a fresh new way.

I always recommending starting with just small amounts of spices because, as my father used to say, "it's a lot easier to put in more pepper than to take it back out." Also, don't feel like you need to add *all* of the ingredients that are recommended, start with just one or two, and then build on that until you find *your* perfect combination.

Whether you like to grill, roast or steam your vegetables, try these and see what you think....

Artichokes - Bay Leaf, Parsley, Oregano, Thyme

Asparagus - Garlic, Lemon, Onion, Chives, Sesame Seed, Tarragon

Beets - Star Anise, Allspice, Basil, Dill, Ginger, Mint

Bell Peppers - Basil, Oregano, Rosemary

Broccoli - Red Pepper, Savory, Turmeric

Cabbage - Caraway Seeds, Celery Seed, Juniper Berries, Tarragon

Carrots - Allspice, Star Anise, Bay Leaf, Caraway Seeds, Cinnamon, Cloves, Ginger, Mint, Sage, Tarragon

Cauliflower - Chives, Coriander, Sage, Turmeric

Corn – Basil, Chives, Dill Seeds, Oregano

Cucumbers - Dill, Mint

Eggplant - Basil, Cumin, Marjoram, Oregano

Fennel - Caraway Seeds, Fennel Seeds, Rosemary, Thyme

Green Beans - Basil, Dill, Garlic, Onion, Savory

Mushrooms - Black Pepper, Marjoram, Nutmeg, parsley, oregano, sage, tarragon, thyme

Onion - caraway seed, mustard seed, nutmeg, Oregano, Sage, Thyme

Peas - Mint, Onion, Parsley, Rosemary, Tarragon, Turmeric

Potatoes - Caraway Seeds, Chives, Dill, Dill Seeds, Paprika, Parsley, Thyme, Turmeric

Spinach - Dill, Nutmeg, Tarragon

Sweet Potatoes - Allspice, Cardamom, Cinnamon, Cloves, Nutmeg

Tomatoes - Basil, Cilantro, Cumin, Fennel Seeds, Garlic, Oregano, Red Pepper, Black Pepper, Rosemary, Saffron, Tarragon, Thyme

Zucchini - Basil, Oregano

Fruit has it even worse than vegetables when it comes to seasoning. Typically them may be tossed with a little sugar and served.

Hopefully these suggestions will help you think beyond granulated sugar. Some may be familiar and others a surprise, but all of them sound delicious. No reason that fruits can't be a bit more on the savory side which also helps balance the natural sugars fond in fruits.

Apples - Cardamom, Cinnamon, Cloves, Ginger, Nutmeg

Berries (strawberries, blueberries, black berries and raspberries) - Black Pepper, Mint, Star Anise

Cranberries - Cloves, Ginger

Mangoes - Cilantro

Oranges - Cardamom, Mint, Thyme

Peaches - Cloves, Nutmeg

Pears - Bay Leaf, Black Pepper, Cardamom, Cinnamon, Star Anise

Pineapple - Cloves, Ginger, Lemongrass, Mint, Rosemary Leaf

Plums - Cinnamon, Cloves, Nutmeg, Star Anise

Homework Assignment #5
The Home Chef's Spices

- Go through your spices & check any that you already have.
- Highlight any you are missing and want to add
- Add any unlisted spices in the black spaces, below.

___Allspice Powder
___Basil
___Bay Leaves
___Black Pepper, Coarse
___Cardamom Powder
___Cajun Seasoning
___Cayenne Pepper
___Chili Powder
___Chinese Five Spice
___Cinnamon
___Cloves, Ground
___Cloves, Whole
___Coriander Powder
___Cumin Powder
___Curry Powder

___Furikake Seasoning
___Garam Masala
___Garlic Powder
___Ginger Powder
___Hickory Salt
___Mustard Powder
___Nutmeg Powder
___Oregano
___Onion Powder
___Red Chili Flake
___Rosemary
___Smoked Paprika
___Star Anise
___Turmeric

~ Notes ~

Chapter Ten
The Home Chef's Toolbox

Julia Child and her famous pegboard

Stocking your Kitchen Toolbox

There's no doubt that having the right tools for the job makes any task easier, and there's no better place to illustrate this than in the kitchen, where having the right cooking utensils can be the difference between creating good meals and great meals.

Many cooks think about major appliances such as the stove and refrigerator when planning to equip their kitchens, but to be a success in the kitchen, you need to have a good selection of cooking utensils in addition to the bigger items.

And don't forget…cooking utensils means more than just spoons; there's a host of small cooking utensils ranging from cutting devices, juicers, graters, and more, that belong in your culinary "toolbox."

Making a List

When thinking about outfitting (*or re-outfitting*) your cook space, think about what you do in a kitchen and about how different cooking utensils come into play for each task:

- **Washing and drying fresh produce** – always easy to accomplish with a strainer and salad spinner. The salad-spinner has gotten a bad rap from comedians over the years, but I can tell you from personal experience...if you don't like a soggy salad, they're a hard-to-beat tool to have around. A good vegetable peeler, with an ergonomic handle is also an important addition to your cooking utensils closet.

- **Slicing, chopping and dicing** all kinds of food and garnishes – a food processor is nice to have (*I have one*), and makes short work of vegetables, but mandolins, knives and graters are more versatile, and don't require electricity. Very helpful cooking utensils to have on hand.

- **Measuring** – cooking doesn't always have to be precise, but likewise, I've found it can be extremely hard to replicate a great dish that I've just flung random amounts of ingredients into. Baking, on the other hand, is as much science as art, and recipes should be followed as precisely as possible so measuring dishes, cups (*both wet and dry measures*), and measuring spoons are invaluable cooking utensils.

- **Weighing** – depending on what you like to cook, you may want to add a food scale to your shopping list of cooking utensils. Such a tool can be excellent for portioning meat and other products that have cooking times affected by weight. Small digital scales are easy to use, don't take much space, and can be found fairly inexpensively at just about any grocery store these days.

- **Temperature** – as important as measures are temperatures, which can affect the success of your kitchen endeavors. An oven or meat thermometer is key to having properly cooked meat that is safe to eat, and should be included in your pantry of cooking utensils.

- **Mixing** – no kitchen would be complete without a cadre of mixing bowls in its cooking utensils cupboard. Having a selection of bowls in assorted sizes is essential to fast, efficient cooking.

- **Manipulating, poking, prodding, lifting and stirring** – perhaps what most often comes to mind when you think of cooking utensils are implements used to move food: spoons, forks, knives, spatulas, , pastry blenders, tongs, salad lifters, slotted spoons, wooden spoons, serving spoons and more.

So, do we really need ALL of this stuff?

Probably not, few do. But by visualizing the tasks you do every day in the kitchen, you'll get a better idea of the cooking utensils you should consider keeping on hand. Think about every stage of the food preparation process, from storage and cleaning, to prep, cooking and presenting.

Other cooking utensils you may or may not need: pastry brush, kitchen shears, rolling pin, salt shaker, pepper mill, cutting board, ramekins, flour sifter, rotary beater, ladles, juicer and a can opener.

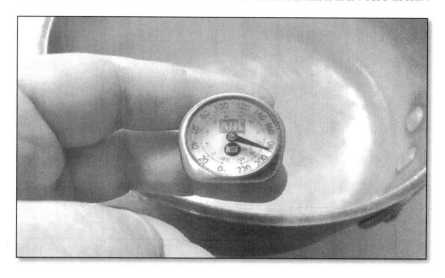

How to calibrate an instant read thermometer

Have you every followed one of those "cook to XXX temperature" recipes to the letter, and ended up with an undercooked or overcooked dish?

What the heck?

Let me ask you this…when was the last time you calibrated your instant read thermometer?

These little stick thermometers that look so cool in the pocket of a chef's jacket are also infamous for sliding up and down from "true" zero at the drop of a hat. This will, of course, give you a false reading, high or low, on your food.

Luckily, it's pretty easy to test if your thermometer is reading correctly, and even easier to get the little bugger to tell the truth again. Water boils at 212F*, so a probe held in boiling water should read 212F. If it doesn't, you need to calibrate it.

First: write down how many degrees (*plus or minus*) your needle is off.

Second: turn your thermometer over, and you should find a little hex nut right at the base of the probe.

By turning this nut left or right, with a small pair of pliers, you'll move the needle right or left.

This thermometer, which ended up rattling around in the bottom of a gear box for a while, was reading thirty degrees low...which would make me want to pull my dish off the heat 30 degrees too late...imagine *that* roast turkey...ugh!

So I let the needle return to room temp, and then turned the nut until the needle reads thirty degrees lower than the original reading at room temp. Finally, retest your probe, if it now reads 212, you're done!

Seriously, it's just that easy!

Make sure to test your thermometers on a regular basis, more often the more you use them. Every little bump, and even just regular handling, can knock it off true, and even 5-10 degrees can have a significant effect on your recipe.

Be sure to adjust those thermometers before starting your next big meal!

Water boils at 212°F at sea-level. Each 500 foot increase in altitude causes a drop of about 1° in the boiling point. The reason that water boils at a lower temperature at a higher altitude is because the pressure exerted upon it from the atmosphere is less at higher altitudes and so it is less "held together".

Check your altitude on this chart, and adjust accordingly.

Approx. Boiling Temperatures of Water	
Altitude	Temperature
Sea Level	212 degrees F
984 ft.	210 degrees F
2,000 ft.	208 degrees F
3,000 ft.	206 degrees F
5,000 ft.	203 degrees F
7,500 ft.	198 degrees F
10,000 ft.	194 degrees F
20,000 ft.	178 degrees F
26,000 ft.	168 degrees F

Copper, Steel or Cast Iron…are all pots crated equal?

When you cook meals in one pot, you realize that not every pot is created equal.

Your big stainless soup pot and equally big cast iron Dutch oven simply do not produce identical results. All sorts of variables come into play.

This can be frustrating, especially if you didn't plan on some of the things that can happen. As they say, forewarned is forearmed. The fact is, different recipes for one pot meals call for different pots. Being forewarned about this will help you choose the proper pot for the dish. Let's take a look at a few types of pots to see how they would be good, or bad, in certain instances.

Stainless Steel

You most likely have a set of pots and pans, with at least one very large pot that you use, perhaps, for boiling spaghetti.

One advantage to these pots is they are relatively light in weight (when compared to cast iron), which means you can have a very big pot and still be able to move it around. They go right into the dishwasher, too. The lids are usually pretty tight fitting. Stainless steel is a 'nonreactive' material, which means you can cook acidic foods without worrying about pitting or stripping the surface.

These pots, however, are not good heat conductors. Most of the heat will be on the bottom of the pot, with little heat traveling up the sides or being retained there. That means a slow simmering stew may be bubbling on the bottom, but not bubbling on the surface and in the middle.

This is a pot that needs watching if you're trying to maintain a slow simmer throughout the contents.

Raw Cast Iron

Often referred to as a Dutch oven, these pots are used for roasting or braising meat, and for making thick stews.

The advantage to these pots is they are very durable. The better models heat evenly on the bottom and up the sides and retain the heat well, and when put on low heat, the contents will simmer slowly. A cast iron pot is also naturally non-stick if seasoned and maintained properly.

Food cooked in raw cast iron also has an added benefit of absorbing iron, a necessary nutrient. These pots are, however, very heavy.

They are also 'reactive' meaning acidic foods may pit or damage the surface, and boiling food in water in a cast iron pot is not recommended. They take a longer time to heat up and to cool down, which can be both an advantage and a disadvantage, depending on the situation.

Very inexpensive models may have 'hot spots' on the bottom. Raw cast iron pots need to be seasoned and re-seasoned routinely to maintain their natural non-stick coating.

NEVER put a cast iron pot in the dishwasher.

Enameled Cast Iron

One way manufacturers have eliminated the problem of the cast iron pot being 'reactive' is by applying an enamel coating.

These pretty pots have all the benefits of cast iron without the problems associated with maintaining the interior and protecting it from acid and other detrimental elements.

They are available in a wide range of sizes, shapes, and colors and make a pretty addition to any kitchen.

Now for the down side. They can be very expensive. However, average priced cast iron manufacturers have upped their game and are producing enameled cast iron pots to compete with the more expensive brands. Of course, these pots are very heavy.

Aluminum

This is a lightweight material that also heats up fast and conducts heat well throughout the pot.

Aluminum pots are also relatively inexpensive. The bad news is, aluminum is very reactive to acidic foods, making it susceptible to pitting and discoloration. It is also rather soft and may scratch easily. This causes health concerns if used over time. To solve this problem, look for anodized aluminum.

It's more expensive than raw aluminum, but the benefits are well worth it if you're considering buying aluminum.

Copper

These are pretty pots that conduct heat very well. They are available with stainless steel linings so you can have the shiny copper outside with a non-reactive inside for cooking.

Yes, copper is a reactive cooking surface if not coated with stainless. Any acidic ingredient will actually transfer a metallic taste to the food you are cooking, and in some cases a gray discoloration. But, again, with a stainless interior, a copper pot can be a good choice if you want a pot that heats well, is lighter in weight, and cooks food evenly.

Also, copper needs polishing, which may or may not make a difference to you. It's just another thing to keep in mind.

When it comes to choosing a pot to use for your one pot meals, you have many choices. Read through the advantages and disadvantages for each and decide what's important to you.

Think about the dishes you most often make, consider the price, weigh the quality and convenience, and then go out and get the pot you need to start creating those delicious one pot meals.

Chapter Eleven
The Home Chef's Knives

Preparing meals that are a cut above the ordinary will be easier if you start with the right knives.

Well-designed knives are engineered with style, safety and performance in mind. A smartly constructed knife is fashioned of forged high-carbon stainless steel and chromium for optimum rust and stain resistance.

> *Slicing a warm slab of bacon is a lot like giving a ferret a shave. No matter how careful you are, somebody's going to get hurt.*
>
> *~ Alton Brown*

When choosing a knife, look for heavy forged bolsters between the blade and the handle.

These bolsters provide greater balance and safety by preventing fingers from riding up on the blade. A full tang blade, extending from the tip of the knife to the end of the handle, provides additional strength, balance and control.

Pick the knife up and hold it, roll your wrist around, let it rock between thumb and forefinger. If it feels comfortable, ask for a cutting board and go through the motions of slicing, chopping, and dicing. If it doesn't feel comfortable, like an extension of your own hand, put it down and ask to see another knife.

I don't want to get all Jedi-knight on you, but you'll know when you have the right knife in your hand.

You'll feel it.

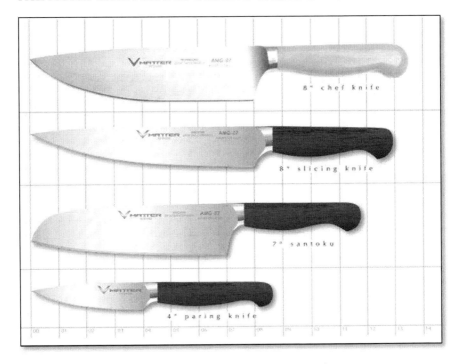

You ask four chef's about knives, and you're going to get six different answers. Personally, I've found I can do most jobs with the four above. I do like to keep a large heavy cleaver for cutting through bone, as well as a 12" serrated commercial slicing knife.

Another option, depending on the specifics of your work, would be a flexible boning knife, and of course a heavy pair of kitchen shears.

A recipe has no soul. You, as the cook, must bring soul to the recipe.
~ Thomas Keller

I'll admit, up front, that I am a completely biased Henkel man, who was raised by a biased Henkel man, who was ALSO raised by a biased Henkel man.

Both dad and granddad were professionals and, while they might be swayed on their religion, they were steadfast and puritanical in their knife faith.

My family has always had a religious bent towards knifes...

Me, I'm not as much a disciple, as I'm inexperienced in other brands. I grew up using my father's knives and he bought me my Henkel's as a wedding present. They've been flawless for over 20 years, so I've seen no reason to experiment.

I realize that this is the high-end of your budget, but, as my dad liked to say, "Buying your knives is like getting married, you only want to do it once."

'Course – he was also divorced three time...so...

BTW, in my not-so-humble opinions, "steak knives" are for bad restaurants...cook the steak right, and all you need is a standard dinner knife.

Don't waste the extra money buying a knife set with a bunch of serrated steak knives.

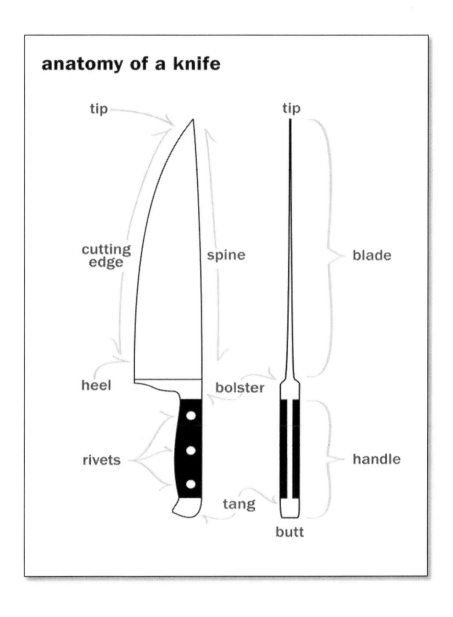

Knife Safety

A bad cut is my biggest fear in teaching the kids and, thank you God, not one I've faced yet.

It is hard to determine at what age a child is ready for using a knife, or how much supervision they require. Knife safety is important and if we feel a child is not ready, we skip this lesson, and pre-cut everything for them.

- Always use a cutting board. It is safer to cut and better for the counter tops. Use a large board to allow more space.

- Always have adult supervision.

- Use a good sharp knife. Dull knives are more likely to cause an injury.

- Curl your fingers under/tuck them in when you are holding whatever you are cutting. For example, when cutting an apple tuck your fingers you are using to hold the apple in.

- Be careful when carrying a knife always carry it point down.

- If a knife falls, step back and let it fall don't try to catch it!

- Place things on a cutting board to cut. Don't cut holding things in your hand.

- Pay attention to what you are doing. Don't get distracted, and always keep your eyes on your cutting.

- Never leave your knife in a sink where someone can reach in unaware and grab it. It is best to clean, dry and put away knives after they are used.

- Point the knife blade away from you. Do not cut towards yourself or your fingers.

- Never store knives in a block, or loose in a drawer. The first is unsanitary (*when did* you *last clean those knife slots?*), the latter isn't good for the blades or for fingers reaching in a drawer.

- Hold the knife in a pinch grip use a rolling motion when you cut.

- You could even put tape on the knife where your fingers are supposed to go as a guide.

If you do cut yourself, run the cut under cold water. When it stops bleeding dry with paper or cloth and use a band aid. If it is a deep cut or doesn't stop bleeding apply pressure to it, hold it above your heart and seek medical attention.

By the way…I cut myself fairly regularly. My fellow chefs buy me novelty band aids to bust my chops about it. It's not that I don't know proper knife technique, it's just that I have a dangerous combination of big clumsy hands and severe A.D.D., and I tend to forget that I'm at the cutting board until it's too late (*I have the same trouble driving.*) You're talking about a guy who flunked typing class all four years of high school, and later wrote three novels and several cookbooks largely using just his index fingers.

Caring for your knives

Nothing gives me the heebiddy-jeebies quicker than seeing a bunch of knives thrown haphazardly into a kitchen drawer.

Your knives should be in a block, or (*preferably*) hanging on a magnetic rack.

However, I also understand that for some folks those options just aren't feasible.

If you *must* store knives in a drawer, make sure they're protected from other utensils, and the blades are covered to keep them safe from dulling and nicks.

Commercially made knife covers can range in price from a few bucks to ridiculous. Most professional knife sharpening stores will send your knives home with temporary covers (*pictured center, below*), or sell you a few for under a buck.

For the super-cheap... er ... do-it-yourselfers out there, you can make perfectly acceptable blade protectors from heavy paper or cardboard paper-towel tubes, folded over the blade, and taped.

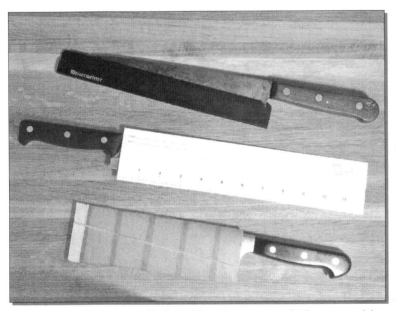

The tubes tend to be a little wider than most knives, so either cut them to fit the blade, or use a rubber-band to hold them in place (see picture.)

Taking good care of your knives is not only an important safety issue, but it can also mean the difference between good cooking and great cooking!

> *Japanese chefs believe our soul goes into our knives once we start using them. You wouldn't put your soul in a dishwasher!*
>
> ~ *Masaharu Morimoto*

A work of art: the proper way to chop

If you're going to spend any time in the kitchen, you're going to have to learn how to chop vegetables. Proper chopping, slicing, and dicing techniques help us reduce waste, stay safe, and improve the taste and texture of our dishes.

Those of us who grew up under tyrannical chef-fathers, toiling away in the Dickens-esque sweat-shops of their prep kitchens (*sorry Dad, just trying to make a point...*), may have spent months, or even years, doing little else than chopping veggies, and take the techniques required in stride.

For those who grew up playing outdoors, with other children, in the sunlight...the following steps will walk you through how to prepare almost any fresh vegetable for cooking, in your own kitchen.

Getting Ready

First, we need to prepare our veggies for chopping, as necessary, by rinsing, peeling, trimming, discarding roots etc.

It doesn't matter how pretty, clean, or pristine they looked at the grocery store, there's always the chance of residual contaminates from chemicals, pesticides, "color enhancers", and, of course, that teenage stock-boy's hands. *Rinse your veggies!*

Next, make sure to use the right knife for each job.

A paring knife has a 3-4" long blade and is used for peeling and paring fruit and vegetables, and for trimming where a larger chef's knife would be unwieldy. A good chef's knife will typically have a blade 8" – 12" long. This is the one you'll use for slicing, dicing, chopping, mincing, and keeping nosy in-laws out of your kitchen.

The side of the blade is great for crushing garlic, as well.

Now, before we start whacking away at our veggies, how do we want the final result to look?

Are we going for cubes, sticks, julienne, or brunoise (*for solid veggies*) or coarse or finely chopped, for leafy ones? Feel free to vary the size of your cuts each time you make the dish (*but keep them consistent for each experiment*). You may find that you enjoy the texture and flavor of one cut size, more than another.

Chef's Note: *Julienne* is a culinary knife cut in which the food item is cut into long thin strips, similar to matchsticks. Sometimes called shoe string , as in *shoestring fries*.

Common items to be julienned are carrots for Carrots Julienne, or potatoes for Julienne Fries. Once julienned, turning the subject 90 degrees and dicing finely (*equal to other dimensions*) will produce brunoise cut. Perfectly even 1/8th by 1/8th brunoise-cut vegetables are one standard by which the proficiency of a professional chef is judged.

A good example is coleslaw. Some folks like a super-fine dice on their slaw, but I prefer a rough chop, so I really get the taste and feel of the cabbage…it's all about personal taste.

Start Chopping

Put your veggies on a dry, clean cutting board. (*I suggest having multiple boards that are dedicated to either meat or veggies, to avoid cross-contamination between the two*).

With your non-dominant hand, hold the vegetable firmly in place.

Firmly grasp your chef's knife at the handle, keeping your index finger and thumb at either side of the upper part of the blade to ensure stability.

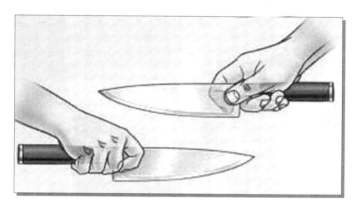

You want most of the pressure on the knife to be between your thumb and index finger, while the handle simply rests in your palm.

Move the knife to the right side of the vegetable (*assuming you're right-handed*), cutting from the "point" to the "root", and keeping the blade parallel to the knuckles of your free hand, with your fingertips slightly tucked under.

Cut straight down (*we'll save those fancy bias cuts for later*), and try to be consistent when in the size of your cuts.

A good sharp knife will do most of the work.

 To see these steps in action, **Google:** *hautemealz basic knife skills*

Here's another cooking tip: if you're having to exert what seems like a lot of force to cut a carrot, celery, or tomato (*jicama and turnips are another matter*)…it's time to have your knives professionally sharpened.

For smaller diameter veggies, like carrots, celery, etc...practice cutting with a rocking motion (*you've seen the TV folks do it*) where you keep the point of your knife touching the cutting board at all times, while you raise and lower the back end, feeding the veggies through like a chop-saw.

This technique is fun, fast, and impresses the heck out of your guests, but BE CAREFUL...it's easy to get enamored with the rhythm of your own cutting and end up with one less nail to paint!

So, there you have it, these basics of how to prepare vegetables will get you through almost any recipe you'll find.

Cutting Boards

There are heaps of cutting board options to choose from – wood, glass, marble, plastic...it can be a confusing choice.

Let's get two out of the game right away...glass and marble style cutting boards may be pretty, but they play havoc on your knives.

These too-hard surfaces will quickly blunt your knife and damage it's edge. Keep your glass and marble boards for serving food (*or for pastry and baking prep*). When it comes to wooden and plastic boards, even the experts are divided as to which is best.

It comes down to personal preference. I like bamboo.

One of our MY KITCHEN students learning to make Pico de Gallo, during the knife skills class.

Chef Perry's Fresh Pepper Pico

Some folks aren't fans of the heat, like I am...so I developed this recipe to allow me to minimize the fire by cutting out the jalapeno and some of the white onion (*yes, some folks find white onion to be "too hot"*) but still retain the contrasting crunch of those crisp, raw veggies with the fresh tomatoes. This attempt got major kudos from the "Mild Not Wild" portion of the family.

2 fresh Roma tomatoes, chilled
1/4 cup fresh cilantro
1 Tbs fresh squeezed lime juice
1 Tbs fresh jalapeño (opt.)

1/4 large white onion
1/2 large orange bell pepper
1 Tbs fresh garlic
Salt & pepper to taste

Mise en Place:

Dice tomatoes, onion, & bell pepper. Chop cilantro. Dice bell pepper. Roll and quarter the lime. Mince the garlic and jalapeño.

Prepare the dish:

Combine all ingredients and refrigerate at least 1 hour before serving.

The leftovers make an AMAZING omelet the next morning!

Add some pepper-jack cheese (inside) and topped with a dollop of Mexican crema... *very* nice!

A Gift for You...

As a thank you for buying and reading (*at least the first half*) of this book, I'd like to say thank you with a little gift:

chefperryp@gmail.com

That's my *personal* email address. Feel free to use it any time to ask me any food or cooking related questions (*no MLM offers, please*) ;)

I'll research and answer your questions, either in a direct reply, or with a how-to video on my website.

I look forward to cooking with you!

~ Chef Perry

> *You don't have to cook fancy or complicated masterpieces...just good food from fresh ingredients.*   ~ *Julia Child*

Homework Assignment #6

The Home Chef's Toolbox

Basic Gear List

____ 8" Chef's knife

____ 8" Slicing knife

____ 7" Santoku knife

____ 4" paring knife

____ Kitchen shears

____ Cutting Boards* (Bamboo)

____ Instant thermometer

____ Oven thermometer

____ Tongs, metal, long

____ Tongs, metal, short

____ Tongs, metal, silicon tip

____ Metal/wood mixing spoons

____ Strainer (1 metal, 1 plastic)

____ Food processor

____ Wire whisks*

____ Metal & plastic slotted spoons

____ Whisks, silicon coated

____ Box grater

____ Digital food scale

____ Meas. cups/spoons (up to 1 cup)

____ SS mixing bowls*

____ Meas. cup, Pyrex (up to 8 cups)

____ Metal casserole dishes*

____ Pyrex casserole dishes*

____ Wire racks (for casseroles)

____ SS pots & pans*

____ Non-stick pots & pans*

____ Steam baskets for pots

____ Grill and/or smoker

____ Manual Juicer

*Assorted sizes

Optional (*but nice to have*)

____ Mandolin

____ KitchenAid Mixer

____ Zester

____ Candy Thermometer

____ Cast Iron skillets*

____ Food Mill (for purees)

____ Enameled cast-iron cassoulet pot

____ Rice cooker

____ Pressure Cooker

____ Immersion Blender

____ Parchment paper/Silpats

____ Mezzaluna

Next Level Gear

____ Immersion circulator/Sousvide

____ Ninja Blender

____ Slow cooker (Ninja)

____ Countertop deep fryer

____ Pasta Maker

____ Paella pan

____ Spiralizer

____ Tajine

____ Steam baskets

~ Notes ~

"The best way to execute French cooking is to get good and loaded and whack the hell out of a chicken."

-Julia Child

Part Four
Let's Cook!

In Paris in the 1950s, I had the supreme good fortune to study with a remarkably able group of chefs. From them I learned why good French food is an art, and why it makes such sublime eating: nothing is too much trouble if it turns out the way it should.

Good results require that one take time and care.

If one doesn't use the freshest ingredients or read the whole recipe before starting, and if one rushes through the cooking, the result will be an inferior taste and texture--a gummy beef Wellington, say. But a careful approach will result in a magnificent burst of flavor, a thoroughly satisfying meal, perhaps even a life-changing experience.

Such was the case with the sole meunière I ate at La Couronne on my first day in France, in November 1948. It was an epiphany.

In all the years since the succulent meal, I have yet to lose the feelings of wonder and excitement that it inspired in me. I can still almost taste it.

And thinking back on it now reminds me that the pleasures of table, and of life, are infinite--toujours bon appétit!

~ Julia Child, My Life in France

Gourmet Cooking

Gourmet cooking is a style of food preparation that deals with the finest and freshest possible ingredients, and preparing your dishes as soon as possible after purchasing these fresh ingredients.

Not only do you want to purchase the freshest ingredients (*with the exception, or course, of pickled or fermented items, or things like dry-aged beef*) when cooking gourmet meals, but you also want to make sure that you're purchasing ingredients of the highest possible quality.

When it comes to gourmet cooking those are really the only hard and fast rules. All else rests on your sense of adventure and taste.

Of course, it's not just about buying the freshest and highest quality ingredients...you also have to know what to *do* with them. For this, the number of personal instructors, from home chefs to Michelin Star professionals, waiting to help you, stretch from your kitchen to past the horizon, and all you have to do is fire up your computer and type in "Google" or "YouTube." Also, you need to learn what ingredients are fresh in your area at any given season. The greatest gourmet dessert recipe does you little good if it's January and the only fresh raspberries are those tasteless wannabes from Mexico.

Once you learn what is fresh locally throughout the year, you can start saving recipes or ideas (*others or your own*) in folders according to the month(s) that the key ingredient is at its peak of freshness.

Layering Flavors

A very important technique when cooking gourmet food is the art of layering of flavors. This type of cooking allows you to taste the meat or seafood as well as each of the vegetables, herbs, and spices that comprise your final dish.

A classic example of layering flavors can be found in the French beef stew, *boeuf bourguignon*. Cubes of beef are salted and seared on all side, mushrooms and onions are sautéed with a little salt. Carrots and celery are browned quickly in butter. Then it's all combined in a pot with red wine and water to slowly simmer for hours, and then served with boiled or mashed potatoes on the side. The thick broth takes on a delicious marriage of all the flavors and the wine, while each component maintains it individual flavor and texture.

To try this dish as home, follow the directions above, in combination with the recipe from the great lady herself.

Youtube: Julia Child boeuf bourguignon

It's an amazing dish, and one of my very favorites.

Chef's Note: To take this already fantastic recipe to an even higher level, serve it with Joel Robuchon's *"Puree de Pomme"* (*potato puree*).

Presentation is the final key in gourmet cooking. It's not enough to have the food simply taste good, it must be visually appealing or striking" as well.

We'll discuss this more in the section on "Sexy Food", but suffice it to say, it's not difficult of make food look good. A nice black or white plate, an artful placing of the food, and some contrasting colors in the garnish; green onion tops, parsley, cilantro, or chives for light or beige foods. Sesame seeds, cream or cheese based sauces for darker foods, and maybe a striking red, orange, or green vegetable to round out the color scheme.

With the right presentation even meals that were easy to make can become a gourmet feast. Keep this in mind whether your dinner plan is a fancy gourmet dish, or just an everyday family favorite.

Some of the greatest meals you'll ever eat, started with someone asking, "I wonder what would happen if I..." Even if it's not a gastronomic knock-out, it's not like you're putting it on a menu, or bought hundreds of pounds of ingredients. Tomorrow you start with a clean slate and another shot at greatness.

The Home Chef always asks "what if" and always seeks to improve their skills.

'I DON'T THINK THERE'S
ANY CHEF THAT IS BORN
GREAT LIKE IN MUSIC OR
IN SPORTS. YOU HAVE TO
BURN YOURSELF.........
MESSING UP MAKES YOU

A BETTER
CHEF.'

- DAVID CHANG

How to Read (*and write*) a Recipe

Always read a recipe completely through before starting to prepare and cook. In fact..read it twice!

If you know how to read a recipe it will make your cooking experience easier. Make sure you have everything on hand and available. Reading through your recipe will also give you a chance to understand each step.

Sometimes recipes can be confusing and trying to understand what to do in the middle of preparing them may be difficult.

- **Title: Basic Egg Salad**. The example begins with a title. This can be an explanation of what you are making or a title that is just for fun. For example, *Goopy Eggs* could be the name of this recipe but it doesn't explain anything about the recipe except that it has eggs in it.

- **Servings.** Sometimes recipes include a serving size. This will help in cooking to know how many people the finished product will serve or for baked goods, like cookies, it will help you know how many dozen it should make. This is a guideline and is not always accurate or included. In this recipe it tells you that it makes one serving.

- **List of ingredients**

> 2 hard-boiled eggs   1 tablespoon mayonnaise
> 1 tablespoon yellow mustard   Dash of salt and pepper

There are some key factors you need to know about how to read a recipe in regards to the list of ingredients. A list of ingredients is usually included at the beginning, but sometimes ingredients are listed within the recipe itself. You'll need to know about measurements, tablespoons, cups, etc. *(or depending on where you live, Liters and milliliters.)*

Sometimes directions are included within the list of ingredients.

Do not be afraid of cooking as your ingredients will know, and misbehave. Enjoy your cooking and the food will behave; moreover it will pass your pleasure on to those who eat it.

~ Fergus Henderson

For example; 1 onion, chopped, would mean you would need to chop the onion before adding it to the recipe. In this recipe example, 1 1/2 cups raspberries fresh or if frozen, thawed, means you will need to make sure your raspberries are thawed before adding them into the recipe. 1 1/2 cups sliced bananas, means make sure you slice the bananas before adding them to the smoothie. Another thing to look for in the list of ingredients is the word *optional*. Recipes sometimes include ingredients such as raisins or nuts that are not essential for the recipe but can be added in if desired.

So, it will say 1 Cup raisins, *optional*. In this recipe example you will see fresh raspberries for topping, if desired. If desired or optional mean the same thing.

Some recipes will only have a "C" or a "T" or a "t" which would stand for cup, tablespoon, and teaspoon. So, if a recipe called for 1 C sugar and 1/2 t of salt, then you would know that it's calling for 1 cup of sugar and 1/2 teaspoon salt.

- **Directions**

This will give you a step by step explanation of what needs to be done in the cooking process. Read these carefully and follow accurately:

> *Finely chop boiled eggs. Mix in mayo 1 tsp. at a time, so not to add too much. Mix in mustard, salt and pepper. Put egg salad mixture on bread, crackers, on rolls, or on top of a green salad.*

Time: There are two times included in a recipe.

✓ Prep time, that is how much time is estimated it will take to prepare. Again this is just an estimate and may take a longer or shorter time depending on the chef's experience.

✓ Total time, which includes the prep and cooking time. This is more accurate and should be followed.

Example of a standard recipe format:

Easy Caramel Sauce

Prep Time: 25 min
Makes 3 Cups

Ingredients:

1 litre Coconut Milk
½ Cup Maple Syrup
1 Cup Coconut Sugar

Instructions:

1) Place the coconut milk and the maple syrup on the stove on a medium to high heat. (It will bubble but make sure it doesn't boil over) Stirring periodically for about 20 mins.

2) Stir in the coconut sugar and keep on the same heat for a further 5 mins stirring continuously.

3) Remove from the hob and allow to cool.

'COOK.'

Cook as much as you can, wherever you can and under whom ever you can. Learn how the kitchen works, how flavors work together, and how ingredients are able to come together to form something that never existed before.

So cook, cook a lot, and develop a point of view - something you stand for.

Don't be afraid of failure. Every time you try something that doesn't work, you get closer to to figuring out something that does.

Now... GO COOK.

> If you learn a recipe, you can cook the recipe. If you learn the technique, you can cook anything.   ~Michael Symon

Homework Assignment #7

Writing a Recipe

Choose one item that you cook often, but have no written recipes for, and, using the instructions in the previous chapter, create one.

Title:

_____

Description:

_____

_____

_____

Number of Servings:

Cooking Time:

Total Time:

List of Ingredients

_____   _____

_____   _____

_____   _____

_____   _____

_____   _____

Mise en Place:

_____

_____

_____

_____

Cooking Directions:

_____

_____

_____

_____

_____

_____

_____

_____

_____

_____

_____

_____

_____

_____

Notes:

_____

_____

_____

_____

Common Cooking Methods

Okay, first things first...let's talk briefly about a few ways to cook your food. Some of these will be familiar to you, others may not.

When you're preparing any kind of meal from a recipe, it's important to understand some basic methods of cooking.

While there are countless techniques and variations of techniques out there (*and more being discovered every day*)...here are the basic techniques that you're most likely to run into...

Note: I'm deliberately omitting "baking" as, again, that's a whole 'nuther world.

Grilling

If a recipe calls for something to be grilled, it generally means it should be cooked over an open flame or heat. Some variations can include direct grilling, indirect grilling, and charring. More on these later.

Grilling can be done by charcoal or gas - on a barbeque for example - or it can be done using a grill of some sort on the burners of your stove.

If none of these methods are available, you can often substitute with broiling.

Broiling

Broiling indicates cooking by exposing directly to a heat source such as a flame or element. Most ovens have a "broil" setting, which heats an element at the top of the stove rather than the one at the bottom, which is used for baking or roasting. When broiling items in the oven, they should normally be placed on the top rack to give them the proper heat exposure.

Frying vs Deep Frying

Both frying and deep-frying cook foods with a similar process, but the method is a little different in each case. *Frying* can be done over any heat source, such as a stove element or an open flame. Oil or butter is heated and the food is cooked by its heat. The depth of oil can vary from a light sheen, to several inches deep, as long as the food being cooked is not submerged.

Deep frying, on the other hand, also involves oil but in this case the food is completely submerged in the oil. Deep frying is used for foods such as pommes frites (*French fries*), breaded chicken and doughnuts. It can be dangerous, however, because you're dealing with boiling oil so proper equipment and safety precautions must be used.

Sautéing

Sautéing involves cooking food quickly in a small amount of fat. It is similar in process to frying, but because of the smaller amount of fat and faster cooking times, it brings out stronger flavors than frying will. Knowing what is involved with the various cooking methods makes it easier to plan when following a recipe.

Roasting

Roasting uses indirect, diffused dry heat (hot air) to envelope food, which cooks it evenly on all sides. Temps typically range from 300F - 500F from an open flame, oven, or other heat source. Roasting enhances flavor through caramelization and the "Maillard Reaction" (browning the surface of the food). This is a great technique for slow cooking large cuts of meat, whole fowl and fish, and most root and bulb vegetables. Most meats and veggies cooked in this fashion are called roast, or "roasted", often requiring anywhere from 2-12 hours.

This method is usually done in an uncovered pan. When you cover the pan, it's typically…

My favorite "Perfect Pot Roast" Not your Grandma's recipe!

Braising

Braising (*from the French: "braiser"*) is a two-step method using both moist and dry heat. The food is first seared at a high temperature (again, imparting the "Maillard Reaction") and is then finished cooking, covered, at a lower heat with some type of liquid (which also add flavor). Braising meat is often used in conjunction with a slow cooker or crock-pot,, though some chefs will argue that these are two different methods, based on whether additional liquid is added. I choose not to quibble on this one.

My favorite braising recipe is my "Perfect Pot Roast." As I once overheard a favorite Southern chef exclaim, "This is something ya'all should eat in the middle of the night, when there ain't no one up but you and Jesus..."

Google: "chef perry's perfect pot roast" for this step-by-step recipe. It s a bit more work than the old dump and stir method, but totally worth it!

Other Cooking Methods

Here are few more (*though certainly not an all-inclusive list*) of cooking methods that you can research on your own…

Baghaar – a cooking technique used in Pakistani cuisine and Indian cuisine in which cooking oil is heated and spices are added to fry. The oil is then added to a dish for flavoring.

Broasting – a method of cooking chicken and other foods using a pressure fryer and condiments

Coddling – heating food in water kept just below the boiling point. Coddled egg may be prepared using this method.

Confit – a generic term for various kinds of food that have been cooked in fat (duck fat is a favorite)

Flambé - a cooking procedure in which alcohol is added to a hot pan to create a burst of flames. The word means 'flamed' in French.

Jugging – the process of stewing whole animals, mainly game or fish, for long periods in tightly covered containers such as a casserole or an earthenware jug.

Kalua – a traditional Hawaiian cooking method that utilizes an imu, a type of underground oven. Similar to Mexican "Barbacoa." An easier method is to use a "La Caja China" roasting box.

See my site: www.lacajachinacooking.com

Microwave Cooking - Do I really need to explain this one?

Poaching - moist-heat cooking technique that involves cooking by submerging food in a liquid, such as water, milk, stock or wine, at a relatively low temperature (about 160–180F)

Pressure cooking – cooking food, using water or other liquids, in a sealed vessel—known as a "pressure cooker", which doesn't permit air or liquids to escape below a pre-set pressure.

Robata - a Japanese method, in which items of food on skewers are slow-grilled very closely over hot charcoal.

Rotisserie - meat is skewered on a spit and cooked, rotating, over a fire in a fireplace or over a large grill, generally used for cooking large joints of meat or entire animals, such as pigs or turkeys, cooking meat evenly with continuous self-basting.

Searing - a technique used in grilling, baking, braising, roasting, sautéing, etc., in which the outside of the food (*usually meat, poultry or fish*) is cooked at high temperature until a caramelized crust forms.

Simmering - foods are cooked in hot liquid kept just below boiling, but higher than poaching temperature.

Sous-vide (*French for 'under vacuum'*) - food is sealed in a vacuum-sealed pouch and placed in a hot water bath for longer than normal cooking times (*anywhere from 1 to 72 hours*) at an exactly regulated temperature, typically around 131 to 140F

Steaming - cooking using steam, often done with a food steamer, or in a wok. Steaming is considered one of the healthier cooking techniques.

Wok Cooking - a range of different Chinese cooking techniques, including stir frying, steaming, pan frying, deep frying, poaching, boiling, braising, searing, stewing, making soup, smoking and roasting nuts. Wok cooking is done with long-handled utensils called chahn (*spatula*) or hoak (*ladle*).

Let's start with...eggs!

If you could choose to master a single ingredient, no choice would teach you more about cooking than the egg. It is an end in itself; it's a multipurpose ingredient; it's an all-purpose garnish; it's an invaluable tool. The egg teaches your hands finesse and delicacy.

It helps your arms develop strength and stamina. It instructs in the way proteins behave in heat and in the powerful ways we can change food mechanically.

It's a lever for getting other foods to behave in great ways. Learn to take the egg to its many differing ends, and you've enlarged your culinary repertoire by a factor of ten.

~ Michael Ruhlman

History of the Omelet

om·e·let

A dish of beaten eggs cooked in a frying pan until firm, often with a filling added while cooking, and usually served folded over.

Origin

French *omelet*, earlier, from *lemele* 'knife blade', from Latin *lamella* . The association with 'knife blade' is probably because of the thin flat shape of an omelet.

History

The fluffy omelet is simply a refined version of an ancient dish.

The French word *omelet* came into use during the mid-16th century, but the versions *alumelle* and *alumete* are employed by the Ménagier de Paris cookbook in 1393.

Legend has it that when Napoleon Bonaparte and his army were marching through southern France, they stopped to rest for the night near the town of Bessières.

Old Bony feasted on an omelet served by a local innkeeper that was such a delight that he ordered the townsfolk to gather up all the eggs in the village and to prepare a massive omelet for his army the following morning.

Styles

The **French omelet** is smoothly and quickly cooked in a very hot pan specially made for the purpose.

The technique uses clarified butter (*to ensure a high smoke point*), and lots of it.

Drowning in butter prevents sticking and cooks the eggs more quickly...at least that's the story I'm sticking with.

Great with just salt and pepper, it's often flavored with tomato and finely chopped herbs (often tarragon, chervil, parsley and chives) or chopped onions.

The French omelet is typically served a bit wetter (less cooked) that we would typically find an omelet in the US.

Speaking of which...

Cooked in a sauté pan without stirring, the **American omelet/Folded omelet** is definitely a different method than the French.

Fillings are placed on the eggs just before it is finished. Fold it in half and slid it onto a plate. Personally, I prefer a slightly more cooked French-style omelet, as the surface it less toughened than the unstirred, longer cooking version.

A **frittata** is a kind of open-faced Italian omelet that can contain cheese, vegetables, or even leftover pasta. Frittata are cooked slowly.

Except for the cooking oil, all ingredients are fully mixed with the eggs before cooking starts. This is the style I grew up with (*which Dad learned from my Sicilian Nana*) and still a favorite way for me to use up leftovers, especially steak and potatoes.

Hangtown Fry, containing bacon and breaded oysters, is an amazing, if unusual omelet that originated in Placerville, California (*aka "Hangtown"*) during the gold rush (*and it happens to be my all-time favorite breakfast, as well.*)

In 1849, a prospector rushed into the saloon of the El Dorado Hotel announcing that right there in town, along the banks of Hangtown Creek, he had struck it rich. Untying his leather poke and spilling its shining contents of gold dust and nuggets. Turning to the bartender he loudly demanded, "I want you to cook me up the finest and most expensive meal in the house." The Bartender called to the cook who said, "The most expensive things on the menu are eggs, bacon and oysters. Take your choice.

I can cook you anything you want, but it will cost you more than just a pinch of that gold dust you have there." "Scramble me up a whole mess of eggs and oysters," the prospector said, "throw in some bacon, and serve 'em up. I'm starving!" The cook did just that, and thus the Hangtown Fry was invented. Such a meal cost approximately six bucks. As a dollar had the equivalent buying power of around thirty dollars today, this was a hundred-and-eighty dollar breakfast.

The recipe swept the entire Northwest Territory, from California to Seattle, in the mid-1800s. Chef Chris Renner and I have enjoyed this dish in the hometown of its birth, Placerville. Lovely stuff!

Get my own recipe for Hangtown Fry!
Google: "hautemealz Hangtown"

"I don't want to lecture people into the kitchen, I want to lure them into the kitchen with pleasure. That's what brought me into the kitchen.

I'm hopeful there will be a renaissance of cooking, and that it will be different than cooking used to be. It will be cooking as an option, as a choice, and because it's satisfying...not because you have to."

~ Michael Pollan
"Cooked" Season 1: Episode 2 "Water"

Farm Fresh Eggs

A note on "farm fresh": There's a striking visual difference in color between the yolks of your typical store-bought eggs and fresh, local eggs from a small farm.

The key here is in the time elapsed from coup to plate, as well as the more natural diet that small-farm chickens typically have.

The sooner an egg is used, after laying, the better it will be. The ideal egg is cooked the same day it's laid, and never sees the inside of a refrigerator.

Chef's Note: Think you don't have access to farm-fresh eggs? You might be surprised! Ask around at work, you may find one of your colleagues is a hobby-farmer. Secondly check Craigslist. Many small and hobby farms, even in urban areas, sell their eggs online, and they're often cheaper than the "organic" eggs at the grocery store!

This richness in the color of the yolk is just as evident in the flavor of the cooked egg.

Another trick that's often used in restaurant kitchens, both to deepen the color and add a bit more flavor, is to add an extra egg-yolk, for every three whole eggs.

Did you know...

Just before laying an egg, hens add a protective layer called cuticle, or "egg bloom" to the outside of the egg. This coating seals the shell pores, preventing bacteria from getting inside, and reducing moisture loss from the egg – all designed to make the egg last longer.

However, this "bloom" is also water-soluble, and can be removed with even the lightest rinsing, rapidly increasing the speed of deterioration.

Factory eggs at the grocery store are pre-washed, so there's not much you can do about that, but if you buy farm-fresh eggs from a local producer (and you really, really should...) make sure they haven't been washed.

Wiping off a little coop-junk is okay, but for the freshest, safest, and tastiest eggs, don't wash them until right before you plan to cook.

Now you know!

On a side-note, before we bought Bramble Hill (our little farm) and had chickens of our own, we bought eggs from a friend of a friend, and they were always quite nasty on the outside. I'm not talking about a few understandable skid marks (I mean, it did just basically get pushed out of a chicken's ass, after all), but big clumpy chunks of mud and crap.

I found that wiping them with a dry paper-towel, or dry-brushing with steel-wool really helps if you want them a little cleaner before they go in your fridge.

Excessively dirty eggs makes me suspect that someone needs to freshen up their nesting area much more regularly, and if they're too lazy or unprepared to do something as simple as sweep and scatter a little straw, I probably shouldn't be trusting them for something I plan to feed to my family.

For what it's worth.

Basic Filled Omelet

Omelets are one of my favorite meals. It was, like many people, one of my first adventures in cooking. For centuries, the omelet was how a chef tested the skill of a cook seeking to join his line. The interview consisted of, "Make me an omelet!"

If you impressed the chef, you got the job.

My father would cook them on Saturday mornings while I was watching cartoons. When I was older he taught me to cook a classic American filled omelet. Now I am passing this tradition to my daughter. It's also the first lesson we teach the kids in our MY KITCHEN Program.

While I like add things like oysters, and brie, and black truffles, the basics are still the same.

Ingredients

2 eggs	1 tbsp. milk or cream
1 tsp. butter	1-2oz. Your favorite cheese*
1-2oz. Ham	Salt & black pepper

Mise en Place

Grate the cheese. Dice the ham. Crack eggs into a small mixing bowl.

Preparation

Melt butter in a sauté pan over medium heat. Whisk the eggs together with the milk/cream(the milk will help the eggs be a little fluffy) and a pinch each of salt and pepper.

Add the ham and the cheese (reserve a pinch or two of cheese for plating) once when the bottom is firm but still runny on the top.

Here's a quick video recipe showing just how easy a light and fluffy omelet is to make.

Google: YouTube Chef Perry quick fluffy omelet

When the eggs are cooked through, use a spatula to gently fold omelet in half, slide onto a warm plate, and sprinkle the remaining cheese on top.

Serve with a side of fruit and toast.

*For a standard breakfast omelet, I like a blend of Italian cheese, or an extra-sharp cheddar.

When you have made as many mistakes as I have, then you can be as good as me.

~Wolfgang Puck

I taste every dish our students prepare, and give feedback, suggestions, and lots and lots of praise. As they are almost always awesome...it's a pretty tough job!

> *When you acknowledge, as you must, that there is no such thing as perfect food, only the idea of it, then the real purpose of striving toward perfection becomes clear: to make people happy, that is what cooking is all about.*
>
> ~ *Thomas Keller*

Perfect Scrambled Eggs

Scrambled eggs are one of my favorite foods. I mean, really, can it get much better that a good, farm-fresh egg, a little butter, and a kiss of sea-salt?

I think not.

Also, eggs offer some of the easiest "recipes" out there, and are often one of the first that most future cooks (*including myself*) learn to prepare.

After decades of scrambling eggs (*my favorite preparation*), I totally changed up my recipe about a year ago, when I learned, from the great Lady herself, Julia Child (*well, from her cookbook, anyway*) the secret to making the best scrambled eggs…e-ver.

It's pretty simple…DO NOT STIR YOUR EGGS!

Instead, draw your flat-edge wooden spoon slowly across the bottom of the pan, from edge to center, reaching all over the bottom of the pan. Add the cream and continue, drawing eggs to the center every 10 seconds or so. The fat in the cream coats the proteins in the egg white and yolk, preventing the loss of too much liquid and yielding light, fluffy eggs. (*Cooking over low heat is key, as well.*)

Nothing will seem to happen for the first few minutes, and then suddenly the eggs will begin to thicken into a custard-like consistency.

Now leave the eggs alone, allowing them to cook until they have almost thickened to your desired consistency. (*I like to leave them in until the bottoms just start to color*).

> *Cooking is like snow skiing: If you don't fall at least 10 times, then you're not skiing hard enough.*
>
> ~ *Guy Fieri*

Garlic

This is one of those little "Chef Secrets" that can elevate a great dish into the range of freakin' amazing. Slowly poaching the garlic cloves in butter adds an amazingly sweet, deep roasted-garlic flavor without the often accompanying hint of bitterness...and, of course, who doesn't like garlic butter?

I use this technique with mashed potatoes (*just add warmed heavy cream*), in poultry stuffing, to toss with fresh green beans, asparagus, or wilted spinach, and it's my go-to finishing ingredient to brush on steak or pork chops, just before serving. And it couldn't be easier. For four servings of...well, anything...

<u>Butter Poached Garlic</u>
1 cube Sweet Cream Butter
10-12 fresh whole garlic cloves, peeled
1/4 tsp. fine sea salt

In a small pan, melt butter over medium-low heat. Add garlic and salt, and poach for 20 minutes, tossing occasionally. When a fork or knife can pierce the garlic with absolutely no resistance, it's done. Remove from heat, and allow to cool for 10 minutes. Add garlic and butter to a blender, or use an immersion blender or even a fork to mash and mix the garlic together into a smooth slurry. Use immediately, or cover, store and chill for up to a week in the fridge.

Garlic is divine.

Few food items can taste so many distinct ways, handled correctly. Misuse of garlic is a crime. Old garlic, burnt garlic, garlic cut too long ago and garlic that has been tragically smashed through one of those abominations, the garlic press, are all disgusting.

Please treat your garlic with respect. Sliver it for pasta, like you saw in Goodfellas; don't burn it. Smash it, with the flat of your knife blade if you like, but don't put it through a press.

I don't know what that junk is that squeezes out the end of those things, but it ain't garlic.

And try roasting garlic. It gets mellower and sweeter if you roast it whole, still on the clove, to be squeezed out later when it's soft and brown. Nothing will permeate your food more irrevocably and irreparably than burnt or rancid garlic.

Avoid at all costs that vile spew you see rotting in oil in screw-top jars.

Too lazy to peel fresh?

You don't deserve to eat garlic.

~ Anthony Bourdain

Homework

French-Style Scrambled Eggs

Personally, I've found that the recipe below is awesome enough that it doesn't require a yolk-boost, but feel free to experiment!

Here's how I make them...

French Scrambled Eggs
Adapted from "Mastering the Art of French Cooking" by Julia Child

8 eggs (*local, farm-fresh organic, if possible*)
sea salt fresh ground black pepper
2 Tbs softened butter
4 tsp water
2 Tbs whipping cream
1 Tbs shaved Pecorino Romano cheese

Perfecting this recipe is as much (*and maybe more*) about the technique than it is about the ingredients.

Combine the eggs, pepper, and water in a mixing bowl, and beat lightly with a fork, just enough to mix, but not completely incorporate (*you should still be able to define some of the whites from the yolks*).

Add butter to a NONSTICK pan, and heat to medium, until the butter has just melted, but is not yet foaming.

Sprinkle with a little sea-salt, to taste, and stir to coat the entire surface...preferably with a flat-edge wooden spoon.

Pour in the eggs, reduce heat to medium-low, and allow them to set, untouched, in the butter 20-30 seconds.

Slowly begin working your eggs toward the center of the pan.

Nothing will seem to happen for the first few minutes, and then suddenly the eggs will begin to thicken into a custard-like consistency. Now leave the eggs alone, allowing them to cook until they have almost thickened to your desired consistency.

Sprinkle with cheese and remove from heat immediately; the eggs will continue to cook slightly.

Re-season to taste, arrange on plates and garnish with parsley.

No one who cooks, cooks alone. Even at her most solitary, a cook in the kitchen is surrounded by generations of cooks past, the advice and menus of cooks present, the wisdom of cookbook writers.

Food keeps us alive, as we all know. Nourishment allows us to grow and be healthy. But good cooking takes us beyond survival and into the realms of culture and pleasure.

~ Fernando Divina
Foods of the Americas: Native Recipes and Traditions

Chapter Twelve
Stocks, Broth, & Gravy

> **Broth** – *The strained clear liquid in which meat, poultry, or fish has been simmered with vegetables and herbs. It is similar to* **Stock***, which is basically the same thing, but richer and more concentrated.*

A good chicken stock is *the* key to so many great dishes in the kitchen. It's the base for your pan sauces, gravies, flavoring for rice, pasta, and potato dishes, and a fantastic steaming medium for fresh, seasonal veggies.

It's the Chef's go-to for thinning, flavoring, and deglazing pans.

I can't tell you how many times, as a boy, I accompanied my father to a restaurant he was cooking in, in the wee hours of the morning and, after donning jackets and aprons, and checking the inventory lists, the first job of the day was to start making stocks.

Chicken and beef trimmings, carcasses, and bones, leftover from prep done by the staff earlier, would get dumped into giant kettles on the back of the 6-burner. Into each would go 5 gallons of water, a few handfuls of salt, herbs and spices, and another bucket of veggie trimmings, likewise from prep earlier in the day, maybe a couple of peeled onions and a head of celery...a few healthy knobs of butter and each stock was brought to a boil and left to simmer for a few hours before the dinner rush began, skimming every hour or so.

Stock is the super-glue that hold the kitchen together. Mashed potatoes too thick? Ladle in some stock...those chicken breasts starting to look a little dry under the hot lights of the pass-thru?

Squirt a little broth on 'em.

Want to toss that cooked pasta in something to add a little zip?

You guessed it...

The bubbling cauldrons of meaty nectar were also the base for all soups, stews, gravies, and sauces. Much like a good sourdough starter, it was a constantly evolving flavor as it was ladled out, and refilled through-out the night.

> *Always start out with a larger pot than what you think you need.*
> ~ *Julia Child*

Now, it's likely that you're seldom confronted with a cooking situation requiring 10 gallons of hot chicken stock, but a gallon batch will usually cover any need you may have tonight, as well as several future dishes.

Step 1 - Prep the skin, bones and left-over meat for the stock pot.

For a gallon of water, you'll want 1 whole chicken carcass + skin (*store-bought rotisserie chickens are great for this*) or the equivalent.

If you carve out your own baked chicken (*and you really should*) you're ready to go!

Step 2 - Prep/gather the veggies you'll be using.

Whole veggies and/or peels & ends (*onions, carrots, potatoes, celery, mushroom stems, cabbage, etc.*) A lot of times, if I know I'll be making stock later in the week, I'll keep a paper bag in the fridge for saving trimmings during the week. Just wash everything well, and chop it all coarse, as you'll be straining out all the solids anyway.

I like to split a couple of heads of garlic, and maybe a chuck of ginger through the middle and toss it in too. Stems and extra pieces from chopped herbs like basil, parsley, oregano, etc…are very nice in the stockpot, too. This is how you go "nose-to-tail" with your veggies!

Step 3 – Add all to a stock pot over med-high heat (*I toss a couple of lemon-rinds, and some asparagus stems in as well*), cover with water, and season with salt & pepper to taste. Bring to stock just to a boil, then lower heat and simmer at least 1 hour. To help your stock stay clear, and grit-free, use a large wooden spoon to skim off any foam that gathers on top.

Step 4 – Once stock has simmered at least 8 hours (*12-14 are better*) ladle out solids and toss. Then pour the stock through a fine sieve or cheese cloth to clear.

So…you need two cups of chicken stock for that recipe tonight, but you're looking at a gallon of the stuff steaming on the stove…*now* what do you do with it? Here's what I do…

Pick up a couple of cheap plastic ice cube trays, and use a sharpie to write "BROTH" or "STOCK" on both sides (you don't *ever* want to make ice in these again…trust me!) Allow your broth to cool completely, skim off any skin or fat from the top*, and ladle your stock into the ice-cube trays. Freeze, and then pop your "stock cubes" into a zippie bag for easy access later. Next time you need some stock…a few seconds in the microwave, and you'll be ready to cook!

If you're really watching those fat grams, chill that pot of stock overnight, and remove all of the hardened fat that gathers on the top. You'll lose a little flavor, but you'll be able to look your doctor in the eye!

Gravy

It wasn't a proper Thanksgiving or Christmas without Dad showing up early in the day with a couple of armloads of groceries and his knife-roll.

It also wasn't a holiday meal with Mom reminding Dad she was neither his sous chef, nor his wife, that it was *her* kitchen, not his restaurant, and if he wanted the butter he could damn well get it out of the fridge himself…

Here's my recipe for one of my all-time favorite breakfast gravies, "Super Simple Sausage Gravy."

Google: "Chef Perry Sausage Gravy"

Plus we had to get stuff cooking before my hermit Uncle Raymond pulled up in the driveway, wished us a happy day, dumped an ashtray full of silver dollars in the driveway for me to scramble for, while he laughed, and then drove home…never getting out of his car.

We had an interesting family dynamic.

But…back to the point…

One of the amazing things to come out of those grocery bags, were the ingredients for Dad's homemade turkey gravy.

That gravy was, I kid you not, the best part of the dinner. It could have turned a dirty old flip-flop into haute cuisine.

Dad's been gone for almost a decade, Mom for almost three, but I still feel their presence, the friendly bickering, the unspoken loyalty, and the underlying love for each other that neither knew how to express, when I whip up the gravy each year.

You can make pretty much any type of gravy with this recipe, simply by changing up the type of stock or broth you use. It's the simple, old-school way that gravy's been made for hundreds of years.

It's the taste of the happiest parts of my childhood.

...and it's still just as good.

If you're cooking and not making mistakes, you're not playing outside your safety zone. I don't expect it all to be good. I have fat dogs because I scrap that stuff out the back door.

~ Guy Fieri

The Best Roast Chicken You've Ever Eaten

You could probably get through life without knowing how to roast a chicken, but the question is, why would you want to? ~ Nigella Lawson

Of course the very best first step for amazing stocks and gravies is to roast your own chicken, which also leaves you with one heck of a tasty dinner. I wanted to share with you all my super-simple (*and simply amazing*) roast chicken recipe.

Chef Perry's Aromatic Roast Chicken

1 - (5-6lb) roasting chicken
½ C each: sugar and honey
½ sm. gala apple, sliced thin
½ sm. navel orange, peeled/sliced
peeled/sliced
½ sm. sweet onion, sliced thin

¾ of a cup of salt
1 gallon distilled water
½ sm. Asian pear, sliced thin
½ sm. lemon,

3 cloves of fresh garlic, peeled.

Combine salt, sugar, honey, and 1 quart of water, and bring to a boil, stirring. When all solids are dissolved, pour this mixture into your brining pot, and add 3 more quarts of very cold water.

Add your chicken, breast-side down, and brine in refrigerator 8-18 hours. The longer you brine, the more moist and flavorful the meat will be. Remove the chicken from the brine and rinse thoroughly (*this is important, as you must wash away the excess salt*). Pat to dry well, and set on a rack on the counter to continue to dry for up to an hour.

Roasting vs. Baking

Roasting and baking are both dry heat cooking methods. These cooking techniques use hot air to conduct heat, typically at 300°F or higher. However, roasting, typically done without a lid, refers to solid foods like meats and vegetables, while baking is used in conjunction with foods that do not start out in a solid state (things like dough, quiches, etc.,)

*Rule of thumb: you **roast** meat, and you **bake** doughs.*

Add all of the fruit, onion, and garlic to a saucepan. Add about a cup of water and bring just to a boil, covered. Drain, and (*carefully*) stuff the bird (*you'll toss these after roasting*) and truss her up.

Place the chicken, breast up, on a rack into a roasting pan, add ½ inch of water to the pan.

Brush the bird lightly with oil (do NOT salt it!)

Preheat your oven to 425F, and roast the chicken for 20 minutes (rotating once), then turn the heat down to 350F for 90 minutes. Flip to brown the back (personal preference, I like the skin, lol!), then remove from oven and let rest 30 minutes, breast down on a rack, before carving.

Reserve bones and scraps for making stock for *Hainanese Chicken Rice* the next night!

Okay, so for those nights when you're jonesing for a lovely bit of roast bird, but you just don't have two hours and twenty minutes to spare...try Spatchcocking to save a little time! (Plus...you get to use the word "spatchcock", which is awesome.)

Google: Chef Perry Spatchcock Chicken

Why so many foods "taste like chicken."

This reference has been used so often in pop culture that it has become a food cliché.

The most commonly accepted reason for this phenomenon lies in the fact that chicken, especially lean cuts such as America's favorite (*sadly*) the skinless chicken breast, have a bland, almost neutral taste because fat contributes more flavor than muscle. This 'lack of taste" makes it the generic choice for comparison with other neutral tasting proteins.

Also, chicken has lower levels of glutamates that contribute to the "savory" aspect of taste known as umami; processing or tenderizing other meats would also lower glutamate levels and make them taste more like chicken.

This is especially true in first-world countries where we have bred the fat and flavor out of chickens (and cows, and pigs...) with growth hormones and genetic modification breeding. I can personally attest, that in lesser "progressive" countries like Nigeria, where chickens are still grown the "old fashioned way" i.e.: free-ranging and natural foraging, chicken has a very unique, rich flavor that's nothing like the hyper-inflated "food product" we eat here in the states. If you've ever had wild pheasant, it has a similar taste.

BTW, if you're wondering how you can tell if you're getting a "real" chicken, or some HGH Schwartzenagerian cross-bred monstrosity... just check out the boobs. A truly natural chicken will have much smaller breasts and much larger thighs (so...many...jokes...)

This is, in part, because they are chasing food all day, as opposed to factory chickens which spend their brief lives in shoe-box sized cages, and are so "top-heavy" that they can't even stand up.

Chris Nuttall-Smith, food writer for *The Globe and Mail,* writing for Lucky Peach Magazine (*March 2017*), points out that "These chest-heavy, weak-kneed, fast-growing freaks of modern breeding, and ballooned from an average size at slaughter of just more than four pounds in the early 1980s to more than ten pounds at the upper end today. (Chicken breasts can now weigh more than entire chickens did in the 1950s.)"**

One great place that I often (but not always) find "real chicken" is at a Halal meat market, which generally has better quality meats across the board.

So, the next time you taste something you just can't quite put your finger on, instead of saying it "tastes like chicken", tell your dinner companions that it tastes like "corporate greed"...dry, bland, and boring.

Now you know!

**Lucky Peach (my favorite food magazine), has many of their articles, including this one, available for free to read on their website. Google: "Why Slow-Growing Chickens Are the Next Big Thing" it's very much worth the read.*

Dad Perkins' Turkey Gravy

(Makes 10-12 generous servings)

1/2 cup (1 stick) Sweet cream butter   1/2 cup AP Flour
4 cups hot turkey stock (below)   2-4 cups boiling water*

The Roux

Melt your butter in a heavy bottom stock pot over medium heat. When the foam has cooked off the butter, add flour and whisk vigorously to a smooth paste. This is call a "roux." Continue whisking slowly until roux becomes deep brown in color. You know when your roux is done by the roasted nutty smell.

Add hot stock, one cup at a time (*the first will create a thick paste...press on*) whisking in each until smooth. Once all your stock in incorporated, keep whisking at a lower simmer for 10-15 minutes.

Add hot water (again, a cup at a time) until you reach the desired consistency. Taste and add salt and pepper as desired.

*You can also use milk, just make sure it's hot. Rule of thumb - never add cold liquid to a hot one (especially milk, as it will curdle.)

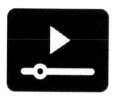

Short on time, and long on holiday recipes?

Check out my video on roasting a perfect turkey in 90 minutes!

Google: YouTube Chef Perry Roast Turkey

Simple Turkey Stock

2 whole turkey thighs, skin on
6 cloves of peeled garlic
1/2 cup butter
4 stalks of celery, roughly chopped
1 stalk each: rosemary, sage, thyme
8 cups of water

Salt and pepper
2 tsp. whole peppercorns
1 lg. yellow onion, quartered
2 lg. Carrots, roughly chopped
2 bay leaves

Preheat over to 350F

Sprinkle thighs with salt and pepper. Roast about 40 minutes, until skin is a deep golden brown.

Meanwhile, melt butter in a heavy bottom stock pot over medium heat. Add peppercorns and garlic and sauté a couple of minutes, stirring, to infuse the butter. Add onion, celery, and carrots, and sauté until carrots begin to brown.

Add water and bring to a simmer. Add fresh herbs (*whole*) and bay leaves. Add roasted turkey thighs.

Simmer uncovered, until liquid is reduced by 1/2. Strain your stock and discard the herb, skin, and veggie remnants.

Roughly chop the meat, and return it to the stock. Taste, and add salt and pepper to your liking.

Homework Assignment #8

Stock & Gravy

- Make "Simple Turkey Stock" (*if you can't find turkey thighs, you may replace with chicken thighs*).

- Once your stock is properly reduced, use it to make Dad Perkins' Turkey Gravy.

 This gravy would be wonderful with some spuds. Here's my favorite recipe… "Crazy Creamy Once-A-Year Mashed Potatoes.

Google: *"hautemealz once a year potatoes"*

~ Notes ~

Chapter Thirteen
The Mother Sauces

Once you learn how to make sauces you can dress up casseroles, use them to top your pasta and even pour them over steamed vegetables.

'Cause, let's face it…like bacon, it's a short list of foods that gravy can't make better.

There are several different types of sauces we will cover in our cooking lessons such as cream sauces, Alfredo sauces, tomato sauces and teach you what the 5 mother sauces are.

And…

It all starts with Roux

Roux (*"roo"*) is a cooking mixture of flour and fat (*usually butter*), used as a thickener for soups and sauces, with roots dating back more than 300 years in French cuisine.

Made by combining and cooking a flour and fat until the raw flavor of the flour cooks out and the roux has achieved the desired color, from a light tan to a deep mahogany (*the darker the roux, the deeper the flavor*)a properly cooked roux imparts silky-smooth body and a nutty flavor while thickening soups and sauces.

Making gravies, sauces, and roux-based stews can be intimidating at first, but building a roux is actually a remarkably simple process that leads to many wonderful dishes.

1. In a large kettle, sauté onions over medium heat, in butter until tender.

2. Add flour, salt, pepper (*and any other spices*); stir to make a crumbled paste. By the way, if you're not working off a recipe, a good rule of thumb is to start with equal parts fat (*butter, drippings, etc.*) to flour.

3. Cook, stirring, 1-2 minutes until roux begins to turn golden and gives off a nutty aroma.

4. Gradually add water, broth, meat drippings, or milk/cream (*I recommend one of the latter*), starting very slowly (*1/4 cup at a time*) stirring constantly to keep smooth. Bring to a boil; cook and stir for 1 minute.

One trick Dad taught me, was to warm whatever liquid you're using to just steaming. This keeps the roux from cooling (*stopping the cooking process*) each time you add liquid to it. Depending on the broth/drippings, you now have an awesome gravy. Flavor check for salt, herbs, and/or spices, and it's ready to serve.

For stews, or chowders, this is where you'd start adding all the goodies, and a bit more liquid (usually stock) to thin. (*FYI...use bottled clam juice for the liquid, and you have the base of an amazing clam chowder.*)

Cook a roux-based sauce for at least 25 minutes to achieve a smooth and silky texture.

Mother Sauces

In the culinary word, the term "mother sauce" refers to any one of five basic sauces, which are the starting points for making various secondary sauces or "small sauces." They're called mother sauces because each one is like the head of its own unique family of sauces.

Béchamel, Espagole, Hollandaise, Tomato and *Veloute*, are the five "Mother" sauces of French Cuisine.

Béchamel is a white sauce made with a roux (equal parts butter and flour (*see more below*) and milk. A Mornay sauce is Béchamel with a white cheese. Cheese sauce (as used in macaroni and cheese, nachos, etc.,) is a Béchamel with cheddar cheese and a variety of spices.

Espagnole, also called Brown Sauce, is a slightly more complex mother sauce. Espagnole is made by thickening brown stock with roux. So in that sense it's similar to a velouté. The difference is that Espagnole is made with tomato purée and mirepoix* for deeper color and flavor. Moreover, brown stock itself is made from bones that have first been roasted to add color and flavor.

Hollandaise is a tangy, buttery, emulsified sauce made by slowly whisking clarified butter into warm egg yolks. So the liquid here is the clarified butter and the thickening agent is the egg. Hollandaise sauce can be used on its own, and it's particularly delicious on seafood, vegetables, and egg dishes such as Eggs Benedict.

Basic Hollandaise

- 2 Tbs. butter
- 2 egg yolks
- 1/4 cup cream
- 1 ½ Tbsp. lemon juice

1 tsp. flour
1/4 tsp. mustard
pinch salt

In a saucepan, melt butter and add flour. Blend together, making a roux. Slowly whisk in milk until smooth. Take off heat and allow to cool 3-5 minutes.

Add egg yolks and mustard. Stir until well blended and eggs have warmed in the heat of the warm sauce. Blend in the lemon juice and salt. Serve.

> *Chefs Tip - If you add shallots, tarragon and crushed black peppercorns to your Hollandaise, you have a Béarnaise Sauce...which will, hands down, beat any steak sauce you've ever had.*

Check out my video, How To Make A Roux, Béchamel, & Cheese Sauce

Google: "Chef Perry Cheese Sauce"

Remaining Sauces

Tomato sauce is, well, just what it sounds like. We teach the kids to make a tomato sauce by reducing fresh diced tomatoes, minced shallots, oil, garlic, and fresh chopped basil with a little salt, and then pureeing it.

 For sauces, it s best to used peeled tomatoes, as the skins won t break down into the sauce. Here s my video on just how easy it is to peel a tomato.

Google: YouTube Chef Perry

Velouté is another relatively simple mother sauce. Velouté sauce is made by thickening white stock** with roux and then simmering it for a while. While the chicken velouté, made with chicken stock, is the most common type, there is also a veal velouté and fish velouté.

* Mirepoix: see the next page…

** A white stock is made by boiling down meat bones with a mirepoix, and a sachet of bay leaf, thyme, peppercorns, parsley stems and whole clove in a square of cheesecloth.

Chef's Tip: *For perfect mashed potatoes, drain your potatoes, then return them to the hot pan, and cover. Let the potatoes steam for around five minutes. This lets the potatoes dry a bit so they'll mash to a beautiful texture and soak up the butter and cream more easily.*

Cooking your potatoes in whole milk, garlic, and a little salt is another restaurant secret.

What is a Mirepoix?

A mirepoix (*meer-PWAH*) is, most typically, a combination of celery, onions, and carrots. There are a lot of regional mirepoix variations, and it can also include additional spices. Mirepoix, either raw, roasted, or sautéed with butter or olive oil, is the flavor base for a wide number of dishes, such as stocks, soups, stews and sauces (*as well as my mama's turkey stuffing*). Similar combinations of vegetables are known as the holy trinity in Creole cooking, "refogado" in Portuguese, soffrito in Italian, sofrito in Spanish,

Though the cooking technique is probably older, the term mirepoix dates from the 18th century and derives, as do many other appellations in French cuisine, from the aristocratic employer of the cook credited with establishing and stabilizing it: in this case, Charles-Pierre-Gaston François de Lévis, duc de Lévis-Mirepoix (1699–1757), French field marshal and ambassador.

According to Pierre Larousse (*quoted in the Oxford Companion to Food*), the unfortunate Duke of Mirepoix was "an incompetent and mediocre individual. . . who owed his vast fortune to the affection Louis XV felt toward his wife and who had but one claim to fame: he gave his name to a sauce made of vegetables and a variety of seasonings"

Traditionally, the weight ratio for mirepoix is 2:1:1 of onions, celery, and carrots; the ratio for bones to mirepoix for stock is 10:1.

When making a white stock, or *fond blanc*, parsnips are used instead of carrots to maintain the pale color.

Homework Assignment #9

Roux & Sauces

I think you can guess what your assignment for this chapter will be.

Choose one of the roux-based sauces listed in the previous chapter, prepare, and serve with an appropriate finished dish.

Sauces are a great way to "fancy up" any recipe. If possible, invite some friends over to enjoy this meal with you (*they can bring the salad and dessert…*)

~ Notes ~

_____

_____

_____

_____

_____

_____

_____

_____

_____

_____

_____

_____

_____

_____

_____

_____

_____

Vegetables

How to Cook Vegetables

Learning how to cook vegetables can be broken down into simple, understandable parts. The essential parts involve cleaning and preparation and the techniques of different cooking methods.

In this class we will cover these basics, as well as taking a look at what methods are the fastest and healthiest ways to cook vegetables.

Cleaning and Preparation

There are two major reasons for cleaning vegetables thoroughly before cooking them.

The first one, which will be obvious to anyone, is that fresh vegetables are often covered in dirt due to being grown in the ground.

There's also a less obvious reason – virtually all vegetables you buy from a supermarket will come from crops sprayed with pesticides.

Chef's Tip: you can increase the lifespan of greens by wrapping them loosely in a damp paper towel and refrigerating them in a re-sealable zip bag. Most will last about four days longer.

These chemicals, while invisible, can be harmful and should not be ingested. Make sure all vegetables are washed thoroughly before you start cooking. This is less important with vegetables that will be peeled, but it's still good practice to do it.

Peeling and chopping are the next elements of preparation.

The recipe should specify how vegetables are to be prepared – whole, peeled, diced, sliced, finely chopped, mashed, and so on. There is a difference between sliced and diced – slicing means a long fine slice in one direction through the vegetable, while diced means cutting the vegetable into cubes.

Some favorite ways to cook vegetables

- **Boiling.** This simply involves placing the vegetables in a pot of boiling water until cooked – you can usually tell with most vegetables when they are cooked because they will be soft when poked with a fork.

- **Sauté.** A sauté involves cooking all the ingredients of a meal in a pan at once, usually with oil or a little fat.

- **Grilling**. You can cook some vegetables on a grill to go with a barbequed meal.

- **Steaming.** As the name suggests, this is cooking using steam. You boil water underneath the vegetables and the steam passes up through a grate to cook them – this method requires the right cooking utensils.

- **Bake.** Many vegetables are best baked in the oven such as baked potatoes, eggplant, squash, or fresh pumpkin.

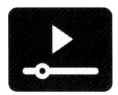

Actually, a great way to "bake" your potatoes while you're away at work (and save a little time on dinner prep) is to use your crockpot (not a phrase I use often). Check out my video!
Google: YouTube Chef Perry baked potatoes

Boiling and steaming, as they only use water, are known to be very healthy methods of cooking vegetables.

Any method that includes using oil, such as frying, tends to be less healthy – although this depends on the type of oil used. Sautéing is next on the list of healthy options after boiling and steaming.

Personally, I think that veggies seldom benefit from being boiled.

Boiling leeches out vitamin content, and is the main culprit in turning vegetables to a gray lifeless, tasteless glop.

So, how then do we proceed?

Depending on the veggies, I prefer steaming, roasting, or sautéing.

All three of these cooking methods leave vegetables full of life, crisp and colorful.

It will also not deplete the vegetables of their vitamin content. By rule of thumb, vegetables will only need a few minutes of heat…i.e.: take them off BEFORE they look done.

If you wait until they look cooked through, they're gonna be soft and soggy when you serve them.

So, get out there and pick up some fresh, beautiful (*or even not so beautiful*) veggies at your local farmer's or produce market, and enjoy them at their seasonal best!

> *The beet is the most intense of vegetables. The radish, admittedly, is more feverish, but the fire of the radish is a cold fire, the fire of discontent, not of passion. Tomatoes are lusty enough, yet there runs through tomatoes an undercurrent of frivolity.*
>
> *Beets are deadly serious.*
>
> ~ *Tom Robbins, 'A Cook's book of Quotations'*

Making Magic with Your Mushrooms

Of all the flavor profiles, umami is my favorite…and of all of the umami foods, roasted mushrooms are high on the list.

Mushrooms are mostly water, so the secret to really getting that deep, earthy goodness from them is to roast out some of the moisture, almost like a reduction, which concentrates and intensifies the flavor.

That's why those thin, almost leathery slices of 'shroom on top of a properly baked pizza are so good!

Here's what I do with just about any mushrooms I'm going to add to a dish like a pasta, eggs, stuffing, soup*, or even for topping a burger or sandwich.

> *An uncooked mushroom is a sponge, so by tossing them raw into a soup, stew, etc., it's going to just soak up whatever liquid it's cooking in, and you'll get almost no "mushroomy" flavor from them.*

- 1 lb. white mushrooms   ½ stick salted butter
- 2-3 lg. garlic cloves, minced   1 tsp. salt, to taste

Preheat oven to 375F. Brush the mushrooms clean or wipe with a (barely) damp cloth, then slice 1/4 inch thick. Any thinner and they'll start breaking apart.

Combine butter, garlic, and salt in a microwave-safe bowl, and nuke until the butter is completely melted. Stir to mix well, and pour over sliced mushrooms in a large bowl. Toss gently until 'shrooms are completely coated.

Spread mushroom slices in a single layer on a foil-lined baking sheet or Pyrex pan. Don't worry if there's a little overlap here and there, you just don't want them in piles.

Roast at 375F for 10-12 minutes, then switch oven to broil and cook another 5-6 minutes, watching closely, until they look like this...

These mushrooms can be used immediately, or stored in a zip bag in the fridge for 2-3 days before using.

Nature's Flavor Enhancer

Monosodium glutamate, also known as sodium glutamate and MSG, is a sodium salt of glutamic acid, a naturally occurring non-essential amino acid. It is used as a food additive and is commonly marketed as a flavor enhancer.

For decades, concerns have been raised on anecdotal grounds, and hypotheses have been put forward, that MSG may be associated with migraine headaches, food allergies in children, obesity, and hyperactivity in children.

Subsequent research by dozens of health centers and universities around the world, however, have found that, while large doses of MSG given without food may elicit more symptoms than a placebo in individuals who believe that they react adversely to MSG, the frequency of the responses was low and the responses reported were inconsistent, not reproducible, and not observed when MSG was given with food.

In the 2004 version of his book, *"On Food and Cooking"*, food enthusiast and author, Harold McGee, states that "[after many studies], toxicologists have concluded that MSG is a harmless ingredient for most people, even in large amounts.

Still, the reports suggest that less than 1% of the population, sensitive individuals may experience "transient" side effects such as "headache, numbness/tingling, flushing, muscle tightness, and generalized weakness" to a large amount of MSG taken in a single meal. So, if you're trying, for whatever reason, to avoid MSG...did you know that the same flavor enhancing proteins, called glutamates, in MSG are found naturally in mushrooms?

Really...is there anything that bacon doesn't make better?

Don't crowd the mushrooms! If you do, your mushrooms will steam rather than fry.

~ Julia Child

This is the Home Chef's secret to expanding the palates we're cooking for…whether they like it or not!

The Rule of 3: Most people will accept a new food when it's introduced with two or more ingredients that they are already familiar and comfortable with…

Examples:

#1: Chicken breast + #2: Peanut butter + #3 fish sauce = Thai Chicken

#1: Mozz cheese + #2: Marinara + #3 zucchini planks = Veggie Lasagna

#1: Fresh corn + #2: butter + #3 Lima beans (or edamame) = Succotash

Not only is this a great way to "soft test" new foods, it's a fantastic (if slightly sneaky) way to get more fruits and veggies into a picky child (or spouse's) diet!

Brussels Sprouts with Bacon & Shallots

I always ask the kids in my classes what their least-favorite vegetable is and the answer is, universally, Brussels Sprouts.

Most adults give the same answer.

In fact, an old friend of ours, Kathy, who is famous for not liking any food that "didn't have a face", was quite polite, but vehement, about her dislike of these mini-cabbages, when we did a dinner at her house.

However, when she tried a small bite of *this* recipe, she came back for seconds.

Many of our kids do the same.

1½ lbs. Brussels sprouts	½ lb. smoked bacon
1/4 cup shallots, diced	1 cup chicken stock
2 Tbsp. butter	Kosher salt to taste

Mise en Place

Trim the stems off the Brussels sprouts, then slice a small "X" in the stem end, about 1/2 inch deep.

Dice the bacon and shallots.

Preparation

Add the bacon and shallots to a cold sauté pan. Heat slowly over medium-low heat, stirring frequently, until the fat starts to render and the meat turns golden brown and crispy but not burnt.

Add the Brussels sprouts and sauté over medium-high heat for a few minutes, or until they're slightly browned. This caramelization will add a lot of flavor to the recipe.

Add the stock, bring to a boil, then lower to a simmer and cook until the liquid is reduced by about half (*5 to 10 minutes*), stirring occasionally.

Stir in the butter, season with Kosher salt and serve right away!

One can get too familiar with vegetables, you know!

~ Chef Skinner, Ratatouille

Chapter Fourteen

Tips from the Restaurant Kitchen

Growing up with a chef for my father definitely expanded my culinary horizons. Dinner (and sometimes breakfast) was often whatever the special had been that night, or what had to be moved out of the walk-in to make room for new stock.

Suffice it to say...things that would have sent some kids screaming into the street, were as common as hotdogs and mac-and-cheese at my house.

However, I also learned many of the techniques that chefs use to make their dishes just a little tastier, a little easier, and a little quicker than the home chef has been taught to do.

Butter it Up!

"The three secrets to French cooking are butter, butter, and butter!" ~ Julia Child

Let's take a look at one simple trick that some of the "high end" steak houses use, to keep folks raving about their beef.

Now, don't get me wrong, the quality and preparation of the cut has a lot to do with how good it's going to taste once it hits the plate, but here's a little something you can do to jack the flavor of even a great piece of meat, up to the next level. This works equally well with beef, lamb, pork, chicken, even fish...

> *I believe it's a cook's absolute moral obligation to add more butter whenever given the chance.*
>
> *~ Michael Ruhlman*

As soon as you plate the meat (*after resting*), give it a smear, end to end, with a thin coating of herb-butter, or "compound-butter" (*recipe below*). This should melt into the surface of the meat almost instantly.

The browning effect that creates that lovely crust on the outside of a steak or chop, also tends to suck all the fat out of that first 1/8 inch.

Chef Tip: *Another of my favorite meat cooking techniques is the "Reverse Sear." In reverse searing, the meat is roasted on a rack in the oven first, then finished in a very hot skillet or pan.*

Cooking your steak in the oven first, dries the outside of the steak (a good thing) while slowly cooking the inside and keeping it tender.

Also, when the surface of the steak is dry, it will then sear faster and more efficiently in a hot pan, forming that ideal crust. For the step-by-step of reverse searing: **Google: "hautemealz reverse sear"**

Fat (*either natural or added*) is a flavor distributor, washing that salty/savory awesomeness throughout all of the taste-buds in your mouth, as opposed to just the ones that come in first contact with the meat.

This effect creates that instant "explosion of flavor" that's so often moaned about during fine dining. Again, you just need enough to coat the surface of the meat (*a tsp or two*), and you want to add it just before serving, so there's still enough coating the meat (*before it's absorbed*) to have this effect.

Secondarily, the herb butter creates a beautiful, juicy sheen to the meat, making all those shades of brown and black deeper and more vibrant. As chefs in all parts of the world are fond of saying…"*we eat first with our eyes*", and thinking of how delicious that first bite *looks*, has an important effect on our reaction when it reaches our mouth.

Here's a simple herb butter that's great on just about anything.

The beauty of making your own is you can add just about anything you want…are you a dill junkie? Add a couple of tablespoons, minced. Chile-head? Toss in some red pepper flake, or fresh minced habanero. If you're going for an Asian flair, a teaspoon of fish sauce and a dash of cinnamon are awesome.

Play with it, make it your own…it's okay, *you're* the chef!

Basic Herb Butter

¼ pound + ½ Tbs. unsalted butter, softened
½ Tbs. minced garlic   1 tsp. minced fresh thyme
1 tsp. minced rosemary   1 tsp. smoked salt
1 tsp. black pepper
In a small skillet or pan, sauté the minced garlic in 1/2 tablespoon of butter over medium heat until just translucent; do not brown (*it makes your garlic bitter*).

Add garlic, chopped herbs, salt, and pepper, cook another minute or two, stirring. Allow this mixture to mix, and then pour it over the quarter-pound of softened butter. (*You want the butter soft, but not melted, so that all of you herbs don't sink to the bottom, but stay suspended throughout the butter.*) Mix well. Scoop into a storage container and cover with a lid or plastic wrap. Refrigerate until needed. Just before serving, spread 1 or 2 teaspoons of seasoned (*softened*) butter on top of each serving.

Note: Butter logs can be kept in the freezer for up to 1 month.

Saving an Over-Salted Dish

We have all, at one time or another, gotten too generous with the salt shaker. Sometimes it's a slip of the hand, and sometimes we just forget to take into account how much a liquid will reduce (*which intensifies the flavors – especially salt.*) First and foremost…

DON'T PANIC!

Aside from the lid of the shaker coming off mid-sprinkle (*and we'll talk about that in a second*) most dishes that have been over salted, CAN be saved.

However, the best advice I can give you is…don't over-salt your food. (*Duh – right?*) Seriously, before we take on the task of un-salting, here are three keys to NOT over-salting/over spicing in the first place:

Taste your dish every few minutes during the cooking. This is a cornerstone of good cooking. The taste, consistency, and intensity of salts, herbs, and spices, can and will change dramatically over the cooking time of a dish. The more ingredients, the more wildly the flavor combinations will vary. Taste often, and adjust with a light hand.

Never add salt (*or spices*) directly from the container.

It's very hard to judge, especially with white salt, how much is actually going onto the food.

Add steam, smoke, etc., and it's nearly impossible. If you watch food TV, you'll notice that most chefs measure a little seasoning into the palm of their hands, and add it to the food from there. This is because they have learned over the years to know exactly what a ½ teaspoon, a teaspoon, a tablespoon, etc., looks like in their palm, and unlike a shaker or container, all that can end up in the pot is what they've pre-measured into their hand.

Plus, you never know if your crack-head line cook screwed the lid back on the container.

If you do the same, you'll virtually eliminate over-seasoning issues in your kitchen. Wait to salt. With most foods, it doesn't really matter at what point during the cooking process that salt is added (*pasta being an exception, as it must be boiled in salted water*), so wait until the dish is almost done, before adding the majority of the salt. That way, issues like natural saltiness, or reductions are less likely to surprise you in the finished dish. Things like pasta and boiled veggies are fairly simple. If you catch it early (*which is why, again, it's important to taste, taste, and taste again, at all steps of the cooking process!*) you can change out the simmering water, with fresh (*unsalted*) simmering water, and that will usually draw the excess saltiness out.

Note: *never, never, never* rinse pasta! Doing so washes off all that lovely starch that both makes your sauce creamy, and helps it stick to the pasta.

For hunks of meat, ground meat, steaming veggies, etc., about all you can do is rinse (*cold food-cold water, hot food-hot water*), pat dry, return it to the pan, and re-season.

Soups, stews, and sauces: peel and slice raw potato (*russets seem to work best*) and add them to a slowly simmering liquid.

The potato will draw in the salty liquid. Remove the cooked potatoes and replace the liquid (with unsalted liquid). Repeat as needed.

Sometimes, in dishes like a casserole, chili, or a pasta dish that's already been combined, about the only thing you can do is add more of the main ingredients (*meat, pasta, rice, veggies*) that have been cooked without seasoning, mix them with the original ingredients, and continue cooking to dilute the saltiness. With this method, if possible, be sure to give the whole dish an occasional stir while it's finishing.

Make sure to add more of your non-salty favoring ingredients (*herbs, spices, etc.,*) so the dish doesn't become bland.

Also, if your dish would be complimented with an acidic component (*and most are*) try adding a little lemon or lime juice, as this will often reduce the perceived saltiness.

If none of that works, serve with lots of beer. ☺ *(I'm kidding...sort of...)*

What about a dish that's too *spicy?*

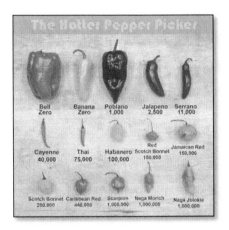

Typically, what sets your mouth on fire, the fault is a compound in foods called capsaicin (*typically found in chili peppers.*)

Both the amount of capsaicin, and the sensitivity of your mouth's taste buds, determine just HOW hot the fire gets.

Much of the capsaicin is in the membranes and seeds of the pepper.

Remove these if you want to limit the level of heat in a dish.

Add Additional Ingredients - Adding more ingredients to a dish dilutes the heat and helps keep the balance the flavor.

Add Dairy - As most of us know, when our mouths are burning, a glass of milk is a nearly sublime remedy. Likewise adding dairy to a dish will reduce the heat as well. BTW, if you're using butter, be sure it's "unsalted" butter.

A daube of sour cream can really tone down a soup, stew, or casserole (plus it tastes great.)

Chef's Note: *The heat of a pepper is rated on the "Scoville Scale."*
The higher the Scoville rating, the hotter the burn. Bell peppers rate a zero; while the Carolina Reaper, measures an inedible 2,200,000. Ouch!

Remember, drinking water or alcohol merely spreads the heat to the rest of your mouth and throat. Stick with the milk!

BTW, if you have issues with dairy, nut butters will often do the trick as well.

Add Sugar - Sweetness can balance out the heat of a dish. Sugar, of course, comes to mind, but don't dismiss honey, molasses, maple syrup, fruit juices, or other natural sweeteners.

Add Acid - A few squeezes of lemon or lime juice helps, tomatoes, vinegars (flavored or unflavored), and wine are all good for dousing the flames.

Of course the very BEST option is add you heat in small increments, tasting as you go (keep in mind, as a dish reduces, both heat and saltiness will increase, so save your salting for closer to the end.)

As my old man used to say (*ad naseum*) "it's a lot easier to add some more than to take some back out."

5 Tips for Perfect Pasta

"The trouble with eating Italian food is that five or six days later, you're hungry again." ~ George Miller

Okay, let's face it…cooking pasta really isn't all that difficult.

Most of the time, just following the package directions will get you a pretty tasty finished product. Still, if you've ever been to a good Italian restaurant, you probably noticed that there's just *something* different about the pasta there, *something* that takes it to the next level.

Here are 5 *somethings* that the Capo Cuoco is doing, back in the kitchen, that makes all the difference…

Salt yes, oil no.

Once your water is boiling, toss in a small handful of sea salt (*about 1 tbsp. per quart*). Your pasta is going to absorb that water as it cooks, so you're effectively seasoning the pasta from the inside out.

Also, regardless of what you learned at home (*sorry, Mom*) never add oil to the water. You WANT your pasta to be sticky, that's what keeps the sauce adhered to each strand. To keep it from clumping in the pot, give it an occasional stir with your tongs. On a related note…for the same reason above, never, ever, *ever*, rinse your pasta after cooking.

Rinsing your pasta is a sin against God.

> *I made lemon spaghetti in an early season of 'Everyday Italian,' and to this day people still come up to me and say they love it.*
>
> *It's very, very simple. Basically, you cook the pasta and mix together Parmesan cheese, olive oil, lemon juice and zest and pour it over the pasta.*
>
> *~Giada De Laurentiis*

Keep a cup or two

When you cook your pasta, save a couple of cups of the cooking water. This salty, starchy pasta broth is a major component in those lovely sauces. Use a little to start your sauce, and a bit more to thin it just before adding the pasta. The starch adds a silky, rich component to your sauce, as well as helping it combine with the pasta.

Pasta goes *in* the sauce!

…not the other way around. I know, I know…we've all seen the picture: a big bowl of steaming pasta, topped with a lava-like scoop of sauce. Try this, next time: Heat a large sauté pan over high heat and, just *before* your pasta is done to your taste, add a serving of sauce and then a serving of hot pasta (*straight from the water with tongs*) directly to the pan.

The picture on the right is a Rachel Ray recipe…just, you know…sayin'…

Give it a flip or two to combine, and pour directly onto the plate or bowl. This step allows the final cooking of the pasta to happen while *in* the sauce, which pulls in some of that additional flavor, and insures that you have sauce clinging to every bite.

For tube or shell-shaped pastas, this step also allows the sauce to "get inside" each piece. If the sauce looks a little thin, let it simmer a couple more minutes to reduce. If it looks a little thick, add a bit of your reserved pasta water.

Butter makes everything better! *(...are you sensing a theme here?)*

A couple of teaspoons each of butter and olive oil, added to the pasta/sauce combo during those last couple of flips in the pan, really pulls your sauce together, while creating a smooth, unctuous mouth feel. Remember, fat is a flavor transmitter.

> *The Italians were eating with forks when the French were still eating each other.*
>
> ~ *Mario Batali*

The big finish...

This last tip is optional, but it really does go a long way in taking a great dish of pasta to a fantastic dish of pasta...the toppings.

Add a healthy sprinkle of fresh-ground black pepper, some shredded or shaved *Parmigiano-Reggiano, or (my favorite)* shredded asiago cheese, and/or a dash of freshly chopped basil and Italian parsley, just before serving.

Not only are these add-ons pretty, and make for a classy looking dish, but they add an extra layer of flavor to those all-important first bites.

Homework Assignment #10
Spaghetti alla Carbonara

If there's one pasta dish that every Home Chef should know how to make, it's got to be the classic *Spaghetti alla Carbonara.*

This is a very old dish that carbonari (*coal workers*), cooked directly over the coal fires from ingredients they could carry in their pouches: eggs, guanciale, pecorino and pasta. If you want to make a perfect carbonara, there's no cheating. Guanciale, not ham. Pecorino, not parmesan, and the freshest eggs possible. It's these details that makes this quite possibly the greatest single pasta dish in history.

Chef P's Spaghetti alla Carbonara
Serves 4

16 ounces guanciale*, diced
4 large egg yolks
1 cup Pecorino Romano, freshly grated

1 pound spaghetti
1 Tbs. coarse black pepper

In a large pan, fry the guanciale over medium-high heat until rendered and crisp, about 10 minutes. Beat eggs and pecorino together in a small bowl with a fork and set aside.

Cook the spaghetti to al dente, then drain, return to pot, toss with guanciale, pepper, and rendered fat over low heat and immediately transfer to four shallow bowls.

Pour egg/cheese mixture over each of the four bowls, add black pepper to taste and quickly mix with a fork to slightly cook the eggs with the hot pasta. The result should be creamy, not dry.

Serve immediately.

*Guanciale

Jowl bacon, or *guanciale (gwan-chalie – doesn't everything just sound better in Italian?)* is an Italian-style bacon made from hog jowl, is a prized gourmet delicacy in central Italy.

Typically, it's dry-cured, hand-coated with fresh cracked peppercorns, and then slowly smoked over cured hickory logs for nearly 24 hours.

The result is a meat with a noticeably richer flavor than typical bacon, and is a popular addition to such classic dishes as spaghetti alla carbonara and pasta all'amatriciana.

If you absolutely cannot find Guanciale, you can replace it with chopped pancetta. But do try to get the pork jowl!

Carl Blake of Rustik Rooster Farms - The Hog Whisperer...

I get mine from Carl Blake, the guru of pig. Carl (who you may have seen on...well...many, many shows) raises Iowa Swabian, and Mangalitsa pigs at Rustik Rooster Farms in Iowa, and (*lucky me*) he happens to be a Facebook buddy of mine, sharing another passion of mine...pig roasting boxes. His own American Hotbox's are the Lamborghini of *caja china* style cooking.

Carl and I talk...a lot, and he knows more about raising heritage hogs than any of us probably want to know. Getting Guanciale from Carl, is like having the Pope say your bedtime prayers with you.

It's a good thing.

Carl sells pork of every shape, size and cut (and lots of other cool stuff) at **www.porkportal.com**, and for the premium quality of the product, his prices are insanely reasonable!

Tell him Chef Perry sent you!

> **" Tutto quello che vedete lo devo agli spaghetti.**
>
> Sophia Loren

"Everything you see...I owe to spaghetti."

12 Things I've Learned Watching "Chopped"

- *Whenever possible, toast grains and rice prior to cooking to add depth of flavor*

- *Skin MUST be served crisp...brown separately, if necessary.*

- *Dessert - when in doubt, incorporate fresh whipped cream and fresh fruit.*

- *Foods that need to be cut, or have bones, should be served on a flat plate.*

- *Keep your station clean.*

- *If you're serving smooth or creamy, consider topping it with a crunchy element for an added texture.*

- *Pickled cucumbers (peeled) are a simple way to add an acid component to a plate.*

- *Oil the product, not the grill.*

- *If you want a finished dish to be mixed or stirred at table, serve it in a bowl, not on a plate.*

- *A dash of Worstershire sauce brings out the umami in sautéed mushrooms.*

- *Taste EVERYTHING, before and after each step.*

- *A perfectly fried or poached egg is seldom a bad accompaniment.*

 Food for Thought...

"Food is like a dog, it can smell fear"

— Anne Burell

joinmykitchen.com

Giving Citrus a Roll

Whenever possible, when preparing a recipe that calls for lemon, lime, or orange juice, I try to go with fresh-squeezed. It tastes *so* much better!

Like many folks, I inherited one of those round "citrus juicers" from my mother's kitchen, but here's a trick *Dad* taught me, for getting the most out of my favorite fruits.

Before you halve your orange, lemon, or lime, place it on a flat surface, and roll it back and forth with the heel of your hand, exerting firm, constant, downward pressure.

You want to press hard enough that you can feel the fruit give a little under your hand, but not too hard…or you'll end up with a pulpy mess, and juice all over your kitchen!

After a few rolls, you should be able to feel the fruit softening, as the pulp inside is crushed (*which releases the juice*).

Now, place the fruit on a small plate or bowl to catch the extra juice, and slice it in half, across the middle, with a very sharp knife.

At this point, you can either use your citrus juicer, a press, or (*what most chefs do*) squeeze the fruit with one hand, and allow the juice to run through the fingers of the other (*to catch any seeds or pulp*) and into a bowl.

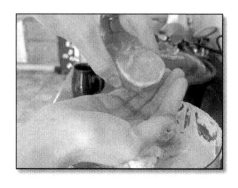

Rotate the fruit ¼ turn clockwise in your hand with each squeeze.

By rolling the fruit first, you'll get a lot more juice, for a lot less effort.

This is also a great job to assign to any junior kitchen assistants!

Try this technique with one of my favorite summer drinks, Brazilian Limeade.

Google: hautemealz Brazilian limeade

Brown is Beautiful!

"Browning is the process of becoming brown, especially referring to food." – *From Wikipedia, the free encyclopedia*

Is that not the greatest definition ever?

Okay, seriously…browning, or searing meat in oil over high heat, and doing it correctly, is a major tool in the chef's bag-of-tricks for getting an amazing richness and depth of flavor out of steaks, chops, stews, casseroles, and soups.

By browning the meat before cooking it with additional ingredients, you get fabulous flavor and beautiful color.

This makes all the difference to the finished meat and any sauce (it removes a lot of the excess fat from the meat, as well.) So…how does it work?

Chef's Tip: *When cooking a steak, I always start by cooking it on its side, where there is a rim of fat on its narrow edge. This renders all that good, flavorful fat in the pan for the rest of the cooking.*

First, let's look at where all those flavors come from in the first place…

The chemical term for this type of browning is the "***Maillard reaction***" which is a reaction between the amino acids and sugars (*called "caramelizing" when referring to sugars*) in the meat that breaks down large molecules and produces smaller molecules which our senses are better able to perceive as flavors and appetite-pleasing aromas. Uncooked meat (*with the exception of some types of fish*) tends to be pretty bland and flavorless. Browning adds texture and better color and flavor.

It's an absolutely essential step in the deglazing process (*loosening the browned bits or "fond" from the bottom of the pan with water, broth, or wine*), which is the first step in creating a pan sauce, such as in our Filet Mignon with Umami Merlot Sauce recipe (*Google it!*). Browning and deglazing is also one of the secrets to the French tradition of building "layers of flavor" in famous dishes like cassoulet.

> ***Chef's Tip:*** *When you need more oil in the pan when sautéing, add it in a stream along the edges of the pan so that it's heated to cooking temp by the time the oil reaches the food.*

For some soups and stews, however, the additional smoky hint of char that this process lends is pretty amazing…try making a "grilled steak chili" sometime, and you'll see what I mean!

Tips for Browning

Use a good cast iron skillet or enamel-covered cast-iron cassoulet pan. Iron retains the heat better (*and they last a lifetime!*) Non-stick pans don't perform as well for browning as iron, as the "sticking to the pan until done" is an important part of the process. They will, however, work in a pinch.

Don't add cold meat to a hot pan…again, this just cools your pan. Let meat come to room temperature before cooking for best results. (*I know some of you are freakin' out on this one…trust me, 30-60 minutes on the counter isn't going to poison your family!*)

Dry meat. The meat may be a little damp or even wet if it has been frozen, so pat it dry with absorbent paper. WET MEAT WON'T BROWN! This is because the release of water creates steam, which retards the caramelization process by creating a layer of water vapor between the meat and the surface of the pan.

Essentially, you're boiling the meat, instead of browning it.

Also, the pan has to be HOT…if the pan's not hot enough, the meat releases water before it sears and, again, you're boiling it.

Coat the meat with oil rather than adding it to the pan. This is a matter of personal preference, but I do it because it saves oil, and cuts down on splatters (and the resulting burns) that can occur when the raw meat is set in a pool of hot oil.

Heat the pan before you add the meat. Adding meat will cool the pan quickly, and if you have too much meat, or not enough heat, you'll drop the temp below the "browning zone". The oil should be a little hotter than you think it should be, when you add the meat…just below the smoking point. Remember, you're not COOKING the meat, you just need to brown it on all sides.

Don't overcrowd the pan. When you're browning meat cubes for a casserole brown the meat in small batches. Much like our tip, above, about drying the meat, crowding the pan traps in steam. If the meat you're trying to brown is turning gray…it's either wet, or you've over-crowded the pan.

Don't fuss. Flipping the meat, or constantly poking at it with tongs may make food TV more interesting to watch, but it's not helping the meat brown. In fact, it's making it take longer, and drying it out in the process. As meat browns is will typically stick to the bottom of the pan a bit *(this is what creates that delicious fond)*. My father used to tell me, "The pan will let you know when it's done." It's true, when that molecular change from big bits to little bits is complete, the meat will release from the surface. If there's resistance, leave it alone.

So, there you go.

Try these tips at home, and the next time you want to give dinner a big boost of flavor…make it brown, make it beautiful.

Cooking with stainless steel

A friend recently wrote me, asking… *"Just bought 12" stainless steel fry pan w/lid, and now at 70 plus years, I am faced with a great amount of trepidation about using it. Any info on learning to use this will be greatly appreciated. I want to brown some great thick-cut bone-in pork chops I found at a local store. I want this to give me the pan drippings so I can try and figure out how to make a sauce."*

Okay, so first things first…I am answering a specific question, about a specific product, not weighing in (*or asking anyone else to*) on the pros and cons of any type of cookware. I have at least four different styles of cookware in my kitchen, from cast iron to Teflon, and they all have their purpose.

This is about *stainless steel.*

There's a lot of info out there, a lot of do's and don'ts, and if you're going to ask the great and powerful Google, I strongly suggest you stick to the answers written by names you know and trust…and even *they* don't all agree. However, the basics of cooking with stainless steel, that most everyone seems to agree on, are:

ALWAYS preheat your pan before adding food, especially meat you want to brown, and keep the heat at medium-high or below.

Stay at the stove, baby your food, and adjust the heat often until you're familiar with how your pan, works with your stove, and even with each burner. My electric burners all vary, and SS is going to have the least forgiving margin of error.

Pre-heating your pan is key, nothing else will work right afterwards, if you don't. For best performance I suggest using 50/50 oil and butter. The butter is going to give you better flavor and caramelization, and the oil, which has a much higher smoke point, is going to help the butter not to burn. Plus, it's a little healthier.

Chef's Note: The meat IS going to stick, period. Let it! If the meat doesn't move easily in the pan, it's not ready to be moved. Let it cook until the pan releases it.

You WANT the meat to stick to the pan. This is also how the lovely brown "fond" that's the base for your sauce or gravy, is formed.

This is also why "non-stick pans, though not out of the question, are at least less desirable and effective for creating sauces and gravies.

Fond: French for "base" commonly refers to the browned bits and caramelized drippings of meat and vegetables that are stuck to the bottom of a pan after sautéing or roasting. It's often retained as a source of flavor and deglazed with liquid and aromatics like onions and garlic. The fond is the base of a number of classic French pan sauces.

Now, a word to the wise...

I've known folks who have switched from non-stick (Teflon) to stainless steel, and couldn't be happier. I've known others who developed an almost instant hatred of the stuff. If you're fairly new to cooking, non-stick is a much more forgiving material to work with, and I highly recommend that you start out with the best you can afford, and put off stainless steel until you have more experience with the other elements of cooking. Non-stick has a nearly zero learning curve, is easy to cook with, and super easy to clean.

Also, good stainless steel (and you want good stainless steel) varies from really expensive to nose bleed expensive, so, if possible, see if you can borrow a good 12-inch pan from a friend for a week or two, before you blow junior's college fund on a 12-peice All-Clad collection.

Lastly, for my friend who posed this question, here is, undoubtedly, my favorite stove-top pork recipe.

Google: *"Huffington Post Pan Seared Pork"*

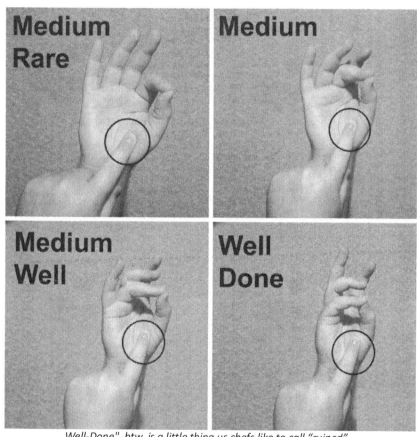

Well-Done", btw, is a little thing us chefs like to call "ruined"...

Giving it a Rest

Have you ever gotten a steak or a chicken breast right off the grill, cut into it with a sharp knife, and had a gush of hot, steamy juices pour out onto your plate? Yeah, me too.

Did you notice, a few minutes later, that that lovely, juicy piece of glorious cow, pig, or chicken had turned into sawdust? Yeah, me too. Once meat is removed from the heat, it's vital that it be allowed to "rest", tented loosely in foil.

Resting allows the meat to relax and reabsorb its own juices back into the muscle fibers, as they cool.

If you cut into that same steak or chicken breast after it's rested under a foil tent for 5-10 minutes, you'll see those same juices bead up on the surface of the meat, but do not pour out of your plate. This means that the whole cut is going to stay moist.

Eating chicken without skin is like riding a bike without wheels

~ Michael Symon

With small cuts like steaks and chops, I think that just a few minutes (5-10) is sufficient.

Some larger cuts of meat, like pork shoulders, leg of lamb, or beef brisket, require foiling or wrapping tightly in foil, and "coolering" for a longer length of time. This allows the internal temp to rise the last few degrees without any additional heat, and without the outside of the meat overcooking.

Here are some good general resting times:

- *Pork shoulders (Butts), & Brisket – 2 Hours*
- *Whole Turkey, Lg. Roasts - 30 minutes*
- *Smaller roasts, Whole Chickens, Turkey breasts 15– 20 minutes*
- *Steaks, Chops, Chicken Breasts, 5 – 10 minutes*

Always tent the meat loosely in foil to keep the surface temperature from dropping much faster than the internal temp. This can lead to drying, as well. Oh, and while those steaks are resting…toss some chopped shallots, a cup of Merlot, a tablespoon of Dijon mustard, and a teaspoon of chopped garlic into a skillet and simmer.

Add any drippings from the steak plate, as well, then pour a couple of tablespoons over each steak, just before serving.

You're welcome.

Roasting Tip: *When in doubt about the correct temperature for baking/roasting a dish, go with 350F.*

Happiness is a Warm Plate

Whenever possible, I warm the plates that I'll be serving hot food on, and chill the plates I'm using for cold food.

Good restaurant chefs warm their diner's plates because, while hot food served on a room-temp (*cold*) plate is fine when it reaches the table, it quickly becomes cold before the end of the meal. This is especially true for light foods such as loose rice, pasta, and other foods that tend to cool quickly.

> *Today is for being grateful for the many blessings each of us have in our lives, from the smallest miracle of a warm plate of food, to the largest gift of unconditional love*
>
> *~ Unknown*

Let's put it this way. Ever been out for a walk on a snowy day? You're bundled up nice and toasty, and then you plop down for a rest on a snow-covered bench. In the instant battle between warm and cold, who wins…the bench or your butt?

Exactly.

Hot food will cool much sooner than the cold plate will get warm. And hot food is simply more attractive, flavorful, and enjoyable to eat. When you're at a restaurant, and your server says "Careful, this plate is very hot"…that's no accident. Nothing frustrates a chef like putting a nice, hot meal on the pass-through, only to have a customer dig into a lukewarm chunk of meat or tepid veggies.

Even in a serve-yourself situation, there's something very comforting and inviting about picking up a warm plate.

In fact, my father *(also a chef)* always made it a point, when he had guests over *(he liked to serve family-style)* to hand each diner a warm plate. It never failed to elicit a smile and a positive comment.

And...it's so easy to do! Honest!

You can warm plates in the oven, microwave, or dishwasher, or just run hot water over them, and then place them in a *(warmed)* towel-lined basket until ready to serve. For the oven, set it for lowest setting (typically 150F) put the plates in the cold oven and allow to warm 2-3 minutes. If you have to stack your plates more than 2 deep, you'll need to "shuffle" them while warming.

(A toaster oven works great too, and uses less energy.)

Run them under some really hot water, or fill the sink with hot water and let them soak a few minutes. Towel-dry your plates just before plating the meal, or before popping them in a basket. If you're a gadget junkie, consider using an electric plate warmer: think of it as an electric blanket for your plates. These typically hold between 6-16 plates and can be a little spendy, but in their defense...sometimes I'm using my oven AND my sink, and I just want some warm plates. When that happens, this gadget is awfully convenient.

Lastly *(and this is the method I typically use for the three of us)* if your oven's in use, and the sink's full already, you can stack the plates on top of the oven between the burners, or on the back "oven vent" burner, if you're warming something inside. I recommend this method unless you've got the oven on high broil, which can heat the stove-top to unsafe temps, especially at the vent. If not, stack 'em up, cover with a dishcloth *(both to hold in heat, and to protect from splatters)* and shuffle them now and then so the bottom plate doesn't get too hot, while and the top one stays cool.

This concept is equally important when serving salads, cold sides, or desserts.

> *Chef's Tip: Here's a good rule of thumb – when plating, you want the temperature of your plates to generally match the ideal temperature of the food that's being served on it.*

Homework Assignment #11
A Proper Steak

- Select a good steak, no less that one inch thick.

  I suggest either New York Strip, or Ribeye, preferably from a butcher shop, or one selected by the butcher from your grocery-store (*ask for "fresh and well-marbled.*

- Nothing that s already been wrapped in plastic!

- Pan-sear a steak, using the instructions in the "Brown is Beautiful" and "Cooking with Stainless Steel" sections, and finish with some fresh herb butter, from "Butter it Up".

- Rest your steak, and serve on warmed plates, perhaps with a rice dish from Making Rice that s Nice (next section....)

Chef's Note: If you can't eat beef, substitute this entire recipe with "Quick Chicken Piccata" a few pages on.

~ Notes ~

_____

_____

_____

_____

_____

_____

_____

_____

_____

_____

Cooking Rice that's Extra Nice

Hi, I'm Chef Perry…I'm a carb-junkie, and I love rice *(every one say, Hi Perry…)*

Seriously, I don't even need it served with anything else; a nice bowl of properly cooked rice, a pinch of salt or a splash of soy sauce, and I'm a happy cook. Admittedly, plain boiled or steamed white rice can be a little bland, but here's a kitchen secret to make your rice extra nice.

I picked this tip up back in my teens, working in a Mexican restaurant: always lightly brown your rice in a little olive oil, before you add water and boil it. Essentially, you're toasting the rice, which, just like when toasting nuts or grains, produces a deep, rich, nutty aroma and flavor. Add a pinch of salt and maybe a little minced shallot *(which gives a mild onion/garlic flavor)* and you have something truly exceptional. I use this step whenever I prepare rice as a side, for risotto, for Spanish rice…pretty much everything but sushi rice, which needs to be stickier than this process allows for.

NOTE: For flavored rice, replace the water with chicken or beef stock, or add spices like curry powder, 5 Spice, Italian seasonings, or a little cumin and chili powder.

Sautéing rice for my Creole Risotto, at the Crawfish Mystery Box Cook-Off. Recipe follows...

Browning works great with all types of white rice, brown rice, and is especially good with a wild rice blend.

Here's the basics...

Heat 1 tbsp. olive oil in a skillet set over medium heat. Add 1 cup of rice (*I prefer jasmine*) and sauté until the ends of the rice are translucent, and it's just starting to color. You can add some finely minced shallots in this step, as well. Combine the rice with 1 3/4 cups water in a heavy saucepan and add salt to taste. Include 1 tsp. olive oil and set the pan over high heat. Heat the water until it comes to a boil.

Reduce the heat to low, stir the rice, and cover the pot. Let the rice cook for 12 to 15 minutes or until all of the water has been absorbed.

Remove the pan from the heat and set aside, covered, for another five minutes. This allows the rice to steam slightly.

Fluff the rice grains with a fork before serving.

Chef's Note: For flavored rice, replace the water with chicken or beef stock, or add spices like curry powder, 5 Spice, Italian seasonings, or a little cumin and chili powder.

My pals Valarie and Linda from Tualatin Chamber of Commerce

Tualatin Crawfish Mystery Box Cook-Off
(with recipes)

I was honored to be one of the six chefs invited to participate in this first annual cook-off, and had a chance to share "the stage" with some major talent from the local restaurant community. Luckily, these guys (and gal) were, to a fault, a heap of fun to work with, and kindly accepted me into their ranks without hesitation.

After donning our snazzy new chef's whites *(thank you Tualatin Chamber)* we opened our mystery boxes to find…well, a whole heap of great stuff.

We each had a "spice rack" butter, and olive oil, as well as a frying pan, pot, and a few basic pieces of kitchen gear.

We were allowed to bring our own knife rolls, as well. Well, as soon as I opened the box *(which I was just SURE was going to have gummy bears, tripe, and diet root-beer in it)* and saw, instead, jasmine rice, onions, cream, and *(thank you Jesus)* bacon I relaxed a little… I had *risotto*, one of my all-time favorite dishes, and one I make often.

So…here's the 1st Place winner recipe (woo-hoo!): *Creole Risotto with Crawfish Étouffée…*

Creole Risotto with Crawfish Etouffee
Chef Perry Perkins

1 cup Arborio rice
2 tbsp. olive oil
1 cup crawfish stock (see below)
1 lb. frozen crawfish tails, peeled
1 yellow bell pepper
3 stalks celery, diced
1 can diced tomatoes, drained
3 Tbs. Creole seasoning
1 lemon
1/4 + 2 tbsp. cup grated Parmigiano-Reggiano

1 cup butter, divided
2 cups clam juice
1 cup heavy cream, divided
1/2 lbs. bacon
1 sweet onion, diced
4 cloves garlic, minced
1 can red beans, drained
1 tsp. red pepper flakes
Salt & Pepper to taste

(Not all of these ingredients were available in the mystery box, but are standard risotto ingredients, and ones I added in the future when preparing this dish! – P)

Mise en Place

Dice yellow bell pepper, sweet onion, celery, and garlic. Drain the red beans, disposing of juice. Slice lemon in half, slice two ½ inch thick rounds from one half, and then cut those rounds in half.

Begin crawfish Etouffee (*below*). While water is heating, melt ½ cup of butter in a deep skillet or pot, with olive oil, over medium heat.

Allow to brown a bit, and then add ½ cup onions, ½ of the garlic, and all of the dry rice. Cook the rice, stirring often, until just golden and aromatic (*the rice will give off a nutty aroma*). Stir in 2 tbsp. of Creole seasoning.

Add ½ cup of clam juice to the rice, stirring constantly until the liquid has been absorbed (about 3 minutes), repeat until clam juice is gone. Add the can of diced tomatoes (*drained*) to the rice, stirring constantly until the liquid has been absorbed (*about 3 minutes*), add ½ cup of crawfish broth/cream mixture to the rice.

> *I like rice. Rice is great if you're hungry and want 2000 of something.*
> *~ Mich Ehrenborg*

Stir constantly until the liquid has been absorbed (about 3 minutes), repeat until only ½ cup of crawfish stock remains. Set that aside.

Add salt and pepper to taste.

Continue adding ¼ cup of hot water, and cooking until absorbed, until risotto just reaches a creamy consistency with still a pleasant bite to the rice (*you don't want it mushy.*) Stir in the ¼ cup of the Parmigiano-Reggiano cheese. Serve immediately.

Crawfish Etouffee

In a heavy saucepan, heat 4 cup of water to steaming. Add frozen crawfish tails, and being back to just steam, turn heat to low, and allow crawfish to rest in the water 10 minutes.

Drain crawfish tails, reserving the broth, and set tails aside. Pour ½ of the crawfish broth into a clean pan, add ½ cup of cream, the remaining butter, and salt and pepper to taste. Bring just to a simmer, and set aside. This is your crawfish stock.

In a heavy pan, cook diced bacon until just crisp. Drain off as much fat as possible, patting the bacon with paper towels. Now, melt ½ cup of butter in that same pan over medium heat, add remaining garlic, diced onions, bell pepper, and celery. Season with salt and pepper, 1 tbsp. Creole seasoning, and red pepper flakes. Cook until veggies have softened but still have a crisp bite to them. Add red beans, remaining crawfish stock, 2 Tbsp. Parmigiano-Reggiano, and remaining cream, simmer and reduce a bit.

Fold in crawfish tails, and squeeze fresh lemon juice over all (from the unsliced 1/2) just before serving.

To Serve:

Spoon equal amounts of risotto onto 4 plates, and spread into a 1-inch thick disk.

Mound ¼ of the warm Crawfish Jambalaya in the center of each.

Add a ½ round of lemon leaned against the jambalaya. Dust all lightly with creole seasoning.

Serve immediately.

Just drop some onion and garlic in olive oil, and your day improves exponentially.

~ Jen Hatmaker

Toasting Toast

We don't know how to toast bread anymore.

You know that buttery, golden brown, super crunchy toast you get in the restaurant? They achieve that by making toast pretty much the opposite of the way most people do it a home. You can't add cold, or even warm butter to hot bread and expect it to become anything but soggy. Even buttering the bread before placing it in a hot pan is problematic, as the butter has to melt, and most of it will just get sucked up into the bread, again...soggy-ville.

What makes that restaurant toast so good is that it actually isn't "toasted" at all...it's *fried*. The correct way to make toast is to get the butter good and hot in a shallow pan (*you don't want to hold any steam in*), over medium heat and THEN add the bread. This allows a crispy crust to form, keeping the bread from absorbing too much butter (*i.e.: getting soggy*), which allows it to brown perfectly. I like to cut thick slices of whole loaf artisan bread for our toast.

Toasters are for home cooks, not you and me. (*Repeat that five times, with your nose high in the air...*)

"Plantxan Olagarro" Basque-style grilled octopus with Mojo Rojo. A traditional tapa at our Christmas dinner. A very sexy dish.

Sexy Food

Okay, we've talked about this idea before, but let's really take a look at it a little closer... *people eat first with their eyes.*

Open your favorite cookbook, flip on your favorite foodie TV channel, or sit down at a "nice" restaurant, and you'll see they have one thing in common: no matter what they're serving, outside of prison, nobody's just slingin' it on the plate.

Beautifully plated dishes, studiously presented...sexy food...it sells the dish before you ever taste it.

(Just a note, sexy presentation will never, ever make bad, or even mediocre food, good. It will, however, make good food better, and great food amazing.)

So, there are three basic elements to consider when plating food…the shape and color of the food, the shape and color of the plate, & the position and spacing of the food(s) *on* the plate.

Owner and Executive Chef, Dee Elhabbassi, of my favorite restaurant, Dar Essalam Moroccan, in Wilsonville, Oregon is a master of sexy dishes (like this pie and ice-ream) with a simple squirt-bottle technique, she takes it to the next level!

The Rules

A couple of simple rules of thumb:

Square food = round plate. Round food = square plate

Light food = dark plate. Dark food = light (white) plate.

Personally, I'm not a fan of multicolored plates, so I typically stick with black or white, as it keeps the focus on the food. Also, your plate/bowl/platter is your *frame*, so make sure you leave a good margin around the edges to highlight the food.

This in one reason that restaurants like to use over-sized plates, as it allows each item to be "framed" separately on the same dish.

The Tools

A biscuit-cutter is a great tool for sexy food, and a pair chop-sticks are great for placing garnishes and toppings.

Here, Chef Terry Ramsey used a soup can, opened at both ends, to create these beautiful "cake towers"...

Also, think in three dimensions.

Sure, I can plop that steak down next to the mashed potatoes, and just pour sauce over the whole thing...OR, I can center the potatoes, rest the steak *(sliced or whole)* at an angle against one side, top with a little color, and drizzle it artfully with sauce *(an inexpensive squeeze bottle or two is another must-have tool for pretty plating.)*

> *It's so beautifully arranged on the plate you just know someone's fingers have been all over it.*
>
> ~ *Julie Child*

Lastly, for a little extra eye-candy, give it a sprinkle of fresh chopped herbs, shredded or shaved cheese, or toasted sesame seeds.

Celebrity chef Gordon Ramsey, in an issue of the BBC's *Olive* magazine, offers this advice, as well:

- *Keep your presentation clean and simple*

- *Use an odd number of ingredients on the plate to avoid symmetry*

- *Avoid moving things around once they're on the plate, as this will simply make a mess. Visualize what your dish will look like before you start arranging it on the plate*

- *Don't clutter the plate*

- *And, of course, don't serve the food cold because you spent so long dressing it.*

One last tip: if you have a somewhat colorless entree, like this tilapia filet, borrow some color from your veggies and use the less visually exciting component as a "frame within the frame."

Likewise, a little diced fresh tomatoes, and/or chopped fresh herbs are very pretty on the brown backdrop of a nicely seared steak, chop, or chicken breast.

As with almost any kitchen rule…you're the chef, so do what you think looks good.

Whatever you do, take your food presentation to the next level, have some fun with it, and eat sexy!

"Food Porn": A Quick Rant

I have to pause here for a moment, before we move on from the idea of sexy food, to indulge in a little rant...luckily, you're used to that by now...

Yes, it's currently a hot phrase, great for SEO, catching the eye of man-bun wearing food-hipsters everywhere and, yes, I've used it in the past...but I wish I hadn't, and I don't anymore.

I don't like it. I want people to think of my food in terms that ascend towards the heart and mind, not descend into the groin. The older I get, the less tolerance I have for crudity and crassness, what Stephen King might refer to as the talk of "low men in yellow hats." Maybe it's because I've mellowed and matured, more likely it's because I have a little girl now.

(Have her catch you, just one time, belting out "Fat Bottom Girls" when you forgot she was in the backseat...it changes you.)

Contrary to popular belief, the term "Food Porn" was not originally coined in reference to still-shots of delicious-looking food, but to videos of delicious food being cooked, plated, or eaten. Close in, often in slow-motion, shots of steam, and oozing cheese, and dripping butter...making obvious reference to its similarities with the sad industry of actual pornography. I don't like it because it's about fetishizing things that the average person will likely never experience.

It's self-gratifying voyeurism, watching other people do things that we don't really believe we could ever do. Too many people already live in a self-constructed (*and media encouraged*) fantasy world.

It's a waste of life, not having the bravery and determination to create a real world that satisfies you. I hate waste, I hate the cowardice of un-attempted potential, whether it's actual pornography, or just food-porn.

Both have everything to do with insecurity and instant gratification, and nothing to do with a self-worth, courage, or love.

The difference between sexy food, and food porn?

One is alluring…the other is simply lurid.

Pan Sauces

A lot people, when they sear a nice steak, or chop, or chicken breast, they take that pan and toss it in the sink to wash.

That is another sin against God.

In doing so, they are throwing out some of the best flavor of the meal. Those nice, crispy bits left in the bottom of the pan…are called the fond. Fond is the residue of the natural sugars that have been cooked out of the meat and caramelized to the bottom of the pan.

Chef's Tip: *Taste what you make before you serve it. I'm amazed that people will follow a recipe but not taste the dish to see if it needs more salt, pepper, or other spices. Also, never add salt to a liquid that's going to be reduced until <u>after</u> reducing it, as the flavors (and the saltiness) will get much stronger during the process.*

This fond is the foundation of most of those wonderful sauces that you get at your favorite high-end restaurant and one of the foundations of fine cooking in almost every cuisine. The basics of a pan sauce include:

- A fat – olive or other oil, butter, or both
- A fond from sautéed beef, chicken, pork, or fish.
- Vegetable(s) – onion, shallots, garlic, mushrooms, fresh herbs, etc.
- Deglazing liquid – wine, juice, meat or veggie stock, liquor
- An acid – citrus juice, vinegar, pineapple juice
- Salt & spices (opt)

After frying your protein in a pan over high heat, remove meat and reduce the heat to medium, and add the fat to the pan. Sauté the vegetables for about five minutes. Add the herbs and sauté for another two minutes.

A student from our MY KITCHEN Program, learning to deglaze.

Turn heat back up to high, deglaze* the pan with your deglazing liquid of choice, and cook until reduced by half. At the end whisk in a little butter, your preferred acid, and remove from heat, allowing it to thicken slightly.

[290]

> **Deglaze:** *loosening the browned bits or "fond" from the bottom of the pan by heating the pan (after removing the meat) and adding water, broth, or wine.*
>
> *Deglazing works best in a cast-iron, or stainless steel pan. "Non-stick" pans do not produce adequate fond to deglaze, or create a pan sauce.*

Now, this isn't a cookbook, I have those, you can find them online.

This is a book *about* cooking.

Still, I have a few dishes that I've felt were important to share with you, and this is one of my favorites, using many of the techniques we've talked about. Again, this was one of dad's recipes...

Growing up with a chef as a parent is a mixed blessing. On one hand, my old man could throw down some amazing food. On the other hand, after putting in 60 or 70 hours a week on the line...the last thing he wanted to do at home, was cook. That meant that if I wanted in on the good stuff, I had to go to the restaurant, which meant that my dad got free slave labor, and a grunt that couldn't hire a labor-lawyer when he'd smack me in the head with a ladle for not having enough "hustle." Still, it must have been pretty epic food, 'cause I kept coming back for more. Maybe I just wasn't too bright.

Let's say it was the food.

One of the recipes that brought me back, time and again, was Dad's clam chowder. This stuff was freakin' famous. Dishwashers would work a second shifts, and owners would come in of their day's off just to get a couple of bowls. A steady stream of compliments and tips *always* flowed from the front of the house, on chowder night.

Dad's workin' that big six-top in the sky now...so the threat of getting smacked with a kitchen implement has somewhat lessened, and I've worked up the courage to post his extremely popular and guarded recipe.

If he tossed in some fresh steamed baby oysters and green mussels, it became *seafood chowder*. FYI...nothing even remotely healthy about this recipe, and if you try to substitute olive oil for the butter, low-fat milk for the 1/2 & 1/2, or some other act of sacrilege and profanation, I hope the old man comes back and smacks you with a ladle. To quote my sweet old father... *"You want healthy? Go home and make a f*****' salad!"*

Dad Perkins' Clam Chowder

1 ½ lbs. Yukon gold potatoes
1 lg. onion, diced
½ cup of butter (*1 stick*)
dash of red pepper flakes
½ lb. fresh bay scallops
2 cups bottled clam juice
¼ cup fresh Italian parsley, chopped

2 cups chicken broth
2 cloves of garlic, diced
2 tsp. coarse black pepper
4 anchovy fillets, diced
½ cup flour
32 oz. roughly chopped clams
1 cup ½ & ½

Rinse potatoes, halve, cover with chicken broth, and bring to simmer. (*Add water to cover, if necessary*). Melt 1/2 cup of butter in a large skillet over medium heat, and sauté garlic and onion until softened. Add red and black pepper, scallops, and anchovies, and continue to cook, stirring, until scallops are just done, about 5 minutes.

Remove scallops and set aside. Increase heat and add flour to skillet, stirring to create roux.

4th generation cook and clam digger!

[292]

Allow flour to cook, stirring often, until the flour begins to brown and smells nutty. Slowly add 2 cups of clam juice, stirring constantly to keep the roux smooth, next add ½ & ½, again stirring.

If you're using canned clams, reserve the liquid and add it now, to bring broth to desired consistency. If not, add enough water to do so. Add parsley, and cook at a bare simmer, 10-15 minutes.

While broth is simmering, remove cooked potatoes from water, and allow to cool slightly. Quarter. Add cooked potatoes, scallops, and clams to broth and stir.

Cook 5 more minutes, and serve hot with warm baguette slices.

Quick Chicken Piccata

Serves 1

It's quick, delicious, and easy to fix, and we always get the same response from our students… "I can't believe *I* cooked that!"

½ s/b chicken breast or 2 tenders
salt & ground black pepper to taste
1 ½ tsp olive oil
2 Tbsp. apple juice (unsweetened)
1 Tbsp. fresh lemon juice
1 ½ tsp fresh Italian parsley

cayenne pepper, to taste
AP flour for dredging
¾ tsp capers
1 Tbsp. water
2 ½ tsp cold unsalted butter

Mise en Place

Drain capers, squeeze lemon, cut butter into 1/4-inch slices, chop parsley

Prepare the Dish

Place chicken between 2 layers of plastic wrap and pound to about 1/2-inch thick. Season both sides of chicken breasts with cayenne, salt, and black pepper; dredge lightly in flour and shake off any excess.

Heat olive oil in a skillet over medium-high heat. Place chicken in the pan, reduce heat to medium, and cook until browned and cooked through, about 5 minutes per side; remove to a plate.

Cook capers in reserved oil, smashing them lightly to release brine, until warmed though, about 30 seconds. Pour apple juice into skillet. Scrape any browned bits from the bottom of the pan with a wooden spoon.

Cook until reduced by half, about 2 minutes.

Stir lemon juice, water, and butter into the reduced juice mixture; cook and stir continuously to form a thick sauce, about 2 minutes. Reduce heat to low and stir parsley through the sauce.

Return chicken breasts to the pan cook until heated through, 1 to 2 minutes.

Serve over angel hair pasta, with sauce spooned over the top.

Layering Flavors

The "layering of flavors" is a professional technique that any Home Chef should master. It's all about combining, expanding, and deepening flavors in a dish with spices, vegetables, meats, liquids, and seasonings.

Reader's Digest version: layering flavor simply means, while "building" your dish, you add different, yet complementary tastes to add to the complexity of your basic ingredients.

The technique works with everything from the fanciest to the most simple of dishes. Layering flavor has become a favorite foodie buzzword recently, as layering flavors is a foundational technique used by professional (*and celebrity*) chefs.

It should be foundational in the Home Chef's kitchen, as well.

Browning, sweating, sautéing, and caramelizing, all of which change the chemical composition of you ingredients, and layers of flavor for soups, vegetable dishes, sauces, and stir-frying. Once you understand the different flavors each of these cooking styles can create, you can whip up some pretty next-level dishes.

Chef's Tip: *Flash Grilling*

If you want to up your dish's flavor profile by several notches, try this – whenever possible "flash grill" the meat and/or veggies over live fire (or on your gas grill), before cooking according to the recipe.

Soups, stews, casseroles...any "one-pot" dishes are especially great for this. From pork tenderloin, to stew beef, to shrimp, to hot dogs...a sprinkle of salt, and a few seconds per side, on a SUPER HOT grill (just long enough to get some char-marks, but not to cook much) will add a smoky, flame-kissed edge that really brings out the natural flavors of the ingredients, and that works its way through the entire finished dish.

Try it...you'll like it!

Here's one of my very favorite recipes that uses the layering of flavors to create a dish that far, far surpasses the sum of its parts.

Chicken Veggie Soup using Asian Techniques

The reason for this recipe is that after much happy experimentation, I am of the not-so-humble opinion, that "Asian" cultures are the gods of broth and stock-based soups (*cream soups and bisques, stews and chowders, I might give the nod to France, but this ain't that recipe...*)

That said, what makes the soups of Japan, China, Thailand, Vietnam, etc., etc., so amazing is more about *technique* than ingredients... though they certainly have some amazing ingredients... the most basic difference between how "they" make soup, and how "we" make soup, is technique, most importantly the technique of prepping each individual ingredient separately for optimum taste, instead of simply tossing them in a pot (*or, God-forbid, a slow cooker*) to become a one-note burbling homogeneous cauldron of meh.

Example: If you've ever seem a properly prepared bowl of pho being made, and you really should, it's amazing...you'll note that the bowl is first loaded with cold cooked noodles, cold cooked meat, and raw veggies, then, filled with boiling-hot stock, to bring everything to a balanced temp.

This allows each ingredient to maintain its own specific flavor and uniqueness, but still maintain the crunchy texture of the veggies, the perfect texture of the meat (*brisket and tendon, please*) and the chewy elasticity of properly cooked noodles (*this, btw, is the same reason that ramen is best when the noodles are cooked, cooled, and then dipped in hot stock at the last moment, on the way to the mouth*).

So, I said to myself, "Self…what if I tried this classic style, this "cook first, and then assemble" technique, of Asian-style soup cooking, with that most classic of Western soups, Chicken Vegetable. (*The fact that my wife and daughter are sharing a horrific cold this week, didn't hurt in the decision making process of the test subject, either…*)

Chicken Veggie Soup

Debone one whole rotisserie chicken, save bones for stock, and meat for soup. Roast celery, carrots, and onions on at 450F oven until browned (but not burned). Combine chicken bones, skin, roasted garlic, ginger, parsley, lemon, fennel seeds, bay leaves, salt and pepper.

Add roasted veggies, cold water to cover, and bring to a simmer.

Dice carrots, celery, shallot, ginger, and set aside. Strain meat and veggies from stock, and whisk in butter. Pan-sear diced carrots, celery, shallot, and ginger in a little stock, until just starting to soften.

Add a little salt and pepper to taste. Assemble pulled chicken, sautéed veggies, and raw corn in a bowl. Ladle simmering broth over the top of the veggies, taste for salt and pepper, and top with fresh chopped Italian parsley.

Optional additions: Rice noodles, soy sauce, Thai fish sauce, jalapeno slices, Sriracha sauce.

You can see this recipe, with step-by-step photos, here.

Google: hautemealz Asian Techniques

Poaching

Even after four decades of cooking, the work "poaching" still makes me think of my favorite childhood book, *Danny the Champion of the World* by Roald Dahl. However, I'm not talking about sneaking out to bag the greedy landowner's pheasants, here (*though I'm not, strictly speaking against that*)...but instead, the technique of cooking by simmering in a small amount of liquid, typically water or stock.

Poaching is a moist-heat cooking method which uses a sautoir (French for a straight sided, as opposed to curved, sauté pan) or other shallow cooking vessel, heat is transferred by conduction from the pan, to the liquid, to the food. Shallow poaching is best suited for boneless, naturally tender, single serving size, sliced or diced pieces of meat, poultry or fish.

Cold poaching liquid is then poured in until the product is partially submerged then heated. The liquid should never be allowed to boil but kept as close to boiling as possible. ~ Wikipedia

My favorite version...Sweet Thai Chili Chicken Breasts

12 Minute Microwave Chicken

I love doing this recipe in my cooking classes, just for the look on my students faces when I tell them we're going to make "microwave chicken." But really, we're making *poached* chicken, we're just using the microwave as the heat source. This is a great technique to shave some time off dinner prep, by multitasking while the chicken cooks.

These are also a great first step for reverse-seared chicken on the grill *(more on the in the BBQ & Grilling chapter)*

- 2-3 boneless skinless chicken breast
- 2 cups of stock, flavored* as desired.

Place the chicken breasts in a microwave safe baking dish, and pour the broth over the top, bringing the liquid at least ½ way up the side of the meat. Do NOT cover the meat with liquid...we're not boiling, we're poaching. Seal the dish with plastic wrap, and microwave on high for four minutes. Carefully flip each chicken breast, reseal, and microwave *another* four minutes. Then, leave the whole thing in the microwave (off) for a final four minutes. This creates an amazingly juicy, tender, and flavor-packed piece of chicken that you can use in a wide variety of dishes, or just eat as is.

*What spices you add to the stock determine the flavor profile of the finished dish. Going for Asian? Try a little soy sauce, rock sugar, and

Chinese 5 Spice. Italian? Some basil, oregano, garlic, and a little tomato paste. The options are endless. Take a look in the spices chapter for the best spice combinations from around the world.

BTW, if you're using some of those truly frightening "Dolly Parton" chicken breasts they're growing nowadays, you might need to add a minute to each step.

Holy Moly!

The holy trinity, a term attributed to the great Chef Paul Prudhomme, is the Cajun and Louisiana Creole variant of mirepoix. Traditional mirepoix is 2 parts onions, 1 part carrots, and 1 part celery, whereas the holy trinity is 3 parts onions, 2 parts celery, 1 part Green bell pepper. Now, don't get me wrong, I love my Cajun food, but over the years I've developed my own Holy Trinity that I found myself using, over and over, in a wide variety of recipes. Here it is:

- 2 med shallots, sliced
- 6 cloves fresh garlic, sliced
- 1/2 cup pancetta*, diced
- 2 Tbs of sweet cream butter (or…more.)

*Pancetta is bacon's sexy Italian cousin. Ask for it in the deli section.

Sweat (very low sauté) the pancetta, shallots, and garlic until all are soft (but not yet brown.) This combination will take any recipe, be it eggs, a baked potato, soup, pasta, or even just a lowly sliced chicken breast, right into the stratosphere!

Homework Assignment #12

Poaching

Simple Poached Salmon with Lemon-Parsley Orzo

Here's my favorite salmon recipe, one which Chef Chris and I have done many times for cooking demos, and a family favorite...

The Salmon

4 five-ounce salmon fillets
2 sprigs parsley
4 tablespoons butter
Lemon juice to taste

1/4 cup dry white wine
2 sprigs tarragon
Salt and pepper to taste

Season the salmon pieces with salt and set aside.

Choose a heavy pan just large enough to fit the salmon snugly in one layer and add the wine, tarragon, and just enough water to come halfway up the salmon pieces (*but do not add the salmon yet*).

Chef Chris and I, poaching lots & lots of salmon for a MY KITCHEN fundraising demo.

Season with a good pinch of salt and bring to a boil. Once boiling, immediately turn the heat to very low so it's barely simmering. Add the fish pieces and cook for 3 1/2 minutes (add an extra minute or two if using steaks), then carefully turn the pieces over and cook for 3 minutes more to finish. Ensure that the water never gets hot enough to boil..

Remove the fish pieces to a warm plate then turn the heat to high to reduce the liquid by half. Whisk in the butter and season to taste with salt and lemon juice, if necessary.

Pour the sauce over the fish and garnish with a little chopped parsley.

Orzo with Lemon and Parsley

1/2 cup extra-virgin olive oil	2 garlic cloves (thinly sliced)
3/4 lbs. orzo (cooked)	1 lemon, juice & zest
1/2 bunch of flat leaf parsley	salt & freshly ground pepper

Cook orzo in large pot of boiling salted water until tender but still firm to bite, stirring occasionally.

Drain. Rinse with cold water; drain well.

In a small Dutch oven over medium-low heat, warm the olive oil. Add the garlic and sauté until fragrant but not browned, about 2 minutes. Gently fold in the cooked orzo, lemon zest, lemon juice, parsley, salt and pepper until well mixed.

Transfer the orzo to a serving bowl and serve warm.

~ Notes ~

Chapter Fifteen
Grilling & BBQ

Let's get this out of the way, right off the bat…"barbecue" is not a piece of equipment, it's a method of cooking, and the items cooked that way. What's sitting on your deck is either a grill or a smoker, either of which can produce barbeque.

Grilling is done over direct heat, quickly searing at high temperatures.

Barbecue is cooked slowly, over coals at low temperatures using indirect heat by pushing coals to one zone of the cooker and the meat to another zone.

Spanish conquistadors reported seeing Taino-Arawak and Carib natives in Hispaniola roasting, drying, and smoking meat "on wooden frameworks high over small beds of smoking coals. The framework was called a babracot, which the Spaniards turned into the word "Barbacoa."

Most importantly: putting "bbq sauce" on something does not make it barbecue any more than poring motor oil on my dog would make him a Lamborghini. There…now we're clear. I feel better. I was five or six years old, and we were having a family get-together at Uncle Vern's house.

My Uncle Raymond, who was, almost assuredly, several mason-jars into whatever my grandfather brewed up in that oil tank behind the barn, decided that the charcoal in the battered old Weber - which was sitting on a plywood-covered, screened porch – *(them's my genes, folks!)* wasn't heatin' up as quickly as he'd like.

Indignant, he walked over, peered blurrily at the coals for a moment, and then nonchalantly tossed the contents on his half-full cup of white-lightening onto the open flame. I was five…and I remember the fireball. I also remember Uncle Vern and my father grabbing up the garden hose and dousing the smoldering mosquito netting that surrounded the porch.

I'm pretty sure they were speaking in tongues… at least a tongue that I wasn't familiar with at that tender age.

Taking your Grill-Skill from Tragic to Magic

We've all seen it…the flaming hot dog, the carbon-crusted hockey-puck that was once a hamburger patty, the black-on-the-outside, frozen-in-the-middle steak that comes off the grill like saddle leather, only with less flavor… So why do so many well-intentioned grillers turn so much good meat into bad food?

What do those smug bastards with their instant-read thermometers, and monogrammed aprons know that WE don't? What's the secret? There's no secret to good barbecue, but rather a number of simple skills. None of these tips here are about the price of the meat. Grilling and, to a greater extent, barbecue, is all about taking the cheap *(and sometimes throw-away)* cuts, and making them not just edible, but incredible.

You don't need to serve $30-a-steak rib-eyes, or fresh Maine lobster-tails, to make a great meal on the grill…

When in doubt…brine!

In cooking, brining is a process similar to marinating, in which meat is soaked in brine before cooking. Brining makes cooked meat moister by hydrating the cells of its muscle tissue before cooking, via the process of osmosis, and by allowing the cells to hold on to the water while they are cooked, via the process of denaturation.

(Thank you, Wikipedia!)

How long to brine depends on the size and type of meat you've got.

Larger meats like a whole turkey need more time for the brine to do its magic. Small pieces of seafood like shrimp shouldn't sit in brine for more than half an hour, or so.

Be sure not to brine meats that have already been brined before you buy them, such as "extra-tender" pork, which has been treated with sodium phosphate and water to make it juicier.

Meats that improve on the grill with a good brine:

- Chicken & turkey (*whole or cut*)
- Rabbit (*or any non-red game meat*)
- Pork (*especially boneless picnic ribs*)
- Salmon

Fatty meats like beef and lamb are generally not improved by brining.

My basic brine = *3/4 cup coarse Kosher or sea salt + 1 cup sugar (white or brown) + 1 gallon purified water.*

Bring water to a high simmer, add salt and sugar to dissolve, and allow to cool to room temp before adding the meat. You can increase or decrease the amount of brine, as long as you have enough to completely submerse the meat, by modifying the brine ingredients in these proportions. How much brine do you need?

Here's a tip: put your meat in the container you're going to soak it in, and fill it with purified water until completely covered. Remove the meat, and use this water to make your brine. Clever, huh?

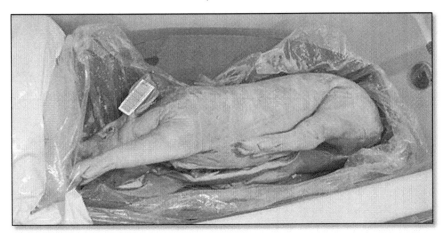

Chef Note: *When thawing a whole hog, prior to brining, warn your wife, in advance, that she's going to find a big dead animal in her apartment bathtub...trust me on this...*

One caveat with brining is that whatever you put the meat in, needs to fit in your refrigerator or cooler. Both the meat and brine need to stay below 40F at all times.

This isn't a big deal with a couple of pork chops, but can present some logistical headaches when you're roasting half-a-dozen turkeys, as I did last Thanksgiving. In this case, your best bet is to sterilize a cooler that's big enough to fit the meat, brine, and a couple of bags of ice.

General Brining Times

- Whole Chicken, Salmon fillets - 4 to 12 hours
- Chicken Pieces, Pork Chops - 1 to 1.5 hours
- Whole Turkey or Pork Shoulder - 24 hours
- Turkey Breast, Rabbit - 5 to 8 hours
- Cornish Game Hens - 1 to 2 hours

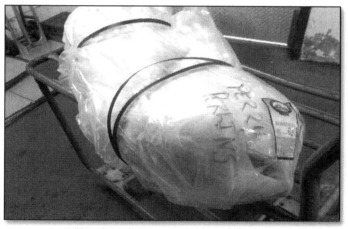

Happiness is your name on a pig's butt...

The beauty of a good brine is you can add whatever you want to it!

I often add quartered lemons and chopped garlic to my whole chicken brine, and Chinese 5 Spice to my pork brine. The best flavored brines are often the simplest...citrus juice and dried mint will add a nice Mediterranean flavor to chicken, while cracked black pepper and red wine vinegar provide a rich French flair. Having said that, the best turkey I've ever eaten was roasted by my business partner Terry Ramsey, using Alton Brown's ingredient-heavy brine from his *Good Eats Roast Turkey* recipe.

That was some next-level bird, brutha!

After brining, always rinse your meat and dry it well before cooking.

Otherwise, your dinner is going to be super salty, likewise, don't salt the meat before, during, or after cooking, nor any sauces or gravies you make with the residual broth (*which, btw, is freakin' awesome.*)

Lastly, make sure to keep a close eye when grilling meats that have been brined. Brining adds sugar to the meat and can cause it to burn faster, another reason to use a 2-step grilling method.

4 Common Grilling Problems (*& how to avoid them.*)

With grilling it's usually one, or a combination, of four problems…

Too high of heat for the food.

A lot of time we crank it up and either the outside burns before the inside cooks, or the inside is raw when the outside looks perfect.

Always keep an "indirect heat" area on your grill, with one burner on med-low (*or with just a few coals*) and if the internal temp of the meat isn't high enough and you're concerned about burning, move the food to that area and tent loosely in foil until the temp comes up to your desired doneness.

Not enough "babying."

Unlike food cooked on the stove-top, which often needs to be "left alone", food on grills are at the mercy of flare-ups and temp spikes.

You have to be constantly monitoring your food. Is there too much flame under the food? (move it or use a spray bottle of hot water).

Is one area of the grill cooking faster? (rotate the food between all areas of the grill). This is referred to in grilling lingo as "multi-zone cooking" (more on that in a moment.)

Was the food prepped correctly?

Food that is still chilled in the center (especially with bones) is going to cook unevenly, and this is especially true on the grill. Some folks don't like to hear this in our sterilized, bacteria-phobic society, but most meats need to be removed from the refrigerator and allowed to rest at room temp at least 30 minutes (*and up to an hour, depending on thickness*) if you want them to grill evenly. A chilled chicken leg is basically a hunk of meat wrapped around an ice-cold spike. The outside layers *will* burn before the bone warms enough to allow the meat touching it to even start cooking.

Saucing too soon.

Traditionally, barbequed meats do not require sauce, as the flavor of salt and smoke are enough flavoring (*this is what we like to call the "right way" of doing it*). Sauce, is used at all, should be served on the side, warm.

That said, if using a sauce on grilled meats (*perfectly acceptable, btw*), keep in mind that most sauces are heavy in sugar, either natural or added, and sugar burns quickly at high temps.

Food should basically be cooked through, the grill temp lowered, the food sauced (*I like the dunking method over the brushing method*) and then the food returned to the grill, turning often and re-dunking as needed, until the sauce has glazed.

This is another good place to alternate between multiple zones.

Direct vs. Indirect Grilling

I don't have much patience for people who are self-conscious about the act of eating, and it irritates me when someone denies themselves the pleasure of a bloody hunk of steak or a pungent French cheese because of some outdated nonsense about what's appropriate or attractive. ~ Anthony Bourdain

What is the difference between grilling over "direct" and "indirect" heat?

Most experts will tell you that **direct grilling** really works best for foods that take less than 20 minutes to cook, such as steaks, chops, boneless chicken breasts, burgers, and hot dogs.

Personally, except for maybe the burgers and dogs, I think that direct grilling is nearly always the 'Step 1" in the a 2-Step process, used to seal the meat and make those beautiful charred grill marks.

Typically, I would then move the meat to indirect heat to finish cooking. For example, a 2-inch-thick steak, or a well brined chicken breast, can be seared or browned over direct heat for a short period of time, and then moved to the indirect heat area to continue cooking internally without burning.

[313]

Indirect grilling refers to foods are not cooked directly over the heat. With charcoal grilling, the hot coals are moved or "banked" to opposite sides of the grill, this is known as a 2-Zone Fire. Often a drip pan with water, beer, or juice is placed on the bare grate, below the meat.

Grilling my "Dragon Claws" at Chicago's Grill-Fest for Sears/Kenmore, With my pals Robyn Lindars (Grill Girl) and Ty Pennington, was a hoot. Four cameras in my face the whole time....not so much.

 | ***Google: "Perkins Dragon Claws"** for the recipe!*

When grilling with gas, the burners are all pre-heated, and then one or more are turned off, and the meat is placed directly over the "off" burners. I do with this chunks of meat as large as pork shoulders (*aka Boston Butt*) to sear the outside and seal in all the yummy juices.

Again, I believe that indirect heat is best used for finishing foods that need to be cooked for a longer time like roasts, whole poultry, ribs, and other large cuts of meat.

Except for fish and shellfish, if a piece of meat is too thin to grill over direct heat first, it probably shouldn't be cooked on the grill at all. Lastly, never take a piece of meat off the grill when it looks done. By then, it's too late. The time to plate your entrée is a couple of minutes before it's done. Known as "hold-over cooking", the external heat will continue to cook the insides to meaty perfection.

This is especially true of thin meats like hamburger patties

Hitting the Sauce

Many grillers, myself included, either eschew sauce altogether, or serve it on the side. Too often, all we taste in our bbq is bbq sauce, and I want to enjoy that wonderful flavor of grilled meat! Also, sauce is probably the #1 leading culprit in burned bbq. Many folks don't realize how much sugar there is in a typical bbq sauce, nor how quickly those sugars will caramelize, and then burn.

The one meat that I do invariably sauce is chicken. I especially like a nice, sticky bbq or teriyaki sauce on a big mess of grilled chicken legs and thighs. The same goes for pork. Beef - not so much. Of course, this is a matter of personal opinion, not religious doctrine, so, to paraphrase one of my favorite foodie personalities, "If it tastes good…sauce it!" If you do want to sauce your chicken, turkey, or pork, you'll do it towards the end of the cooking time, and do so after you've moved the meat to indirect heat, otherwise you run the risk of the sugars in the sauce burning. One exception to this rule (*and of course there's an exception*), is when I'm "finishing" slow roasted ribs. Once they come out of the smoker (*or oven*), I like to sauce them thinly, and slap them down directly over hot coals for a few seconds, flip, and repeat the process 4-5 times.

Speaking of slow-roasted ribs, if you have a smoker or Traeger, check out my video for these sweet, juicy, elbow-drippin' "3-2-1" pork ribs:
Google: "Chef Perry ribs on Traeger"

This layering of charring and saucing, over and over, creates an amazing and complex depth of flavor.

> *"My doctor told me I had to stop throwing intimate dinners for four unless there are three other people."*
> *-Orson Welles*

EXTRA TIP – An Awesome "Steak Sauce".

While those steaks are resting…toss some chopped shallots, a cup of merlot, a tablespoon of Dijon mustard, and a teaspoon of chopped garlic into a skillet and simmer.

Add any drippings from the steak plate, as well, then pour a couple of tablespoons over each steak, just before serving. *(You'll thank me.)*

Try these four simple steps and I guarantee that you will see an instant, and significant improvement in your 'Que.

No more wiener flambé, carbonized steaks, or particle-board chicken!

"It is remarkable how much sheer bullshit seems to accrete around the subject of barbecue.

No other kind of cooking comes even close.

Exactly why, I'm not sure, but it may be that cooking over fire is so straightforward that the people who do it feel a need to baste the process in thick layers of intricacy and myth.

It could also be that barbecue is performed disproportionately by self-dramatizing men."

~ Michael Pollan, Cooked

Grilled Sweet Chili Chicken

Sweet, spicy, sticky perfection…the secret lies in pre-baking the chicken first, so you can grill it over very high heat, just long enough to caramelize the sugars in the sauce, without drying out (*or under-cooking*) the meat beneath.

First, rub chicken with some salt and pepper, and let sit on the counter, covered, 1-2 hours to come almost to room temp. Bake in a single layer on a foiled lined baking sheet at 350 degrees for about 50 minutes, or until the internal temp reaches 165F. Finish on a preheated very hot grill, over direct heat. Sear both sides of the chicken first, then dip with the sauce, then turn.

Cook for about 5 to 10 minutes total, brushing with sauce and turning several times, until chicken is done. For the best application of sauce, dip each piece of chicken into a bowl of sauce (recipe below), instead of brushing.

For thicker sauce, repeat 2-3 times while on the grill.

Allow the chicken to rest, and the sauce to set, about 10 minutes, uncovered, once removed from the grill.

"Burnin' Love" Rub *(Shh…it's a secret!)*

- ¼ C fine sea salt
- 2 Tbs garlic powder
- 2 Tbs smoked paprika
- 2 Tbs hickory salt (or seasoned salt)

¼ C light brown sugar

2 Tbs onion powder

2 Tbs coarse black pepper

This is enough for 5-8lbs of chicken.

Sweet Chili BBQ Sauce

- 2 cup Sweet Baby Rays *(Brown Sugar, or Hot & Sweet)*
- 1 cup Thai sweet chili sauce (we like "Mae Ploy" brand)
- 1/2 cup apple cider vinegar
- 1/2 stick sweet cream butter

Combine all, simmer and allow to cool.

BBQ – Low & Slow

Okay, I like to cook with wood and charcoal, but I get a lot of emails asking how to modify my recipes to a gas grill *(yes, I own gas grills)* and even for the oven. Some recipes just can't be adapted, others can with decent results, and some…well, as much as this is going to tick-off the die-hards…*some* you can hardly tell the difference! Here's one of my favorites. Oh, and if you want to recreate a true "Southern pulled pork sandwich", and really take 'em to the next level… be sure to add a couple of tablespoons of our Sesame-Cilantro Slaw (recipe on next page) on top of the meat and sauce.

Pulled Pork BBQ

In the gas grill, oven, or smoker:

1 Pork shoulder (6-8lb) Burnin' Love Rub (see below) Basic BBQ Sauce (see below)

Rub the shoulder with spices. Set it aside for a few minutes and rub again over any wet spots. Keep doing this until there are no wet spots, the heavier the rub, the better. This makes the "bark" of the shoulder. Wrap the whole thing in plastic wrap and fridge 12-24 hours. Take shoulder out of fridge and let sit 60 minutes to bring the temp up.

For the gas grill:

You want indirect heat for cooking, you can easily do this on a conventional gas grill. Just keep the meat as far from the heat source as possible, or it will burn during the long cooking time.

You want to cook this at 250 degrees Fahrenheit; you can go as high as 275, but no higher. You don't want to go lower than 250, as you will start to dry out the meat before it is cooked. Put the shoulder on the "cool side" of the grill, and place a disposable pan with a couple of cups of apple juice underneath it to add moisture and catch the drippings. A spray bottle with 50/50 apple juice and cider vinegar is nice for basting, as well. A lot of folks like to use apple chips, soaked, for smoking. You can add 1/2 cup to a disposable tin pan over the "hot" side of your gill, every 30 minutes for the first 3 hours.

> *Grilling, broiling, barbecuing - whatever you want to call it - is an art, not just a matter of building a pyre and throwing on a piece of meat as a sacrifice to the gods of the stomach.*
>
> *~ James Beard*

Personally, I prefer to use a small, nearly indestructible smoke box, called the "**A-Maze-N Smoker**". One of several smokers designed and sold by Todd Johnson of A-MAZE-N Products, it's a metal-mesh maze that holds your favorite flavor of smoking pellets, and burns slowly enough to allow a three-hour smoke without constantly having to lift the cover and let all of that precious heat out.

It's cheap, and I've used my dozens of times with no visible wear or tear.

Here's a quick video I did on how it works:

Google: Chef Perry A-Maze-N

If you don't trust your on-board thermometer, get a cheap instant read (or better, a digital probe) and stick the probe all the way through a halved potato. Set the potato cut-side down on the grill. This keeps your thermometer off the grates. After three to four hours, remove the shoulder from your grill, and roast (uncovered) in a pre-heated oven at 225F for 10-12 hours. The pork is done when it reaches an internal temperature of 200 degrees. If you don't have an instant-read thermometer (*and you should really get one*), the meat is done when it pulls apart easily with a fork.

In The Oven

Follow the same prep directions as above. Pre-heat the oven to 225F, and roast the shoulder, fat-cap up, <u>uncovered</u>, for 14 hours (yes, I said fourteen. I usually roast mine overnight.) Follow the "Finishing" steps, below.

On the Traeger - Once the shoulder(s) are prepped, start the Traeger on "Smoke" with the lid open until it's cruisin' (4 to 5 minutes). Set temp at 225F and preheat, lid closed, for about 15 minutes. Place shoulders on the grill, fat-cap up, and smoke for 3 hours, spraying with a mix of apple juice and cider vinegar (50/50) every hour after the first three hours.

Put shoulders in a large disposable aluminum foil pan and up the temp to 250F. Roast shoulder for 8 more hours, or until an instant-read meat thermometer inserted in the thickest part, but not touching a bone, registers 190 degrees F. If the skin starts to get too dark, cover it loosely with foil. Remove the pan from the heat, tent shoulder(s) loosely in foil, and let rest for 30 minutes. Pour the juices from the bottom of the pan into a fat separator. Mix broth (*fat removed*) with some salt and cider vinegar, to taste, and pour back over the meat after shredding. Allow to rest an additional 10 minutes to soak up the juices. Serve either as sliders, or with a sauce on the side (*see below*), and some white bread slices to use as edible napkins!

Pulled Pork Tips - For "oven only"...before applying the dry rub, brush the entire shoulder generously with Stubbs (*brand name*) Mesquite Liquid Smoke, allow the surface to dry, and repeat. Then apply the dry rub (while still damp.) **Note:** this is the ONLY liquid smoke that I'll allow in my kitchen. For the smoker, I like a wood chip/chunk blend of 75% oak, and 24% hickory. I only smoke for the first 3-4 hours.

Northern Carolina Vinegar Sauce

Personally, I think this very old, very traditional recipe is the best and only sauce for pulled pork.

2 cups apple cider vinegar	2 Tbs. smoked paprika
2 Tbs. white sugar	4 tsp. fine sea salt
2 tsp. coarse ground black pepper	1 to 2 tsp. red pepper flakes

Combine all, simmer and cool. The longer it sits, the better it is!

How to grill the perfect Hot Dog

Yes, yes…*anyone* can grill a hot dog, but, the "perfect" hot dog?

That's a whole 'nuther thing…

If you're anything like me (*no offense*), you grew up on hot dogs, that favorite of backyard grillers everywhere. Sadly, many a tube-steak that hit our plates were charred on the outside, chilly in the middle, and split and twisted in decidedly unappetizing shapes. But fear not, we're gonna fix that!

Picking the perfect dog

Traditionally, your best bet is going to be an all-natural, all-beef dog, that contains no fillers. My favorite brands are Hebrew National, and Nathan's, and both are 100% all-beef. Don't even think of using a hot dog made from turkey or chicken! When buying your hot dogs, stay away from the 97% fat free choices as they are more difficult to cook and lack flavor.

Another excellent choice is Red Hot Chicago brand dogs. For a real treat, try the "jumbo" sized version of your favorite brand.

For full article & tips on assembling the perfect dog,

Google: hautemealz perfect hotdog

Grilling the perfect dog

1. Allow your hotdogs to come near room temp before cooking, never, never put a frozen dog in, or over, heat.

2. Simmer (very low boil) your hot dogs in water for four minutes before placing them on the grill.

3. Grill them over a low fire just long enough to get those nice grill marks and toasty outside. Once the skin starts to glisten (about 1 minute) turn the dog over and cook for an additional minute on the other side – no more!

Your hot dog is now ready to serve and it will stay hot all the way through for up to 10 minutes after serving.

Wanna to try my version of the classic Chi-dog?
Google: *"Perked Up" Bacon Chicago Dog*

A Better Bacon

First of all, let's get something straight...bacon is not bad for you.

The "healthfulness" of bacon, like most other foods, rests not in the ingredient itself, but in the use and moderation of it. Used responsibly, it's perfectly safe.

Bacon is the candy-apple red hot rod of the food world. We want it, but we also fear it a little, which makes us want it even more. That's why it's a typical ingredient in anything labeled a "guilty pleasure."

Yes, bacon is like a sports car, a handgun, or a beautiful woman...treat her wisely, and with respect, and she is a wellspring of unending umami pleasure.

Mistreat her, and...well...she'll probably kill you.

Bacon is proof that God loves us and wants us to be happy...but it sure made a greasy mess of my kitchen, until I adopted this restaurant technique for cooking a better bacon. This not only tastes awesome, with the meat cooked very evenly (*from above and below*), and a lot more of the grease rendered out...but no stove-top splatters to wipe up, and super easy to toss the foil and clean the pan...*this* is how I cook bacon these days!

One pound of bacon, on a flat foil-lined roasting rack, cook 20-25 minutes in a pre-heated 350F oven...Lovely stuff!

How to grill the perfect Hamburger

Who doesn't love a great burger? *(Besides Vegans and Nazis?)*

There's just nothing like a thick, beefy, juicy hamburger cooked over the fire to make you turn your back on cardboard peddling drive-thru clowns forever. Still, like anything else, there's a right way and a wrong way *(several actually)* to grill a perfect hamburger, and doing it the wrong way can make a day-old Whopper seem like filet mignon.

Here are, in my opinion, the 5 most important tips for turning your ground cow into hamburger heaven. First, let's look at three key elements to making a great burger, before it ever hits the grill...

Fat, cold, and anti-social... *(My nickname in high school, btw...)*

Fat

Fat is flavor, we know this. Fatty meat produces a juicier patty than lean meat. Lean ground beef is flavorless cardboard. You need a good 20-30% fat for the best flavor. You can't have a good medium well burger with 90 lean meat, you need the fat to give you juiciness and flavor at those temps.

FYI…for an out of this world 80/20 beef, try grinding your own using a whole packer brisket. Not only in the flavor amazing…it's cheaper than store-bought ground beef!

Cold

Warm meat = melted fat = dry beef = grilled hockey puck. 'nuff said. Also, after you've formed your patties, salt them generously on both sides (*just try it!*), and put them back in the fridge to cool down again for 30 to 45 minutes.

If you're grinding your own, try keeping the grinder accessories for your KitchenAid (*or whatever grinder you use*) in the freezer until ready to use…you'll notice a difference in the quality of your burger, I guarantee it.

Anti-Social

Think of your ground beef as that wild-eyed guy at the bus stop, who's pacing and muttering to himself. As much as possible, do the smart thing…leave it alone.

Working the meat unduly will cause proteins to cross-link with each other like tiny strips of Velcro, making your finished burgers denser and tighter with every manhandling of the grind.

Personally, I like to take an untouched haystack of ground beef, and use a "burger press." Just gently load with a loose mound of ground beef, and press it softly until the burger is just formed.

You want it to be just-about-to-fall-apart loose – to yield the juiciest results.

Chef's Note: If you're one of those folks who just can't bring themselves to touch raw hamburger, here's a clever way to package it into patties without touching it!

Use an ice-cream scoop or ladle to measure out the right quantity of meat you would like for that perfect hamburger patty. Next, place scooped meat into some kind of inexpensive sandwich bag.

Locate a big jar lid that fits the dimensions of the size patty you would like, and press the bagged meat into the lid to form perfect, untouched hamburger patties that will stack nicely in the freezer and are ready to cook when you need them!

Git 'em HOT!

The hotter the better. You want to sear or char the meat really quickly so you have nice crust, color, and grill flavor. Speaking of flavor, I like to toss some oak wood chips on my coals for added smoke flavor. Make sure to add them near, but not directly under your burgers (*the flare-up zone*). Also, before putting on your burgers, make sure the coals are completely gray, otherwise you risk grease flames, and the meat will scorch on the outside (*yuck*).

Here's a trick: If you're just cooking one or two burger patties, just toss a grill grate over your charcoal chimney! A chimney that's 3/4 full of glowing coals produces a *volcanic* amount of heat, and that kind of temperature does amazing things for burgers and steaks.

Cook until **not quite** to your liking, and then let it rest.

Like any grilled meat, you want to cook your hamburger patty to just shy of your desired outcome, and let "hold-over cooking" take it the rest of the way.

Personally, I like to use an instant-read thermometer.

Note: if your burger patty is too thin to use a thermometer...your burger patty is too thin.

Here's a rough temperature guide:

* **120°F** and below for rare (*red/raw in the center*)

* **130°F** for medium-rare (*pink and warm – this is my burger, baby!*)

* **140°F** for medium (*totally pink, starting to dry out*)

* **150°F** for medium-well (*grayish pink, significantly drier*)

* **160°F** and above for well done (*completely gray, very little moisture. What we chefs like to call..."ruined"...*)

Homework Assignment #13
Fire & Smoke

Choose any one recipe from the previous chapter on BBQ & Grilling (*not including the hamburgers or hot dogs – nice try…*)

Prepare using the recipe, and the techniques of brining, marinating, or applying a rub.

Cook to temp, using direct or indirect grilling, or smoking.

Allow to rest and serve with appropriate side dishes.

~ Notes ~

_____

_____

_____

_____

_____

_____

_____

_____

_____

_____

_____

_____

_____

_____

_____

_____

Fish on! *(the grill)*

A lot of folks these days are looking for healthier grilling options without sacrificing great flavor.

When my readers contact me asking about great-tasting, guilt-free grilling, I always point them to one of my favorite food groups: fish and seafood. It's hard to beat a succulent, tender bite of firm salmon or tuna, with a crispy char on the outside and just a hint of smoke, fresh from the grill. Fish and seafood are so simple to cook outdoors...and, ironically, they're one of those foods that intimidate a lot of backyard chefs. But they shouldn't.

What's sad is that the average American palate has become so lazy and unimaginative, that we're happy to toss really amazing little fish into the ocean to try to catch big mediocre fish

Fish is perfect for the grill. Direct high heat sears fish fast, sealing in moisture and flavor. A simple marinade (or just salt and pepper), a few minutes on each side, and *voila*, you have a delicious, nutritious dinner! The biggest issue with grilling fish or seafood is making sure it doesn't stick to the grates. It's vital to carefully clean and oil your cooking surface, and some folks like to brush the fish with a little oil, as well. There are four methods I like to use for cooking fish and seafood on a gas or charcoal grill: *Direct Grilling*, *Grill Baskets*, *Foil Wrapping*, and *Plank Grilling*, and each of them work great. Go get friendly with your local fish-monger, and see which method works best for you!

Direct Grilling

Direct grilling is best for thick fillets or whole fish. Firmer fleshed fish like salmon, steelhead, and tuna, get great results being grilled directly on the grate.Make sure your oiled grill is as hot as possible before laying on the meat (*this will also help to prevent sticking*). Likewise, when you go to flip your fish, move it to an unused area of the grill, to ensure that the grate is as hot as possible.

Rule of thumb: small fish/fillets = 2 minutes per side. Thick fillets/steaks, or large whole fish = 10 minutes per inch of thickness.

Grill Baskets

The grill basket has become a common barbecue accessory, and more delicate species of fish like trout, tilapia, and sole sometimes fare better when grilled in one of these handy contraptions. Basically, the fish is put in between two grates, which are typically hinged to close together, holding the fish securely inside.

Small sea critters like prawns and scallops are much easier to manage in a grill basket, as well. The main purpose is to keep these more fragile fish from falling into the coals. As fish cooks, the flesh becomes flaky, and can start falling apart (great for eating - tough on the cook). Believe me, I've watched many a hard-won brook trout slip through the grates to become aromatherapy on the hot coals below. For these kinds of fish, a basket is the way to go!

A good grill basket also makes turning your fish, a delicate and sometimes frustrating operation, a breeze. With a basket, just grab the handle and flip the whole rig. The fish stays locked between the grills. Easy-peasy! My favorite grill-basket fish recipe, isn't actually my recipe at all, but that of my friend Tesha Johnson, wife of Oregon Coast fishing guide legend, David Johnson (*DavidJohnsonsGuideService*).

This might be my all-time favorite hot salmon preparation, period.

Teriyaki Bacon Salmon Bites
Recipe by Tesha Johnson

- 1 bottle Lawry's pineapple teriyaki sauce
- 1 can of chunk pineapple, juice and all
- 1lb fresh salmon fillet
- 1lb thin sliced bacon

Slice salmon into 2in cubes, and marinate overnight in sauce and pineapple juice. Drain salmon, boil remaining marinade until reduced by half, and then keep warm. Wrap each nugget with half strip of thin cut bacon. Load 4-5 in pieces into each section of a slider grill basket (pictured) along with an equal number of fresh pineapple chunks, and grill over medium heat until bacon is crispy, basting occasionally with the reserved sauce. Use a toothpick to attach a chunk of grilled pineapple to each wrap, and serve immediately.

...try not to get between your guests and the platter.

Foil Wrapping

While really more like steaming or poaching, than grilling, foil wraps (*or, as we used to call them in Troop 651, "hobo packs"*) certainly have a place in the outdoor chef's bag of tricks. Foil wrapping is great for combining the flavors of fruits, vegetables, fresh herbs, or marinades with your fish, while protecting them from charring or drying out over direct heat. Trout is a fish I'm very familiar with, and the thin skin and flaky meat can be a pain on the grill, but wrapping them in foil (*with a little salt, pepper, lemon slices, and fresh dill*) vastly reduces the difficulty.

You end up with a lot more fish on your plate, and a lot less falling through the grates, by foil wrapping. You'll want to use a piece of foil about twice as large as the fish you want to grill. If it's a large piece of fish, or you're adding lots of other goodies to the pouch, plan to double-wrap it. Start your foil packet on the hot grill, smooth-side down, over direct heat. Cook a 1-2 inch thick piece of fish, unopened, for about 10 minutes, flipping once. Remove from the heat and let rest, sealed, for another five.

Open 'er up and check for doneness (*fish should flake easily*) and either serve immediately, or close back up and keep cooking in five-minute intervals.

[333]

Plank Grilling

We eat a lot of salmon and steelhead here in the Pacific Northwest, and grilling fish on soaked wooden planks (*as the local Native Americans have for thousands of years*) ensures moist, mildly smoky fish. It's super-simple, too, with no danger of disasters from flipping...'cause you don't. It's pretty cool! While salmon is by far the fish most commonly cooked on a wood plank, you can grill just about any kind of fish or seafood you want using this method (*it's awesome for shrimp!*)

You'll want to soak the plank for a couple of hours in clean water, and then bring your grill up to about 400 F (*medium high*). Lay your cleaned and prepped fish, skin side down, on the plank, and set the whole thing over indirect heat (*turn off one burner on a gas grill or moving the coals in a charcoal grill to one side*), and close the lid. Cook for 20 to 30 minutes until the fish is cooked through, or when the internal temperature reaches 135 F. Oh, and don't sweat it if the plank starts to burn, or even catches on fire while grilling. The plank usually chars around the edges, and as long as it doesn't reach the meat, it's all good. So there you go! Hot and healthy, fast and delicious...try these new methods on your own grill and you'll see that fish and fire were made for each other!

One Chef's opinion – *I don't buy any fish that's labeled "previously frozen", unless I know, personally, that it's been thawed within the last few hours, and I'm using it that day. Also, I only buy "fresh" from sources I know pulled it out of the water within the last 24 hours, and stored it properly. Fish that's been flash froze on the boat, that I can thaw slowly at home myself, is always your best bet.*

Homework Assignment #: 14

Cedar Plank Salmon or Foil Trout

- Choose a salmon fillet, or large trout that's fresh that day (*ask the butcher when the next haul comes in*) and that has not been previously frozen.

- Depending on your preference, prepare either the Cedar Plank Salmon, or Foil Wrapped Trout.

- Brine, if required, and season properly.

- Serve hot, with appropriate sides.

Best Books on Barbecue

I like to read about BBQ, about grilling...about food.

Not just cookbooks, though I can spend long hours on the couch perusing those as well, but also books about food, food history, and food culture.

Books like The Belly of Paris by Emile Zola, and The Apprentice: My Life in the Kitchen by Jacques Pepin have changed the way I look at food, and the respect I have for it, and the process that gets it to my table.

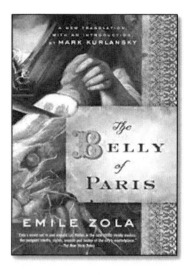

The Nasty Bits by Anthony Bourdain (*regardless of what I think of Tony, personally, it's a fantastic book*) and The Whole Beast, by Fergus Henderson, have sent me on a culinary adventure (*usually flying solo, lol*) far beyond the walls of sterilized, saran-wrapped "stuff marts" into a Wonka-esque world of offal wonderfulness.

Anyway, I like to read about food...and I like to read cookbooks, too.

Especially cookbooks related to BBQ and grilling, and I own a lot of them...a LOT of them, and the list is growing at a rapid rate.

However, if I were told I had 5 minutes to get out of my house and leave everything behind but an armload of my favorite bbq/grilling cookbooks...there are a few that would immediately pop to mind.

Besides my own cookbooks, or course (*wink wink*), these BBQ & Grilling titles would top the list...

The Barbecue Bible *by Steven Raichlen*

A fascinating look at live-fire cooking around the world. Lots more than just a cookbook! A 900,000-copy bestseller and winner of the IACP/Julia Child Cookbook Award, The Barbecue! Bible includes full-color photos illustrating food preparation, grilling techniques, ingredients, and of course those irresistible finished dishes.

A new section has been added with answers to the most frequently asked grilling questions, plus Steven's proven tips, quick solutions to common mistakes, and more.

Following a very close second, is Raichlen's **Planet Barbecue**, self-proclaimed as "the book that will take America's passionate, obsessive, smoke-crazed live-fire cooks to the next level." I love…I LOVE learning about how BBQ and Grilling is done in other countries, and on that subject, Raichlen is the man.

Each country gets a two-page profile, which lists the types of grills and fuels most common to the region, dishes that are a must if you happen to be in the neighborhood, as well as what traditional condiments one might expect to find on one's beef, fish, pork, or vegetables.

Okay…so, let's talk about some good old-fashioned down-home U.S.A. bbq. If I had to pick one, and just one (and that would be tough), I know which book it would be…

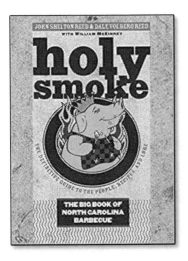

Holy Smoke: The Big Book of North Carolina Barbecue *By John Shelton Reed, Dale Volberg Reed*

Lots of strong opinions, family histories, and great bbq recipes! North Carolina is home to the longest continuous barbecue tradition on the North American mainland. Authoritative, spirited, and opinionated (in the best way), Holy Smoke is a passionate exploration of the lore, recipes, traditions, and people of North Carolina's signature slow-food dish.

Three barbecue devotees, John Shelton Reed, Dale Volberg Reed, and William McKinney, trace the origins of North Carolina 'cue and the emergence of the heated rivalry between Eastern and Piedmont styles. They provide detailed instructions for cooking barbecue at home, along with recipes for the traditional array of side dishes that should accompany it. The final section of the book presents some of the people who cook barbecue for a living, recording firsthand what experts say about the past, and future, of North Carolina barbecue.

Filled with historic and contemporary photographs showing centuries of North Carolina's "barbeculture," as the authors call it, Holy Smoke is one of a kind, offering a comprehensive exploration of the Tar Heel barbecue tradition.

For many of us, cookbooks, as well as books about cooking, are more than just reference material; they're our hobby, our passion, our obsession. They can be the blueprint, the *Bible* that leads the obsessed grilling and pit-master to the promised land of live-fire cooking.

A note from Chef Perry

It's a week before Christmas (2016) as I sit here at my computer doing final edits on this manuscript.

My daughter, in the next room making Christmas ornaments, and watching Rudolf the Red Nosed Reindeer (*is it just me, or is Santa kind of a dill-hole?*) has been home for three days due to snow closures, and is now officially on Christmas break (*Sorry, we don't do "holiday" stuff here, we're hard-core Christmas people!*)

We've made this cocoa three times already, and will make it at least a couple more times before the big day (*our Christmas morning tradition.*)

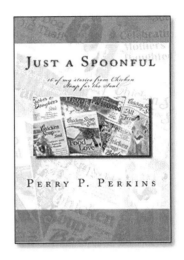

Of the 16 Chicken Soup titles I've been published in, this is one of my favorite stories, and, I think, one of the best all-around books they've ever put out...and they've put out some doozies!

Now, as much as I'd love folks to go buy copies of the book, our hautemealz.com subscribers and followers always get a little extra-special treatment.

So, here's the full story and recipe for your enjoyment!

(BTW - If you don't feel like buying 16 books, you can get all of my stories, and a couple of extras, in one book, "Just a Spoonful" at **www.perryperkinsbooks.com***)*

Mom's Hot Chocolate

One of my earliest memories is of waking up to the smell of camp-smoke and my mother's hot chocolate.

My parents were poor, and we lived in tenement apartments in the Portland suburbs. Dad worked two jobs, and mom was disabled, but that didn't stop them from packing up our sometimes running station wagon and heading into the Cascade Mountains several times each year.

Dad would fish with remarkably poor results, and Mom would read one of the three or four historical novels she went through each week. I, until I was old enough to garner my own interest in not catching fish, would wander around the nearby woods pestering small animals, and doing whatever it is that troublemaking youngsters do to amuse themselves. I was also famous for ingratiating myself to neighboring camps when they were cooking, much to my father's chagrin. One incident that he loved to share was, around age five, discovering me missing, and finding me in another campsite, where I had stood at the fringe while cookies were being baked, and commenting, 'Wow…those sure look *good!*'

On being caught with a cookie in hand, my defense was, *"I didn't ask Daddy, I didn't ask!"*

Our gear was old and worn, and our food was usually cheap and starchy. One thing that we always splurged on, however, was the ingredients for our traditional hot chocolate, a recipe that has been handed down from my grandmother to my mother, and finally to me. There was no store-bought, just-add-water powdered cocoa in our camp!

Mom would set the smoke-blackened and much dented coffee pot at the edge of the fire and slowly warm the milk, adding chocolate and mints, and stirring until the steaming contents had become a thick, rich mahogany, and the aroma of chocolate and mint mixed with the scent of Oregon pine to fill the camp.

More than once I can remember folks that we had just met hours before, wandering into our campsite with mug in hand to enjoy my mother's creation. I can remember blistering hot summer days, freezing spring mornings, and torrential Pacific Northwest downpours that trapped us in our heavy canvas tent for days at a time, but I don't remember ever waking up in the woods without the beckoning smell of mom's hot chocolate wafting into the tent.

Mom has been gone for two decades now. She went home years before I met my wife and started my own family.

Now, when we load up our (*sometimes working*) van and head for the mountains, nestled among the air mattresses, fishing poles, and ultra-light sleeping bags, there are always Hershey chocolate bars and Peppermint-Patties. I still use that battered coffee pot, resting it over a portable camp stove now, as we always bring extra cups for the neighbors that inevitably show up.

I've told my family a lot about Mom, her life, struggles and victories, and it seems like nothing brings back these warm memories better than sitting around the fire at night and sipping sweet hot chocolate.

The Recipe

What I love most about this cocoa, besides drinking it, is that it epitomizes the *idea* of the Home Chef. It's about thinking outside the box (*in this case, a box full of instant cocoa packets*). It's not an *expensive* recipe, it's not a *difficult* recipe...it simply requires some very basic skills and understanding of how food works, to take something that 99% of people out there would consider "good enough", and make something amazing out of it.

That...is what the Home Chef does.

Mom's Hot Chocolate

1 Quart of half-and-half milk.
4 regular milk chocolate bars
1 large Peppermint Patty candy bar

Bring milk to a very low simmer; add milk chocolate & peppermint patty. Whisk all ingredients thoroughly.

Serve hot and enjoy the company!

My "Ah-Ha" Moment

She was a sweet, tow-headed little eight year-old, adorable in a very "Lucy Van Pelt" sorta way.

Chef Chris Renner and I had shown up early, at the battered old rec-center kitchen, to cook for the annual KOIN6 Holiday Magic Store, co-hosted by our pal Amy Roloff, where at-need families could come to "shop" for their children's Christmas gifts.

I loved the concept (*If you've read my "Second Hand Christmas" story, you understand why.*)

Families were invited to come, drop off their kids in the activity room to play, and then "shop" for donated items (*all new*) in a variety from rooms from "Toys" to "Clothes" to "Books", housewares and other necessities were available, as well.

Instead of getting a box of used toys, generically labeled "Boy" or "Girl", these parents could actually pick out specific gifts for their children, knowing they would enjoy them. Parents had a personal shopping assistant to help them out, as well. It was all about dignity and joy, not charity, and I loved it.

The shopping and gift-wrapping portion was followed by a big Christmas Dinner (served from noon until 8pm), which was, of course, where we came in.

Okay...back to the kid.

As I said, we showed up early to do some last-minute inventory (*the night before, cooking alongside Chef Terry Ramsey, we had been slammed*), and there was already a crowd of shoppers on site at 8am. A quick glance in the stand-ups and we realized that we had a bunch of extra eggs, some left-over ham, and cheese that we hadn't used. A bag of onions and bell peppers were located, and, after a lightning-fast run to the local Fred Meyer (*always our heroes*) for fresh herbs and fruit, we had the makings of a slam-up, if impromptu, breakfast menu.

We set to slinging omelets, and whipped through about fifty

breakfasts before we had a chance to breath. As I was taking a quick break from the stove, a little girl came up to the pass-through and shyly flagged me down. I assumed she was interested in the handful of candy-canes in my jacket pocket, but I was wrong.

With a tremulous smile, she stretched out her small hands and offered me a cookie that she had just decorated at one of the kid's craft-station tables.

"I made this for you," she said, "I wanted to say thanks. That was the best breakfast I've ever had."

With a grin and a bow, I took the cookie, pleased as punch. Someone snapped a picture.

But, what she said next changed my life.

"That's the first time we've had breakfast in a week."

Now, those of you who know me know what a cynical, hard-hearted old grump I am (lol), but this was too much, even for me. Eyes swimming, I took the cookie and thanked her. Then, with a silly quaver in my voice, immediately told Chef Cris that I was going to go "get some air", so I could find a place to let me eyes sweat in peace.

That was the moment that I knew, I KNEW, that *this* was what God had built me to do. This was what made me feel right. This was my place.

It may not be glamorous, it's certainly not profitable, and it probably will never earn me "celebrity chef" status, but it's what I do...I feed hungry people.

There are worse jobs.

Part Six: Paying it Forward

Growing up with Hunger

I grew up with hunger. It was a cold, unwelcome monster that slept beneath my bed.

I have a terrible short-term memory, but excellent long-term. I can remember the weeks that we dealt with just having potatoes and bricks of government cheese to eat. Medically my mother wasn't able to work. We didn't even have a car. We were "those people" who lived off your tax dollars.

I remember seeing the look on my mom's face when there wasn't enough food in the house. Though I didn't realize it then, there were many nights when I went to bed with just a little something to eat, but she went to bed without anything. As a parent, I know that if there were only enough for one, my child is going to have it. We get bad times here, and we think, "We have to tough through it, things will get better." I have that hope that if I work harder, things will improve. Some people don't have that hope. They see nothing ahead but a long gray, hungry future.

For parents, the priority is that their kids not go hungry. Not having enough food to give your kids has an effect on the parents in that home. I look at my nine year old daughter and think how would I feel if I had to put her to bed hungry and how would I respond to everything else in my life if I had to do that?

I don't want anyone to go through that. I think there need to be more voices out there bringing this to our attention. There's something wrong with kids going to bed hungry every night in the richest country in the world.

Much of the problem is in a lack of fundamental education. It really doesn't matter how healthy a food is, or how inexpensive, people aren't going to buy what they don't know how to prepare, especially when money is tight and every dollar has to count.

I've had kids in our grocery-shopping field trips tell me that it was the first time they can ever remember being in the produce department, except in passing on the way to the canned, frozen, or "convenience" food sections. Kids in their late teens who couldn't identify a cucumber from a zucchini.

Do you know what Lima beans, Carrots, Pumpkin (fresh), Sweet potatoes, Collards, Kale, Mustard greens, Spinach, Turnip greens, Brussels sprouts, Cabbage, Chayote, Pear squash, Eggplant, Okra, Zucchini, and Yellow Squash, all have in common?

They are among the healthiest, least expensive, and simple to prepare vegetables in the grocery store or market. Just about any person who walks the aisles can afford these ingredients. Simple…that is, if someone has taught you. Otherwise they might as well have been grown on another planet.

But if, like many second and third generation families below the poverty line, your only experience with these foods is mushy school lunch carrots and zucchini, cloying holiday "sweet potatoes", or God help us all…canned spinach…are you going to spend your last few food dollars experimenting with unfamiliar ingredients, or are you going to grab a few boxes of mac & cheese, some frozen chicken nuggets, or maybe some ice cream for a special treat?

And, honestly, do YOU know how to prepare all of these ingredients? Are you willing to bet your child's opportunity to eat this week on it?

Neither are many, many poor families out there, who, faced with the agonizing decision of something that tastes good even though it's killing them, and going to bed without anything at all, make the sad, but logical choice that something, anything, regardless of health concerns, is better than nothing, all too common.

This is where our politicians, big food and (yes, I'll say it) the corporate manipulation of the women's liberation movement of the sixties and seventies, when anything that got Mom out of the "slavery of the kitchen" was progressive and positive (and lined food manufacturer's pockets), has gotten us.

From those first glorified c-rations, to the sugar, salt, and dye loaded poison in pretty packages on our store shelves today - greed and laziness have turned what was once the greatest nation on earth into a wheezing, pill-popping country that pours drugs into our hyperactive babies and stomach staples our teenage girls to combat the growing epidemic of a society happily starving the brains of our future generations, while eating itself to death so that Kraft Foods can see a bump in their stock price, and give their senior executives seven-figure bonuses.

Throughout history, citizens whose nutritional needs were ignored by the rich and powerful for their own gain, from Rome, to Imperial Russia, to the French Revolution, to the genocides of modern Africa, when pushed to the edge of the cliff have universally responded the same way...

Heads rolled, cities burned, and thrones toppled.

We are standing at the edge of the cliff.

"There are people in the world so hungry, that God cannot appear to them except in the form of bread."
~*Mahatma Gandhi*

A great day spent with my pals Amy Roloff and Lisa Dixon, filming an episode of Little People, Big World, and cooking up a Christmas feast for homeless kids.

As we near the end of this book together, I don't need to tell you that childhood hunger is an issue that is near and dear to me.

Some of the things that we do, through the MY KITCHEN Outreach Program, include sponsoring several charities and non-profits that share this goal, including *The Amy Roloff Charity Foundation, The Father's Heart Street Ministry, Sparks of Hope, Impact NW*, and the national *No Kid Hungry campaign*, through financial contributions, volunteering our time and resources, auctioning off our private chef services at fundraisers, and preparing and serving meals for fundraising and outreach events.

Currently, we're working on an exciting new educational outreach program to teach basic cooking skills and low-cost, healthy, grocery shopping, to low income families. The classes will include hands-on instruction, Q&A, and a free cookbook of low-cost "real food" recipes, weekly meal plans, and shopping lists! *You* can do any of these things as well, or support someone who does.

Don't wait, start today. Start now.

Before you eat your next meal...do *something* to make sure that someone else has one, too.

How MY KITCHEN Outreach Works

(The Reader's Digest version...)

Want to help us, help kids?

Our *MY KITCHEN Outreach* has three main goals:

1. Provide meals for children and families in need.

2. Teach basic nutrition, shopping, and hands-on cooking classes for at-risk kids.

3. Support other like-minded ministries and programs by providing the above services to their clients.

You can support and help grow the **MY KITCHEN Outreach**, and receive delicious, healthy recipes, cooking tips, and our free weekly meal plans...<u>and it won't cost you a penny!</u>

Here's the "Reader's Digest Version" of how it works:

By signing up for our free weekly newsletter and meal plans, and visiting our website to view new recipes, articles, and to download your new plans, you'll have the opportunity to see relevant ads from food, lifestyle, business, and outreach related companies on our pages. If you click* on an ad...we get paid for the referral. You don't even have to buy anything if you don't want to!

If you **NEVER** click on an ad...your visit to our website still increases our daily traffic, which increases our rating with Google, and brings us higher paying ads, and more exposure. Either way, you help us increase our funding and ability to feed the hungry, and teach cooking classes for at-risk kids, without taking away from the other important charities and programs you currently help fund!

How's *that* for a win-win?

www.joinmykitchen.com

The "ministry" of the MY KITCHEN Outreach Program

So, I was asked the other day what I consider to be the "ministry" aspect of our MY KITCHEN Cooking Classes.

I gave the question a lot of thought, and I want to share with you the answer I came up with. Many of the kids we work with have severe self esteem and self-worth issues. Many come from a history of abuse, neglect, or abandonment. The world, as they know it, has hurt, marginalized, or just plain abandoned them, and they live daily questioning their worth and wondering if they are "just a mistake" (*as one student told me last summer.*)

These kids have lived much, if not all, of their lives in "survival mode", simply trying to make it through each day without being hurt again, and never having the time, resources, or support to develop the kind of skills, interests, or passions that many of the rest of us take for granted.

Chef Chris Renner, Chef Terry Ramsey, and I, when we teach a child a cooking skill, have seen time and again how at the end of that day, or weekend, or six-weeks...when they successfully flip that omelet, or taste that delicious chicken piccata that THEY made from scratch, and hear the cheers, praise, and compliments of their peers and leaders, they begin to realize that they *can* do something, that they *can* have a skill that is unique to them, and that they, alone own.

In the end, all journeys are spiritual. So go off the main road.

Be givers of hospitality and gracious takers of it too. Accept the serendipitous moments of life because, when all is said and done, you may find out that they were not serendipitous at all.

And know that faith is as real as bread broken among friends.

What you believe will take you far on your journey.

If you search carefully, you will find good food all along the way.

~ Alton Brown

A note from a hero, Amy Roloff...

"I met Chef Perry and his team at a Sparks of Hope auction that was raising funds to make a difference in kid's lives that were facing or had faced BIG insurmountable challenges of physical and emotional abuse, and to provide these precious kids healing, support, encouragement and life-changing experiences of what life should and could be, when others care to reach out, give, and show love. I was there doing my part, on behalf of the Amy Roloff Charity Foundation, as well.

As they stood up in front, with big grins on their faces, offering their expertise, love of cooking, and passion for gathering others around the table, by offering a fun dining experience for the person that would win the auction bid, I thought I need to meet these guys! They take what they know how to do, and what they love best, and turn it into a gift they can give back to impact others.

We have partnered up on many events ever since.

When kids, especially at-risk kids who often feel marginalized, forgotten, and without worth, learn how to shop, and discover nutritional healthy cooking and eating, they'll become encouraged, as well as gain self-respect and a badly needed sense of self-worth.

As they gain more confidence, they can become independent in caring for themselves, and then they can pay it forward, sharing that knowledge and experience with others.

And *that*, changes destinies.

~Amy Roloff, Little People Big World

Final Homework Assignment

Using any number of items from the lists on the following page (*and only these lists*), and using the principles and techniques you've learned in this book, write a menu consisting of one main dish, and two side dishes.

- Create a recipe for each dish, including mise en place, and number of servings. *(You may add any number of spices or sauces, created from scratch) to add to your recipes.)*

- Create a shopping list, then organize that list by store department.

- Shop for your ingredients, first in your own pantry, then at a store *(this is a great time to try out a farmer's market or local produce store!)*

- Prepare that meal.

*Bonus points if you send me a picture of the plated meal!

Bon Appetit!

Chef Perry
chefperryp@gmail.com

Meat

Whole chicken (Raw)
Chicken hearts or livers
Boneless picnic pork ribs
Leg of lamb
Beef shank
Salmon/steelhead fillet
Fresh oysters
Rabbit
Fresh, unpeeled (raw) jumbo shrimp

Bone-in, skin on chicken thighs
Pork tenderloin
Ground pork
Flank/skirt steak
Ox tail
Tilapia/Swai fillet
Sea scallops
Duck

Veggies

Fresh Roma tomatoes
Whole carrots
Sweet corn (on the cob)
Shallots
Celery
Whole white mushrooms
Hot peppers (any kind)
Eggplant
Italian parsley
Radishes
Sweet onion
Leeks
Chinese long beans

Avocado
Brussels sprouts
Sweet potatoes
Whole garlic
Parsnips
Bell peppers
Cabbage
Delicata squash
Fresh cilantro
Green leaf lettuce
Mixed fingerling potatoes
Green onions

Fruits

Honeycrisp apples
Lemons/Limes
Plantain
Cantaloupe
Star fruit
Honeydew Melon

Fresh (*whole*) pineapple
Bosc or Asian pears
Pomelo
Kiwi fruit
Tangerines

Starch

Black Rice
Fettuccini
Fresh baked bread

Wild rice
Orzo pasta

Resources

Knowing what's in your kitchen – a printable fridge & pantry list.

Converting Crock-Pot Recipes for the Oven

Vegetable Cooking Chart

Meat Marinating Chart

Weights & Measurements

7 Tips for Perfect Wine Pairing

Glossary of Cooking Terms

Favorite YouTube Cooking Channels

"Pay to Play" Online Resources

My Recipes

Top 10 Recipes from Around the World

Knowing what's in your kitchen
~ a printable fridge & pantry list.

A favorite saying from the long-gone days of my youth was, "Knowing is half the battle" (*Thanks Joe...*) and this is just as true in the kitchen as it is on the battlefield.

I'm often surprised at the great lengths folks will go to, to clip coupons, drive from store to store to shop loss leaders, face rude crowds and disinterested employees at bulk stores...all to save a couple of bucks on groceries that end up getting pushed to the back of the fridge and rotting there. And, yes...I was a major player in the "40% of food in America goes to waste" scandal myself...until I decided to get *organized* and know what I needed to know to be a smarter consumer and a better citizen of the planet. (*I love that phrase, btw, it makes me feel like Captain America...*)

The second best way you can save money...and protect your food investment is to KNOW what's in your fridge and pantry, what you're out of, and what you're actually using between shopping trips.

Here s a little something to help

Google: "hautemealz food inventory list"

Print this excel spreadsheet, keep it on the door of the fridge, and make a habit to updating it when you take something out, or put something in. It's just that easy! Also, if you have a big family, or go through a lot of a certain items, jot down the number of the item you want to keep on hand if possible, next to the product name. *Example: Tuna (6)* This will help you remember that your total inventory of canned tuna should be six cans, and so you can adjust your shopping list accordingly. Now this is a very basic list, based on what happens to be in my fridge and pantry (*minus a couple of items you just don't need to know about*), so feel free to tweak and customize as needed to fit your family.

Oh, and if you don't have Excel, here's a PDF version. It's not as easily customized, but it'll work! Here's to saving money and reducing waste...you domestic superhero, you!

PS – In case you're wondering what the "first best way" you can save money, and protect your food investment is…well, that's easy…

Stick to a weekly meal plan and itemized grocery shopping list so you always know what you need, what you've got, and what you're shopping for! ~ **www.simplysmartdinnerplans.com**

Converting Crock-Pot Recipes for the Oven

Great news…you can, *absolutely*, cook your crock-pot recipes in the oven, using a Dutch oven, cassoulet pan, or even a cast-iron skillet and some foil*.

We often include crock-pot and slow-roast recipes in our weekly meal plans, so I have a *lot* of practice doing conversions!

Here's an easy conversion chart:

Crockpot time – Oven time

* 12 hours/Low – 3 hours/325° F
* 10 hours/Low – 2 1/2 hours/325° F
* 8 hours/Low – 2 hours/325° F
* 6 hours/Low – 1 1/2 hours/325° F
* 5 hours/Low – 1 hour, 15 min./325° F
* 4 hours/Low – 1 hour/325° F
* 4 hours/High – 2 hours/325° F
* 3 hours/Low – 45 min./325° F
* 3 hours/High – 1 1/2 hours/325° F

*To use a cast iron skillet, follow the same instructions, but (*once the food is in it*) wrap the entire skillet in 2-3 layers of heavy foil, before putting it in the oven.

VEGGIE COOKING cheat sheet

DomesticSuperhero.com

VEGETABLE	BOILED	STEAMED	BAKED/ROASTED	MICROWAVED
Asparagus	Not Recommended	8-10 min	400°F for 8-10 min	2-4 min
Beans	6-8 min	5-8 min	425°F for 12-15 min	3-4 min
Brussels Sprouts	Bring to a boil, simmer 5-7 min	8-10 min	400°F for 20 min	4-6 min
Broccoli	4-6 min	5-6 min	425°F for 15-18 min	2-3 min
Cabbage (shredded)	5-10 min	5-8 min	400°F for 30 min (wedges)	5-6 min
Carrots	5-10 min	4-5 min	400°F for 20-30 min (baby carrots)	4-5 min
Cauliflower	5-10 min	5-10 min	400°F for 25-30 min	2-3 min
Corn on the Cob	5-8 min	4-7 min	350°F for 30 min, husks on	1.5-2 min
Eggplant	Not Recommended	5-6 min	425°F for 25-30 min	2-4 min
Mushrooms	Not Recommended	4-5 min	400°F for 25 min	2-3 min
Onions (sliced)	30-50 min (whole, outer layer removed)	5 min	425°F for 25-30 min (halved)	Not Recommended
Peas	8-12 min	4-5 min	400°F for 20 min	2-3 min
Peppers	Not Recommended	2-4 min	450°F for 15 min or until black (peel skin after)	2-3 min
Potatoes (cut)	15-20 min	10-12 min	425°F for 20 min	6-8 min
Spinach	2-5 min	5-6 min	450°F for 3-6 min	1-2 min
Sweet Potato (cubes)	20-30 min	5-7 min	350°F for 20 min	8 min (whole)
Zucchini	3-5 min	4-6 min	450°F for 12-15 min	2-3 min

MARINATING TIMES

PROTEIN	MIN	MAX
FISH SHRIMP	**15** MINUTES	**30** MINUTES
TOFU	**20** MINUTES	**12** HOURS
CHICKEN	**30** MINUTES	**6** HOURS
LAMB BEEF PORK	**4** HOURS	**12** HOURS

These are approximate times that can vary based on the acidity of the marinade and the thickness of the cut.

Measurements & Conversions

from the chefs at hautemealz.com

Cup	Fluid Oz	TBSP	TSP
1/16	1/2	1	3
1/8	1	2	6
1/4	2	4	12
1/3	3	5	16
1/2	4	8	24
2/3	5	11	32
3/4	6	12	36
1	8	16	48

1 Tablespoon

3 Tsp
1/2 oz
15 ml

1 Pint

2 cups
16 oz
32 TBSP
96 TSP

1 Quart

2 Pints
4 Cups
32 oz

1 Gallon

4 Quarts
8 Pints
16 Cups
128 oz

www.simplysmartdinnerplans.com

Weights & Measurements

Liquid Measurements vs. Dry Measurements

Nobody, with the possible exception of Alton Brown, *really* understands the conversion process between weight and mass measurements. (*That outta get us a bunch of "It's really very simple…" responses from the math nerds…*) You see, in cooking measurements, all liquids are liquid measurements, but most dry ingredients are also listed in liquid measurements…but not all.

So, first of, let's clarify the difference between a "Liquid Measurement" and a "Dry Measurement".

Liquid Measurements

In the United States, liquid measurement is not only used for liquids such as water and milk, it is also used when measuring other ingredients such as flour, sugar, shortening, butter, and spices. Hence, a "cup is a cup" be it milk or sugar.

Dry Measurements

Dry measurements can be listed in liquid amounts (tsp, Tbs, cup) though the two usually branch off at this point, with dry ingredients being listed in fractions of, or whole pounds, and liquids listing as pints, quarts, and gallons. Even then, there is some cross-over, especially when measuring fresh produce (e.g. berries are sold by the quart, apples by the bushel, or peck).

Here's where you really start to develop a twitch…

"Do not confuse the ounce of weight with the fluid ounce, because they are not the same; there is no standard conversion between weight and volume unless you know the density of the ingredient. To make matters worse, there are different kinds of weight measurement; Avoirdupois weight, Troy weight, and Apothecaries weight. In the U.S., when someone refers to pounds and ounces of weight (especially in cooking) they are usually referring to Avoirdupois weight."

Good grief…I think I'll just order a pizza!

Okay, maybe it's not *really* that bad. With most cooking, you can get pretty close with some simple conversion charts, and, unlike baking, in *cooking*, close is usually good enough. This is why I don't bake…our dough-master

Chef Terry does the meticulously measured baking, while I lounge about casually flinging handfuls of stuff into a sauté pan. Cooking is much more forgiving, and being off 1/16 of a teaspoon of salt in a recipe isn't going to be noticeable in the final dish. Here are a couple of more great charts I found, which should help you get into the ballpark without needing a slide-rule and a scientific calculator...

	teaspoon	tablespoon	fluid ounce	gill	cup	pint	quart	gallon
1 teaspoon =	1	1/3	1/6	1/24	- - -	- - -	- - -	- - -
1 tablespoon =	3	1	1/2	1/8	1/16	- - -	- - -	- - -
1 fluid ounce =	6	2	1	1/4	1/8	1/16	- - -	- - -
1 gill =	24	8	4	1	1/2	1/4	1/8	- - -
1 cup =	48	16	8	2	1	1/2	1/4	1/16
1 pint =	96	32	16	4	2	1	1/2	1/8
1 quart =	192	64	32	8	4	2	1	1/4
1 gallon =	768	256	128	32	16	8	4	1
1 firkin =	6912	2304	1152	288	144	72	36	9
1 hogshead =	48384	16128	8064	2016	1008	504	252	63

7 Tips for Perfect Wine Pairing

#1: Serve a dry rosé with hors d'oeuvres

#2: Serve an unoaked white with anything you can

squeeze a lemon or lime on

#3: Try low-alcohol wines with spicy foods

#4: Match rich red meats with tannic reds

#5: With lighter meats, pair the wine with the sauce

#6: Choose earthy wines with earthy foods

#7: For desserts, go with a lighter wine

Food for Thought...

**"I cook with wine.
Sometimes I even add it
to the food."
–W.C. Fields**

joinmykitchen.com

Recommended Reading

As with everything else I've said, every chef will have a different, and hotly contested, opinion of what books are absolutely essential, and which are worthless. And, like them, I couldn't care less if they agree with me.

I will always prefer the story, over the tech manual, and my list will reflect that preference. I offer these in no particular order, and with the promise only that I've read each of these and found them valuable as a chef and lover of food and cooking...

- *Mastering the Art of French Cooking* by Julia Child
- *The Making of a Chef* by Michael Ruhlman
- *The Whole Beast* by Fergus Henderson
- *Kitchen Confidential* by Anthony Bourdain
- *The Sharper Your Knife* by Kathleen Flynn
- *The Soul of a Chef* by Michael Ruhlman
- *Yes Chef* by Marcus Samuelsson
- *Ad Hoc at Home* by Thomas Keller
- *The Omnivore's Dilemma* by Michael Pollan
- *The Apprentice* by Jacque Pepin
- *Kitchen Counter Cooking School* by Kathleen Flynn
- *On Food & Cooking* by Harold McGee
- *The Nasty Bits* by Anthony Bourdain
- *Cooked* by Michael Pollan
- *Momofuku* by David Chang & Peter Meehan
- *My Life in France* by Julia Child
- *Salted* by Mark Bitterman
- *A Cook's Tour* by Anthony Bourdain
- *White Heat* by Michael Pierre White
- *The BBQ Bible* by Steven Raichlen
- *The Raw & The Cooked* by Jim Harrison
- *Food: A Love Story* by Jim Gaffigan (just for fun)
- *Medium Raw* by Anthony Bourdain

Favorite "Cooking Movies"

As a predominately visual learner, watching cooking shows and movies is both educational and inspiring for me, and I typically have a notebook and pen at my side for taking notes.

Here are a few of my favorites:

Burnt, (R) 2015

When a rock star chef's (Bradley Cooper) bad attitude destroys his career, he finds a crew to help him battle the odds and open a new restaurant that could earn him a third Michelin Star.

Big Night, (R) 1996

A failing Italian restaurant run by two brothers (Stanley Tucci, Tony Shalhoub) gambles on one special night to try to save the business.

Chef, (R) 2014

Jon Favreau leads a hilarious all-star cast in this inspiring comedy about a gifted chef who teams up with his ex-wife, best friend, and son to launch a food truck business. *(Some great cameos in this one!)*

The Hundred-Foot Journey, (PG) 2014

In a village in France, there's a famous - and quintessentially French-Michelin star rated restaurant, owned by a perfectionist restauranteur (Helen Mirren).

A refugee Indian family arrives in the village, and they open the "Maison Mumbai" restaurant across the road.

Julie & Julia, (PG-13) 2009

A culinary legend provides a frustrated office worker with a new recipe for life in Julie & Julia, the true stories of how Julia Child's (Meryl Streep) life and cookbook inspired fledgling writer Julie Powell (Amy Adams) to whip up 524 recipes in 365 days.

Ratatouille, (G) 2007

In one of Paris' finest restaurants, Remy, a determined rat, dreams of becoming a renowned French chef. Torn between his family and his true calling, Remy and his pal Linguini set in motion a hilarious chain of events.

Tortilla Soup, (PG-13) 2001

A widowed chef's life is complicated by his three grown daughters and the attentions of an obnoxious-but-beautiful woman who has set her sights on him.

Cooked, Netflix 2015

This list would be incomplete without adding a mention, again, of the amazing Netflix four-part series based on one of my all-time favorite books, "Cooked" by Michael Pollan.

I've watched each episode several times, and am still learning new techniques with each viewing.

Cooking Terms Glossary

Chef's Tip: For step-by-step how to videos on these techniques, search "What is" or "How to" followed by the glossary term, on the YouTube homepage.

A-B

Al dente- The pasta is cooked until tender but still has a firm, chewy texture.

Bake-To cook in the oven.

Baste-To brush liquids such as fat, meat drippings, marinade, water, or juices over meat during roasting to add flavor and to prevent it from drying out.

Batter-A mixture of flour, butter, shortening or oil, and liquid. Batter usually describes cakes, cookies or muffins. A batter is different from dough because dough can be formed into a ball and it keeps its shape.

Beat-To beat means to stir or mix ingredients with a whisk, spoon or a mixer.

Blanch- To blanch food immerse fruit or vegetable in boiling water for a minute or so, remove and place in a bowl of ice water. This is often used before freezing fruits or vegetables. Or you can blanch a fruit or vegetable such as tomatoes or peaches to remove their skins.

Blend- Similar to beat. Add ingredients together and blending them with a spoon or a mixer.

Boil- To cook a liquid such as water or broth so it reaches a boiling temperature. You will see bubbles in the pan.

Braise- To tenderize meat, you brown meat or poultry in oil. Then place in roasting pan and cook in the oven or place directly in the crock pot.

Bread-To bread something is to coat it with bread crumbs, cracker crumbs, or other crumb mixture before cooking it.

Broil-To cook meat or other food under the heat source. This seals in flavor.

Broth-Broth is a liquid made by cooking meat, vegetables or seafood with herbs, bones and water.

Brown-Sauté meat or vegetables in a frying pan with oil or butter until it turns brown in color.

Brush-To brush food is when you use a pastry brush and brush the top of the food with melted butter or egg white.

Bundt pan-Tube baking pan.

C-D

Caramelize-Browning sugar over medium heat.

Chill-Place in refrigerator.

Chop- To cut food into pieces with a knife, food chopper, blender, or food processor.

Coat-To cover both sides of a food with flour, crumbs or batter. See definition for bread.

Coats a spoon- When stirring liquid in a saucepan the liquid will cover a metal spoon.

Combine-Adding ingredients together and stirring.

Core-To remove the inside of a fruit. Apples or pears are an example of a fruit that is usually cored.

Cream- Mixing butter, shortening or margarine with sugar until smooth and creamy.

Crush-To crush a food into tiny pieces with a rolling pin or kitchen mallet.

Cube- Cutting foods such as vegetables or meat into pieces with 6 equal sides.

Cut in- Blend or cream butter or shortening into a flour mixture.

Dash-To add a dash of something in cooking is less than 1/16 teaspoon. Since there is no 1/16 teaspoon you use a pinch amount.

Deep Fry- To cook food completely covered in hot oil.

Deglaze-After cooking or roasting meat you add liquid such as milk, broth or water to dissolve the juices stuck to the bottom of the pan. Often deglazing is used when making gravy.

Dice-To cut food into small cubes.

Dilute- To thin a liquid by adding more liquid, usually water or milk, to it.

Direct heat-Direct heat is when food is placed directly on a cooking source such as toasting or grilling.

Dissolve- To dissolve something is to blend food together to make a liquid. For example, combining water and sugar, and stirring until sugar is dissolved.

Dot-Add small pieces of ingredients over food for even melting. (usually butter.)

Dough-A dough is a combination of flour, liquid and other ingredients to make a firm mixture usually for bread or cookies.

Dredge-To lightly coat food with flour, bread crumbs or cracker crumbs. See "coat" above.

Drippings-Drippings are what is left in the bottom of a pan after roasting meat.

Drizzle-Pouring a liquid over food in a slow, light trickle.

Dust-To sprinkle food with flour, spices or sugar. For example before kneading bread dust the counter top with flour.

E-H

Egg wash-Blending eggs with water and then coating or brushing baked goods.

Entrée-The main dish.

Fillet-Remove bones from fish or meat.

Firm ball stage-In regards to making candy. This is when a drop of boiling syrup dropped in cold water forms a ball that will give slightly when squeezed.

Flake-Breaking food apart with a fork usually used for fish.

Flambé-To light a sauce or liquid with flames.

Flute- To press edges of a pie crust together in a decorative way.

Fold-To combine ingredients together carefully by stirring through the mixture and bringing the spoon back up to the top gently.

Fry-To cook food in hot oil or butter until browned or cooked through.

G-L

Garnish-To add an edible decoration to make food more attractive.

Gel-To let a food set or become solid by adding gelatin.

Glaze- To coat food with a mixture that gives a shiny appearance. For example, a sugar glaze on a doughnut.

Grate-To shred food into tiny pieces by rubbing against a grater.

Grease-To coat or rub a pan with oil or shortening. For cakes, you grease and dust the pan with flour.

Grill-To cook food over direct heat in a grill or direct flame.

Grind- To crush food with a food processor, blender or grinder.

Hard-ball stage-In regards to candy making, this is when syrup has cooked long enough to form a solid ball in cold water.

Hull-To remove leaves and core from fruits such as strawberries.

Ice-To spread a glaze or frosting on a cake. or to cool food down by placing on ice.

Julienne- Cut food into long thin strips.

Knead-Massage dough with your hands in a back and forth pressing, and folding motion for several minutes until dough is smooth.

Lukewarm- A temperature of about 95°F, not too hot and not too cold.

M-P

Marble-To swirl food together.

Marinate-To season food by placing it in a flavorful mixture called a marinade.

Mash-To press food to remove lumps.

Meringue-Egg whites beaten until stiff. Then add sugar to the egg whites. This is used for topping pies or other baked items.

Microwave-To cook food in a microwave.

Mince-To chop in tiny pieces.

Mix-Stirring ingredients together with a spoon, or a mixer, until well combined.

Moisten-Adding liquid to dry ingredients to make wet but not too wet.

Pan broil- To cook food in a skillet over high heat by itself and removing fat from pan as it cooks off meat.

Pan fry-To cook with a small amount of oil or butter.

Parboil-To cook food partly in boiling liquid. Also called blanching.

Parchment- Heat-resistant paper used in cooking.

Pare-To peel or trim a food, usually vegetables.

Peaks-Egg whites whipped until stiff peaks form or they stay upright.

Peel-To remove the outer skin of fruit and vegetables with a knife or vegetable peeler.

Pinch-To add less than 1/16 teaspoon. See definition of dash.

Pipe-To use a pastry bag, or plastic bag with a corner cut off, to decorate food.

Pit-To take out the stone of a fruit such as cherry or peach.

Poach-To simmer in boiling liquid.

Pressure Cooking-To cook using steam trapped under a lid at a high temperature.

Proof-The process of adding yeast to warm water or milk.

Punch down-In regards to baking bread, you push down risen yeast dough with your fist.

Purée- To blend food together until it becomes completely smooth.

Q-R

Reconstitute-Adding water to dried food to return it back to its original consistency.

Reduce-To boil liquids down to enhance flavor or thicken.

Rehydrate-To soak or cook dried foods in liquid.

Roast-To cook in an oven uncovered.

Roux-A thickened paste made from butter and flour, usually used to thicken sauces.

Rub-A mixture of ground spices that is rubbed over meat, which is then cooked.

S

Sauté-Cooking food in hot oil in a pan.

Scald-To cook just under the boiling point.

Score- Cut diagonal slits on the top of meat.

Sear-To cook meat in a frying pan over high heat to seal in juices. The meat is usually finished in the oven after searing.

Season-To flavor meat with salt, pepper, or other seasonings.

Set- Allowing food to become solid.

Shred-To cut with a knife, tear with your hands, or use a grater to cut food into long strips. For meat, two forks can be used to shred cooked roasted meat.

Sift-To remove lumps from dry ingredients with a mesh strainer or flour sifter.

Simmer- To cook over low heat so food or liquid doesn't reach the boiling point.

Skim-To take the top layer of fat from soups or other liquids with a slotted spoon or other utensils.

Skewer- Used for cooking on a stick, usually wood or metal.

Steam- To cook food in a covered pan with a small amount of boiling water, covered.

Steep-To soak dry ingredients in liquid until the flavor is infused into the liquid.

Stew- Cooking meat and vegetables in broth. This works best with less tender cuts of meat.

Stir-To blend ingredients together.

Stir-Fry-Frying cut meat and vegetables on high heat with a small amount of oil.

Strain-To use a colander or strainer to drain liquid off cooked food.

T-U

Thin- To add more liquid to food.

Toss-Mix ingredients gently together to combine.

Unleavened-Baked goods with no baking powder, yeast, or baking soda.

W-Z

Water Bath-To cook a dish that is set in a larger pan. The larger pan holds boiling water.

Whip- To beat ingredients together quickly with a fork, whisk, or mixer until light and fluffy.

Whisk- To mix together by beating with a whisk or mixer.

Zest- To remove the outer part of citrus fruits with a small grater.

Favorite YouTube Cooking Channels

Chef Perry
Google: "YouTube Chef Perry"

Well, of course I'm going to start with mine! Check out my channel for a couple of dozen (*and growing*) recipe, tips, and technique videos!

Gordon Ramsay
https://www.youtube.com/user/gordonramsay/videos

MasterChef USA judge tones down the language (although there are occasional lapses) and condenses his lessons into short clips.

With sharp editing and quick cuts, Ramsay's YouTube channel will teach you everything from chocolate tarts to skinning and deboning fish, and it won't even take up much time doing that.

Cooking with Dog
https://www.youtube.com/user/cookingwithdog

While a mysterious Japanese chef cooks a variety of popular Japanese dishes (*smooth silken tofu, steamed pork buns, summer somen noodles*), a Yoda-like gray poodle named Francis sits calmly next to her and "narrates" the recipes in English. It's an oddly soothing and wonderfully weird experience—enjoy.

Jamie Oliver
https://www.youtube.com/user/JamieOliver/videos

Oliver runs an active YouTube channel he likes to call "Food Tube", updating it multiple times every week — and recently, he's also started a "Drinks Tube" sub-channel. Oliver is super energetic, talking fast, doing a million things, yet making you understand everything he's saying and demonstrating it in a way that makes you think you can do it too. The best part about this channel is that he almost never uses fancy ingredients and the food used is something you will likely find at your local grocery.

Mario Batali

https://www.youtube.com/user/MarioBatali/videos

Batali stays true to the core of Italian cuisine but sticks to the basics. The How-To Tuesday section has one guide or lesson every week, from chopping onions to saucing pasta. Usually, the lessons are by accomplished chefs chosen by Batali, but sometimes, Batali himself jumps into the fray. What makes this channel stand out is the excellent production quality (the camera is zoomed into the food and the preparation, it's not about the chef) that gives you valuable lessons usually in 2 minutes or less.

Tastemade

https://www.youtube.com/user/tastemade

This global super channel features an array of video series from around the world. Watch Day Tripper to follow along as Australians travel to scenic destinations in Sydney, pausing to cook meals such as spiced lentil lettuce wraps and marinated pork with green apple salad.

Coastal features chef Bryon Talbott visiting and cooking in different seaside towns: clamming in Cape Cod, cooking striped bass in Providence, Rhode Island, and finding the best lobster roll in Portland, Maine.

America's Test Kitchen

https://www.youtube.com/user/americastestkitchen/videos

ATK is relentless in testing every recipe, checking out the best equipment for your kitchen, and coming up with ingenious ways to make your cooking life easier.

Alton Brown

Google: "YouTube Alton Brown"

Alton Brown, the celebrated host of Good Eats, is now on YouTube and sharing some of his greatest tips and tricks in the kitchen in a new channel called Cook Smart. Only good things lie ahead here and only a fool would even think of not following this channel.

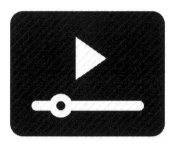

Pay to Play Online Resources

The websites and videos I tag in the book are all free to use/view.

However, there's certainly nothing wrong with paying a reasonable amount for some dedicated courses from a reputable chef. If that interests you, here are a few I recommend:

Andrew Zimmern's Kitchen Online Cooking Course
https://andrewzimmern.thebigknow.com

In this fun and self-paced online course, award-winning TV Host and chef Andrew Zimmern helps you cook world-class food right in your home. Offers course discussions between students.

Course 1: Essential Cooking Techniques
Course 2: Essential Cooking Techniques II

Each course covers a multitude of techniques, and comes with a dozen recipes that pertain to the class instruction.

Cost: $19/course.

Gordon Ramsay Teaches Cooking
(Coming Early 2017)
Google: "Gordon Ramsay Teaches Cooking"

Chef Ramsay invites you into his home kitchen to learn the techniques that have earned him 6 Michelin stars. Gordon will teach you everything from buying the freshest ingredients to constructing unforgettable dishes. Learn the expert-level skills that will take your cooking to the next level. Your kitchen apprenticeship starts now.

15+ exclusive video lessons.

A downloadable workbook accompanies the class with lesson recaps and supplemental materials.

Full refunds up to 30 days after purchase.

No expiration: Take the class at your own pace and in your own time.

Cost: $90.00

Sur La Table Cooking Classes Online
www.surlatable.com (*Under the "Classes" Tab*)

Learn at your own pace as you discover new recipes, develop your skills and practice timesaving techniques with Sur La Table Chef Shannon Cook.

Individual courses, take only the classes that interest you. Each class includes video instruction on techniques and recipes that fall within that category. (Ex: The "Pizza 101" class covers: Pizza Dough, Calzone, Margherita, Potato Bacon, Peach Prosciutto, and Sausage Broccoli Deep Dish.) Online cooking class (class run time: 1 hour, 40+ minutes)

Unlimited access to downloadable step-by-step recipes and all supplemental course materials

On-demand step-by-step video tutorials

Cost: $29.95/class

Top Chef University
www.topchefuniversity

This interactive course created by professional chefs and taught by former *Top Chef* contestants is a graded course that comes with a certificate of completion.

Cost: $25/month or $200/year

ChefSteps
https://www.chefsteps.com

ChefSteps, out of Pike Place Market in Seattle, has courses and mini-tutorials on why things work and how things work, as well as technique tutorials and some basic free recipes.

You can get instruction on certain aspects of molecular gastronomy like how to centrifuge strawberry juice or the science of spherification. It's may not be something you'll want to do as a beginner, but it's definitely great knowledge to have stored away, and you can learn a lot of fun, advanced things to do in the kitchen.

ChefSteps Premium means unlimited access to tons of inspiring recipes, advanced techniques, and all video classes, plus exclusive offers.

More than a dozen free course videos, and 80+ more for Premium Members.

Cost: $24

In the end, all journeys are spiritual. So go off the main road.

Be givers of hospitality and gracious takers of it too. Accept the serendipitous moments of life because, when all is said and done, you may find out that they were not serendipitous at all. And know that faith is as real as bread broken among friends.

What you believe will take you far on your journey. If you search carefully, you will find good food all along the way.

~ Alton Brown

My Recipes & Cooking Tips

Here's a list of favorite recipes from my blog at **hautemealz.com**.

Just enter the name of the recipe into the search box, and enjoy.

Feel free to contact me with any questions at chefperryp@gmail.com

Bacon

Tequila Beans & Bacon
Bacon & Shrimp Soft Tacos
Shelf Life of Cooked Bacon
Kale Bacon Slaw
Bacon Tacos

Bacon Apple Cheddar Dutch Baby
Bacon Wrapped Dates on the Grill
Rigatoni with Bacon & Mushrooms
Green Bean Bacon Bundles
Cheddar-Bacon Hushpuppies

BBQ/Grilling

Garlic-Ginger Chx Thighs
Smoked Honey Swai
Sake-Soy Manila Clams
Smoked Mac & Cheese
St. Louis Style Dry Ribs
Tandoori Chicken Thighs
"Dragon Claw" Appetizer
Chx. & Mushroom Sauce (GF)

Perfect Ponzu Pork Steaks
Sweet-Soy Cedar Plank Salmon
Traeger Steaks with Fresh Herb Butter
Creating Your Signature Rub
3-2-1 Baby Back Ribs (Video)
How to BBQ a Pig (Video)
NY Strip with Horseradish
Breakfast Quickies (GF)

Beef

Sloppy Joe Bashed Potatoes
" Real Deal" Beanless Chili
Gourmet Hot Dog Recipes
Cook Perfect Meatballs
Filet Mignon w/Umami Merlot Sauce
Flank Steak, Asparagus Stir Fry
Hamburgers & Sweet Potato Fries
Steamed Cheddar Bacon Burgers

The Chili-Cheese Torpedo
Po'boy Sandwich
"Gringo" Taco Meat
3 Cheese Italian Meatballs
Roast Beef Pretzel Subs
Beef Short Ribs with Snow Peas
Flank Steak Salad
Steak on the Cheap

Breakfast

Taylor's Pork Roll Breakfast Biscuit
Truffle Flower Eggs
Sweet Southern Oatmeal
Garden Scramble "Everything Bagel"
My favorite breakfast: Hangtown Fry
Cheesy Chipotle Egg Biscuits
Caramelized Onion Frittata
Nana's Green Chile Egg Puff, Dixie Sherman

Bacon-Manchego Bagel
Sriracha-Bacon Pancakes
Au Gratin Haystacks
Breakfast Quickies
Easiest Poached Eggs
Sausage Roll-Ups

Fish & Seafood

Twice-grilled oysters (GF)
Blackened Tilapia Sandwich
Hawaiian Poke
Poached Salmon w/ Lemon Orzo
Twice-grilled oysters
Citrus Salmon w/ Honeyed Carrots
Broiled Salmon w/Thai Cuke Salad

Thai Shrimp Boat Recipe (GF)
Salmon Curry w/ Couscous
Dad Perkins' Shrimp n' Grits
Shrimp Pico Salad
Tilapia Ceviche Tostadas
Thai Shrimp Boat Recipe
Prawns & Pickled Cuke Salad

Healthy Eating

Smokehouse Maple Salmon
Diabetic-friendly BBQ Sauce
Deconstructed California Roll Salad
The Perfect Turkey Sandwich
Amazing Oven-Roasted Chicken Thighs
Creamy Peanut Butter Spread
Orange Chicken & Broccoli Recipe
Farro & White Bean Salad with Chicken Apple Sausage
Crispy Grilled Chicken and Tomatoes with Strawberry-Spinach Salad

Braised Lamb Shank Tacos
Simple Broccoli-Tomato Salad
Sweet Potato Gratin Stacks
Simple Paleo Salmon Salad
Turkey Meatballs 3 Ways
Easy Slow-Cooker Brown Rice

Holiday Cooking

Easter Ham Dinner
Holiday Veggies on the Grill
My 5 Favorite Leftover Ham Recipes
The Perfect 90 Minute Roast Turkey
Thanksgiving Turkey Explosion Recipe
4th of July Awesome Dog
Valentines Grilled Steak
How to Roast Chestnuts in the Oven
Tips for Thawing Your Turkey
Perfect Thanksgiving Wine Pairings
Making Thanksgiving Extra Special
Sweet & Spicy Ham Sandwich
3 Leftover Easter Egg Recipes

Corned Beef & Cabbage
Ultimate Christmas Feast
Peach-Ginger Smoked Ham
Best brined turkey recipe. Ever.
Roast Turkey Risotto
Red Velvet Heart Pancakes
Bacon Roses for your Valentine!
Thai Turkey Soup
Giblets (& what to do with them)
Surviving Holiday Buffets
De-stressing Thanksgiving
Easter Dinner (and leftovers!)
Reheating Turkeys and Hams

International Cuisine

Skillet Gyros with Tzatziki Sauce
Potage Parmentier (Potato/Leek Soup)
Ramen, the Right Way
Pesto Penne w/ Italian Sausage
Poisson Meuniere
Perfect Chicken Marsala
Pork Meatball Pho
Chicken Parmigiana Flatbread Pizza

Ground Lamb Gyro Gorditas
Gyros vs. Shawarma
Oxtail Miso soup
Hawaiian Recipe
Pho Deviled Eggs
Green Chile Chicken Enchiladas
Thai Chicken w/ Peanut Sauce
Portuguese "Pigs in a Blanket"

Lamb
Braised Lamb Shank Tacos

Poultry
Garlic Chicken Bacon Bake

Grilled Chicken w/Succotash

Teriyaki Turkey Tenderloin (Sousvide)

Chx Georgia w/ Garlic Caulif.

Spatchcocking Chicken

Pork
The "Vermonter Cubano"

Easy Oven Pulled Pork

Perfect Oven Pork Ribs

Grilled Brat Gazpacho

Bratwurst Pretzel Sliders

Pork and Sweet Potato Curry

Garam Masala Pork Chops

Pork Wellington with Apple Sage Sauce

Honey Baked Ham with Roasted New Potatoes

Sauces & Such
Best Chicken Baste Ever

Lemon Dill Yogurt Sauce

Make your own Taco Seasoning

Snacks, Sides, and Sandwiches
Garlic-Parm Baked Chicken Wings

Terrific Taco Sliders (leftovers)

Peach Pumpkin Fusion Chicken Tacos

Bays English Muffin Pizzas

Roast Beef & Cheddar Quesadilla

Cheddar-Bacon Hushpuppies

My favorite Fried Rice, ala Amy Roloff

Caprese Grilled Cheese Sandwich

Honey Ham Grilled Cheese

Old Fashioned Russet Potato Pie

Once-A-Year Mashed Potatoes

Low & Slow Baked Beans

Quiche Lorraine Tartlets

Big Kahuna Baked Sammies

My Mama's Deviled Eggs

Perk's Flying Pig Dip

Corn Tortillas at Home

Golden Potato Fans

Slow Cooker Baked Potatoes

Shrimp Dip, Dixie Sherman

Perk's Canadian-ish Poutine

Goat Cheese Naan, Dani Ramsey

Balsamic-Honey Goat Cheese Dip

Spam Musubi

Brown Rice Spaghetti (GF)

Gluten Free Hoisin Sauce

Basic Mac & Cheese (cooking with kids)

Soups
Dad's Old Fashioned Split Pea Soup

Soba w/ Mushrooms & Kale

Thai Turkey Soup

Butternut Squash Soup

Valencian Paella Tomato Soup

Sweets

Sweet Butter Rum Plantains
Blackberry Banana Smoothies
Banana Nut Muffins
Sweet Cranberry Brie Puff Pastries
Blueberry Slush
Chocolate Peanut Butter Pot de Crème
Mayan Hot Chocolate

Mint Oreo Truffles
3-Berry Cobbler
Apple Pie Burritos
Banana Bread Muffins
Caramel Apple Crisp
Almond Roca, Melanie Zallee

Veggies

Veggie Burgers & Mock Brisket
Cranberry Balsamic Brussel Sprouts
Southwestern Butternut Squash Soup
Portobello Mushroom "Pizzas"
Easy Southern Greens
Pasta w/ Zucchini/Shallot Sauce
Mushroom Pan Sauce
Roasted Brussels Sprouts
Tangy Carrot & Cilantro Salad
Wild Rice & Mushroom Pilaf
Garlic Mashed Cauliflower (GF)
Homemade Flax Wraps with Hummus, Amy Sedgewick

My favorite Italian "Salad"
Pretty Honey Ginger Carrots
Delicata Squash
Choosing and Storing Avocados
Simple Sautéed Carrots
Awesome Green Beans
Pearl Couscous Florentine
Sesame-Cilantro Slaw
Garlic Roasted Asparagus.
Caprese Cherry Tomato Bites

For a bit more adventurous eating, visit deependothepool.com and search for...

Shoalwater Breakfast Oysters
Frog Leg's on the Grill
Asian Grilled Chicken Hearts
Sautéed Rabbit Offal in Garlic & Tarragon Cream Sauce

Bacon Wrapped Squirrel
Spam Musubi
Whole Beef Head Barbacoa

Top 25 Recipes (so far) from Around the World

(See HomeChefBook.com for links to these recipes)

Angola ~ Muamba de Galinha (Muamba Chicken)
Australia ~ Sunday Lamb Roast
Brazil ~ Moqueca (Fish Stew)
Canada ~ Poutine
China ~ Salad Rolls, Hainanese Chicken Rice
Cuba ~ Cuban Pork Tenderloin & Soffrito Rice, Cigar del Pinar
El Salvador ~ Salvadoran Sopa de Pata
England ~ Chicken Tikka Masala, Bangers and Mash
France ~ Beouf Bourguignon, Pork & Chicken Cassoulet
Germany ~ Pork Schnitzel and Spatzel
Ghana ~ West African Meat Pie
Hawaii ~ Huli Huli Chicken, Salmon Poke, Spam Musubi, Lau Lau
Italy ~ Cacio e Pepe con Pollo, Braciole (beef steak roll)
Korea ~ Korean Short Ribs
Mexico ~ Lamb Tacos
Morocco ~ Carrot Salad with Paprika and Cumin
Nigeria ~ Eugusi Stew and Pounded Yam
Paraguay ~ Dumpling Soup
Philippines ~ Chicken Adobo & Biko (coconut rice)
Puerto Rico ~ Pastalone de Carne
Russia ~ Chicken Kotletki with Sour Cream Mushroom Sauce
South Africa ~ Bunny Chow
Thailand ~ Thai Laab
United States ~ 3-2-1 Pork Ribs
Vietnam ~ Pork Belly Pho

Cooking is a caring and nurturing act. It's kind of the ultimate gift for someone, to cook for them. It creates all this beautiful stuff, conversation, appreciation, romance. All the most important things in life you do around a dinner table. ~ Curtis Stone

---

Epilogue

To cook or not to cook is the consequential question.

Though I realize that is putting the matter a bit too bluntly.

Cooking means different things, at different times, to different people. Seldom is it an "all or nothing" proposition. Yet, even to cook a few more nights a week than you already do, or to devote a Sunday to making a few meals for the week, or perhaps to try every now and then to make something you always ever expected only to buy. Even these modest acts will constitute a kind of vote.

A vote for what exactly? In a world where so few of us are obliged to cook at all anymore, to choose to do so is to lodge a protest against specialization, against the total rationalization of life, against the infiltration of commercial interests into every last cranny of our lives. To cook, for the pleasure of it, to devote a portion of our leisure to it is to declare or independence from the corporations seeking to organize our every waking moment into yet another occasion for consumption.

Cooking has the power to transform more than plants and animals, cooking I've found, gives us the opportunity to rare in modern life, to work directly in our own support and the support of the people we feed. In the calculus of economics, doing so may not always be the most efficient use of an amateur cook's time, it is beautiful even so.

For, is there any practice less selfish, any labor less alienating, any time less wasted, than preparing something delicious and nourishing for the people you love?

~ Michael Pollan, Cooked

It's time to step back from the edge of the cliff.

> *"Nil desperandum! Across the desert lies the promised land..."*
>
> *~ W.W.*

Author's Biography

Chef Perry Perkins, lives in Washington State, and is a third generation professional chef, an author, and a food blogger.

Perry writes regularly for La Caja China, Latin Touch, Grilling is Happiness, and is a member of the International Food Blogger's Conference's advisory board.

He operates SimplySmartDinnerPlans.com, which offers a free weekly recipe and meal-planning service and blog that's designed to help consumers maximize their grocery dollars, reduce food waste, and prepare simple, healthy meals at home.

Perkins also teaches cooking classes as part of his non-profit's **My Kitchen Outreach Program**, a charity organization that teaches the basics of nutrition and money-saving shopping, as well as hands-on cooking classes for at-risk youth and special needs youth.

Blog: **www.joinmykitchen.com**

Facebook: **www.facebook.com/MYKITCHENOutreach/**

Bookstore: **http://www.perryperkinsbooks.com**

Index

Congratulations on completing your first step to becoming a Home Chef!

FYI...we've just gotten started!

"The Home Chef: Transforming the American Kitchen" was your overview of the basic concepts and tips for taking your cooking to the next level, but let's face it, you can only fit so much information into one book!

Moving forward, we will be publishing a series of smaller "satellite" books, or *Home Chef Guides*, each delving more deeply into the professional quality recipes and techniques of specific cooking styles and cuisines. The guides are based on the foundational principles you've just learned in this book, and how to put them into practice in specific, niche cooking styles.

Here are just a few of the Home Chef titles on the horizon...

The Home Chef's Guide to:

Cast Iron Cooking
Gourmet on a Budget
BBQ & Grilling
Camp Cooking
Dutch Oven Cooking
Seafood

Mastering Sousvide
Quick & Heathy Cooking
Bacon!
Cooking with Kids
Tapas
Dinner Parties

See them all at: **www.homechefguides.com**

Now that you've got the basics, let's delve deeper into the type of cooking YOU want to master!

Let's cook!

Chef Perry
chefperryperkins.com

PS - Have an idea for a new title, email me at chefperryp@gmail.com. If I use your idea, you'll get a special thank you, and a free copy of the book!

47599421R00221

Made in the USA
San Bernardino, CA
03 April 2017